Editor
Eric Migliaccio

Managing Editor
Ina Massler Levin, M.A.

Editor-in-Chief
Sharon Coan, M.S. Ed.

Illustrator
Ken Tunell

Cover Artist
Denise Bauer

Art Coordinator
Kevin Barnes

Art Director
CJae Froshay

Imaging
Alfred Lau
James Edward Grace

Product Manager
Phil Garcia

Publisher
Mary D. Smith, M.S. Ed.

Take 5
Fascinating Facts about Geography
Grades 5-8

Author

Ruth Foster, M. Ed.

Teacher Created Resources, Inc.
6421 Industry Way
Westminster, CA 92683
www.teachercreated.com
ISBN: 978-0-7439-3290-5
©2003 Teacher Created Resources, Inc.
Reprinted, 2012
Made in U.S.A.

Table of Contents

Introduction. 2

Using this Book—Choosing the Country for Daily Instruction—It's Not Here!—Internet Linkages—The Book Is Wrong!

Continents of the World

Africa. 7

Antarctica. 40

Asia 43

Australia. 91

Europe 95

North and Central America 127

South America. 145

Writing Your Own Entry. 163

Bibliography 165

Our World Map 172

Index. 174

Introduction

Fact: There is a country that breaks a spelling rule that every child learning English has been taught. In its name, a *u* does not follow a *q*. In this country, nighttime temperatures are sometimes 50° lower than daytime temperatures.

Fact: People who live in the country where the world's largest river originates have to watch out for the dreaded tsetse fly, a fly whose bite can infect one with sleeping sickness.

Fact: There is a country where once the king tried to ban any young lady over the age of 16 from making lace.

Unfortunately, there are many students today who are deficient in geography skills. Ask them to place countries—sometimes just to the continent—and they are woefully unsure. Africa, a continent, is sometimes mistakenly thought of as a single country; yet this enormous landmass holds over 50 separate nations. It is more than "filled with lions and elephants." It contains the world's largest desert and a diversity of cultures.

Introduction *(cont.)*

The world is getting smaller—telephones and computers link areas that were once difficult or impossible to contact. Through the Internet and electronic mail we can communicate easily with people around the world. News is reported almost instantly, and business has become an international exchange of goods and services.

Now, more than ever, it is necessary for us to know our world neighbors. *Take Five Minutes: Fascinating Facts About Geography* sparks interest in countries to the north, south, east, and west. Written in five-minute lessons, this book promotes classroom discussion and critical reasoning skills. It makes a country located on a map stand out.

Take Five Minutes: Fascinating Facts About Geography is a book that can be used daily to supplement classroom lessons and develop world perspective. It presents countries like Qatar, Uganda, and Belgium in an innovative format. The world is shown to be rich and diverse, with a country's geography playing an important part in its politics and development.

✳ Using This Book

Every teacher has a few minutes a day perfect for a lively discussion: it may be the first five minutes after the bell has rung, it may be directly after lunch when children need to refocus, or it may be at the end of the day when children have grown tired and need to be stimulated by subject matter they are not expecting and is never the same.

Take Five Minutes: Fascinating Facts About Geography presents 140 countries, each a full lesson that requires no further material. Although not every country in the world is included, there are adequate examples from every continent and ocean for students to develop a sense of how the world fits together and where individual pieces lie.

This book is divided into sections based on the seven continents. At the beginning of each section is a title page followed by a map of the continent to be covered in the section. Each country is labeled on the map according to the page number on which it is featured in this book.

Each lesson within each section starts off with a teaser—an interesting bit of data that, when combined with deductive logic, allows students to figure out the name of the country. It must be stressed that "getting the right answer" is not important. This is not a "fact" book in the typical textbook sense. Instead, it is a supplementary text that incorporates facts to develop geography and critical-thinking skills.

Introduction *(cont.)*

❋ Using This Book *(cont.)*

Once the class comes up with the general location of a country or the name of the country, the location of the country can be shown on the map.

At this point, some instructors might want to develop a routine where

- a student points to the country on a large world map
- the map is marked with a pin or some other removable object so that as the year goes by, students can witness the map filling up
- another student locates the country on a globe, in addition to the student who points to it on the traditional flat map, so that students are constantly reinforced as to how the earth can be represented
- students find the country on individual and personal maps containing only country outlines and are asked to bold the border and write in the name
- yet another student is responsible for quickly looking up the name of the country's capital and writing it on the board, along with the country name.

When it comes to the discussion that follows the naming of the country, a teacher has the option of using all or selective points of discussion. Questions that have factual answers, as opposed to opinions, have answers that immediately follow.

Because discussions vary from wildlife, politics, and economics, there may be some questions that a teacher does not find relevant to his or her class or may not have enough time for on that particular day. Leaving out a section does not deter or detract from this book, for each section can stand alone.

There may be some cases where teachers may choose to push their students to explore a little further. For example, one might ask a student to find a picture of the animal, plant, or person discussed. One might ask a student to seek other bits of pertinent information by looking up a particular entry in an encyclopedia or another reference source.

As an instructor becomes more familiar with this book, a teacher might mark specific passages for use at a particular time. In some instances, a teacher might decide to cover several countries in one day— perhaps on Wednesdays and Fridays—and allow time for other activities on other days.

❋ Choosing the Country for Daily Instruction

For clarity and organization, the book is divided into sections designated by continent. Individual lessons cover one country, and they are written so that sequential presentation does not matter. Thus, an instructor has total flexibility when it comes to choosing a daily topic. A teacher might . . .

- take into consideration what is being currently taught in other subjects. For example, if one is covering a unit on the Revolutionary War, one might choose a country like France because that is where both Benjamin Franklin and Thomas Jefferson went to request aid. Or, one might choose the country of Iceland because it is mentioned in one's science text in the unit dealing with volcanic activity.
- have each student take a turn picking out a country. A teacher might want to give students a copy of the paragraph they will be reading out loud a day or two before so they can practice their oratory skills.
- choose a country by what is relevant to current affairs.

Introduction *(cont.)*

✳ It's Not Here!

There are countries and places not in this book. This is not because of lack of importance. It is because of space limitations. It also might be because a country was not yet in existence when this book was written. For example, Eritrea is an ancient land where human settlement goes back thousands of years, but independence was not proclaimed until May 24, 1993. Eritrea is covered in this book; but our world is not stagnant. With political changes, boundaries shift and new countries emerge.

If discussion comes up concerning a country not covered, a teacher might . . .

- encourage his or her students to keep a class list of missing countries that they can add to throughout the year.
- encourage his or her students to think about why and how new countries are created.
- have his or her students write their own entry using the "Write Your Own Entry" guide on pages 163 and 164.

It should be noted that if an instructor chooses to use "Write Your Own Entry" as a writing guide, students are not limited to countries. This same guide can be used for describing cities, states, or specific sights such as a battlefield, fort, or house.

✳ Internet Linkages

Many classrooms have access to computers and use of the Internet. There are sites on the Internet for every country mentioned in this book. Places with more advanced infrastructures have highly developed sites, with linkages to cultural information, history, and tourist attractions. There are other countries where the United States State Department posts travel advisories.

There are times when students "surf" the Internet. Direct them to a country a day! By searching for specific information, the classroom lesson is reinforced. If you are a teacher with computer and Internet access for your classroom, you might do the following:

- ask your students to find a map or a picture of the flag
- if a travel advisory is posted, ask why the advisory is posted
- ask for recent population figures
- ask for a similarity or a difference between his or her country and the one studied
- find literacy rates, etc.
- find a picture or more information about one of the animals, plants, or people discussed.

Introduction *(cont.)*

✳ The Book Is Wrong!

There were times when numbers and figures varied, depending on the resource. For example, two series of very reputable geography books reported different lengths for the Great Wall in China. One put the distance as 1,500 miles (2,414 km) long, while the other listed it as 4,160 miles (6,698 km). In another case, two different numbers were given for the number of Bulgarian Jews saved from the Nazis (48,000 vs. 50,000).

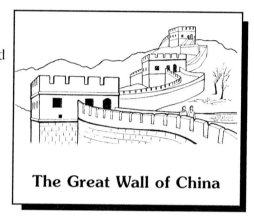

The Great Wall of China

Because this book was not written as a textbook, but rather as a book to develop critical thinking and reasoning skills, actual figures weren't stressed. Facts were always checked though, and generally, the more conservative numbers were used. Even using the lower figure of 1,500 miles (2,414 km) for the Great Wall, the immense distance and enormity of construction was conveyed. In the case of the number of Jews saved by Bulgarians, the lower number was cited, but the point was stressed that the entire Jewish population had been saved, since both sources agreed on that fact.

Developing students are often uncomfortable with statistics that differ. They want concrete answers that are either right or wrong. If, in their own research they find a number that is different from the one printed in this book, they must be assured that they are not wrong. Rather, historians may be using the best information they had at the time. As new information comes to light, numbers change.

Geography is not static. As recently as October 14, 2002, there was an article reprinted in "The Journal and Courier" from *The Washington Post* by Michael Powell who describes a town in Maine where Somali immigrants have begun to settle. The site was chosen by seven young Somali men sent out to find a homeland. Powell writes, "Known as Sahan, this is an ages-old nomadic practice used to find water for the cattle in Somalia's arid hinterland." Powell quotes one Somali elder stating, "The United States is a country made up of immigrants, and one immigrant group came before another. And the Somalis just happened to come . . . now."

Borders change and new countries are created or absorbed. Recent events in the former U.S.S.R. are examples. It is hoped that this book is not viewed as "wrong," but rather as a lesson in the importance of sorting through information, fact checking, and being open to new developments. Most importantly, it is hoped that this book sparks interest and gets students thinking critically when it comes to geography.

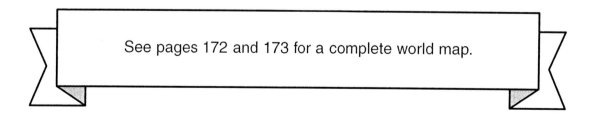

See pages 172 and 173 for a complete world map.

Welcome to Africa!

Map of Africa

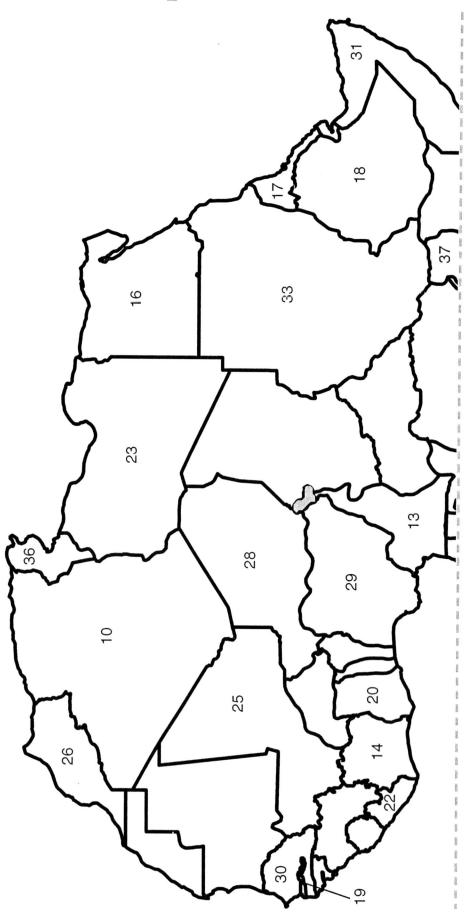

Map of Africa *(cont.)*

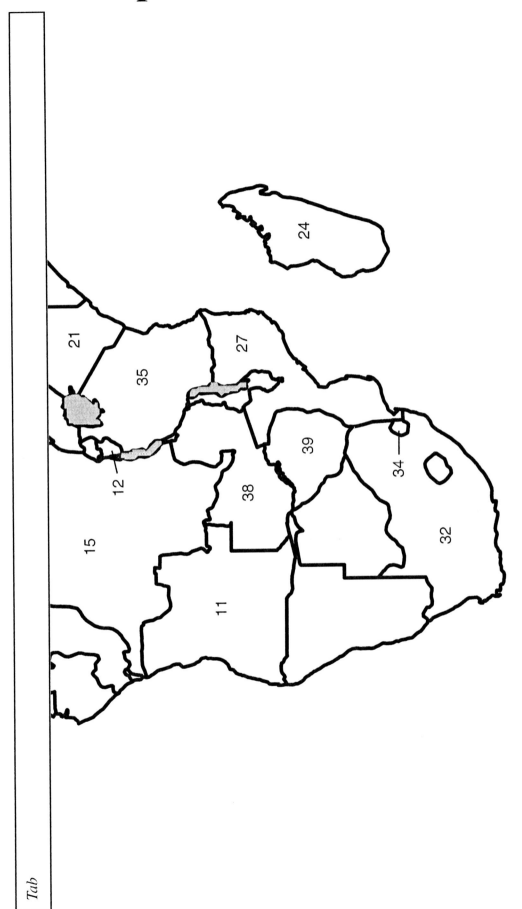

Tab

Africa

You are in the second largest nation on the continent. You would like to be on the fertile coast along the Mediterranean where 90% of the population lives, but somehow you ended up across the Atlas Mountains and are currently roasting in the largest desert in the world. The desert is only getting bigger. The government has tried to curb its encroachment, and at one point they tried to plant rows of pine trees from border to border. Unfortunately, the workers couldn't keep up. The desert spread northward faster than the workers could plant trees. *Where on Earth are you? Can you find your place?*

Algeria

Algeria is second in size only to Sudan on the African continent. The French conquered northern Algeria in 1847 and despite fierce resistance, pushed southward until Algeria's current boundaries were drawn in 1902. Algeria did not gain independence from the French until July 5, 1962. It was a bloody and violent process, partly due to the large number of Europeans (the majority of French origin) who had come to settle there. This produced two economic classes, with the Europeans possessing the principal industrial, commercial, and agricultural enterprises. Although independent, there is still violent unrest in Algeria. Islamic fundamentalists have killed tourists and other foreigners in their attempt to control the country. Islam is the state religion, and Arabic is the national language. The Sahara is the world's largest desert, and it covers 80% of Algeria.

Algeria is big—it is close to one-fourth the size of the United States, or two times the size of Peru. **What percent of Algeria's land do you think is cultivated?** Despite its size, about only 3% of Algeria's land is cultivated, and only 13% is suitable to pasture. Wheat, barley, grapes, olives, dates, and citrus fruits are some of its chief products.

Camels make it possible to travel over long stretches of desert. **One-hump or two, what type of camel is in Algeria?** The one-humped camel is the Dromedary. Bactrian camels have two humps. Here's a trick to remember this: write a capital B and a capital D and turn your paper sideways. The B makes two humps for Bactrian, and the D makes one hump for Dromedary. The Dromedary is the camel found in Algeria.

How do camels keep sand from blowing up their noses? They can shut their nostrils. Camels also have a third eyelid. If sand gets past their first line of defense—really long lashes—the third eyelid comes down like a windshield wiper, moving side to side to wipe the sand away.

Hassiba Boulmerka became the first African woman to win a gold medal at the World Track and Field Championships in 1991 when she won the 1,500 meters. A year later, she became the first African women to win an Olympic gold metal. She ran 1,500 meters in 3 minutes and 55.30 seconds. Boulmerka has been spat on and pelted with rocks by Muslim fundamentalists who feel she has been disrespectful to God by "running with naked legs in front of thousands of men." Boulmerka says, "…my gold medal wasn't simply a victory for the moment. It was a victory for the future." **What you do think Boulmerka meant?**

Africa

Diamonds are the principal mineral resource of this country where one can feel hot on one side of their body and cold on the other. This happens when one stands on the shore where the cool ocean breezes (the result of cold water brought up from the Antarctic by the Benguela current) meet up with the hot desert air coming off the Namib Desert. When the Ovimbundu Queen Nzinga went to negotiate with the Portuguese colonizers at the governor's palace, she knew she would not be offered a chair because of the color of her skin. She was ready for the insult—she brought along a servant who was instructed to kneel on all fours. The Queen sat regally. *Where on Earth are you? Can you find your place?*

Angola

Located on the southwest coast of Africa, Angola is a poor nation that is still troubled from its colonial past. Angola gained independence from Portugal in 1975, but fighting between Portuguese forces and anti-Portuguese nationalists took its toll, as well as the fighting that ensued between rival factions after independence. Angola is the only country on the African continent whose territory includes an enclave. (Cabinda is a small province of Angola that is an enclave.) **What is an *enclave*?** An enclave is a distinct territory that lies totally enclosed within foreign territory. The Democratic Republic of the Congo (Zaire) separates Cabinda from the rest of Angola.

Angola's past haunts it with its legacy of landmines planted throughout the country. When one steps on the hidden mines, if one is not killed, one is often left without arms or legs. Few of the afflicted receive medical care, and even fewer are fortunate enough to be fitted with *prostheses* (artificial limbs). There are some people working throughout the world to ban landmines, especially because the havoc and destruction they inflict continues long after war has been waged. Civilians are maimed forever. **Do you think landmine use should be banned? If so, how would you enforce this? Should companies that produce them be shut down or boycotted?**

Slavery was Portugal's main business in Angola for 300 years. **Where were many of the Angolans shipped?** So many Angolans were shipped to Brazil that it was said that Angola was more of a colony of Brazil than Portugal. Slaves from Angola also worked the cotton plantations of the southern United States.

Though today they are the least in number of all of Angola's ethnic groups, the San (bushmen) were the earliest known inhabitants of Angola. Skilled trackers, the San are able to find food and water in lands that appear dry and lifeless to others. Their language includes distinctive clicking sounds. The Bantu-speaking people who moved down from Central Africa anywhere from 500–1300 A.D. overwhelmed the San. **What did the Bantus have that gave them an advantage?** The Bantus had the ability to smelt iron. They were able to make much more effective tools and weapons than the San.

Angola has a high infant mortality rate, in part due to dysentery. **What is dysentery?** It's a disease characterized by severe diarrhea, often filled with blood and mucus.

Africa

This is a country where conflict resolution is desperately needed. It's landlocked, resource-poor, with over 90% of the population dependent on subsistence agriculture. Over the years ethnic-based violence has resulted in the deaths of hundreds of thousands and the displacement of hundreds of thousands more. It was hoped that the first democratically elected president would help create stability, but it didn't. In 1993, after only four months in office, the president was assassinated. Ethnic violence intensified, and the numbers of people murdered, internally displaced, or who became refugees in neighboring countries only increased. Food, medicine, and electricity are all in short supply. *Where on Earth are you? Can you find your place?*

Burundi

Located in east central Africa, Burundi's troubles started centuries ago and are intertwined with neighboring Rwanda's ethnic conflicts. Before the 7th century A.D., Pygmy-like hunters named the Twa lived in Burundi's forests. From the 7th–10th centuries, groups of Hutu, a Bantu people from the Congo River Basin, migrated into the region. They introduced a culture of farms and villages and dominated the Twa. Beginning in the 15th and 16th centuries, northern Tutsi migrated into Burundi and the neighboring country of Rwanda. The Tutsi, though in the minority, dominated the Hutus. They set up a complex system based on cattle herding where the Hutus were reduced to the status of serfs and the Tutsi were the rulers or the nobles. When independence was granted in 1962, the Tutsis, still a minority, remained in power. In neighboring Rwanda, the Hutu majority had managed to seize control, and Tutsis fled to Burundi, adding to the resentment of the Hutu workers. Violence erupted in the late 1960s when the Tutsi started arresting Hutu leaders and killing even those Hutus who could read and write. The Tutsis have been accused of attempting *genocide*. (Genocide is the systematic killing of a particular race or group of people.) Violent confrontations continue today.

Is there really a difference between a Tutsi and the Hutu? The ancestors of the Hutus came from Western Africa, while the tall Tutsis originated in the Nile regions to the north and east in Sudan and Ethiopia. Despite our ancestry, what is important is that we are all human beings. **What laws in your country help people to get along?**

What does Burundi have in common with the Red Sea and the Dead Sea? Answer: the Great Rift Valley. Formed over millions of years as Earth's surface plates were slowly pulled apart, the Great Rift Valley is filled in parts by the Red Sea, the Dead Sea, and Lake Tanganyika, a lake Burundi shares with several countries.

Why is erosion such a problem in Burundi? Majestic forests of towering hardwoods once covered Burundi, but today Burundi is one of the most deforested countries in tropical Africa. The trees that remain are small and scrubby, and they cover only 2.5% of Burundi's area. The hilly topography adds to the erosion. **Replanting is a long-term solution, but if you needed fuel to cook your meal today and in the following weeks, wouldn't you be tempted to chop down a young sapling?**

Africa

This country is named for the great number of prawns that the 15th century Portuguese explorers found when they first entered the estuary of the Wouri River. *Camaroes* is the Portuguese word for prawns. In the late 18th century, this country was a focal point for transporting slaves, and in the late 19th century, it became a German possession. After WWI, it was divided between the British and the French. The French territory became an independent colony in 1960, and in 1961, the southern part of the British territory joined with the former French part, while the northern part joined with Nigeria. *Where on Earth are you? Can you find your place?*

Cameroon

Cameroon is a tropical country located on the west coast of Africa. With over 200 different ethnic groups and 24 major African language groups, Cameroon is linguistically diverse. Because of all the different dialects within a language group, it is not uncommon for a village to be called three different names. French and English are the official languages, though French is more commonly used. Most of the African languages in Cameroon are tonal languages. **What are tonal languages?** In tonal languages, the tone of the voice actually changes the meaning of the word. In English, the word *dad* has the same meaning, whether we say it with a level, rising, dipping, or falling tone or pitch. In a tone language, certain pitches belong to certain words. The tone or pitch we use would determine the meaning of *dad*. **Do you think it would be easier or harder to make a mistake while learning a tonal language?**

About 90% of Cameroon's food is produced on small farms by about 75% of the people. Its chief products include cocoa beans, coffee, bananas, peanuts, palm oil, cotton, and livestock. Grains like millet, rice, maize, and sorghum are also grown for consumption, as is cassava, a starchy root. Cassava is one of the most common vegetables found in all of West Africa, but it actually came to Cameroon from South America (like potatoes and maize). **How did it get to West Africa?** Most probably on returning slave ships. Cameroon also produces petroleum, natural gas, bauxite, and timber.

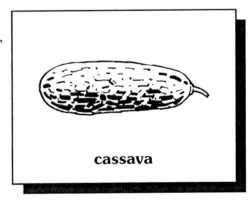

cassava

Some spiders in Cameroon—like the palm-spider—can grow as big as a saucer. **Are spiders insects?** All insects have six legs; spiders have eight. Spiders are actually arachnids.

In Cameroon, the government owns all of the radio and television stations. **How can one tell if news is unbiased or uncensored? Within your own country, are some stations more liberal or conservative than others? Should a government be able to censor news?**

Few virgin forests remain in Cameroon, and experts believe that timber is being felled at a rate that cannot keep up with replanting. Part of the problem is bribery. Logging companies that pay the biggest bribes are often the ones to get the logging contracts. **How can bribery be stopped? Is one solution only to buy products from reputable companies? What if this means a higher cost?**

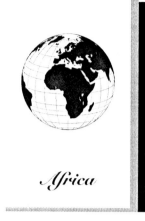

Named for elephants, this country was a French colony until it received its independence in 1960. Sandbars, some as long as four miles (6.4 km) long, lie along the coast. Many coastal cities have developed in this area where the sandbars or barrier islands are separated from the mainland by narrow lagoons. *Where on Earth are you? Can you find your place?*

Africa

Cote D'Ivoire (Ivory Coast)

Located in West Africa along the Atlantic Coast, Ivory Coast was so named over 500 years ago by Portuguese traders who came for ivory elephant tusks. Elephants are still found in Ivory Coast today, but their numbers have greatly diminished. Before French rule, the Ivorian economy was primarily a subsistence economy. The French introduced new crops like cocoa, bananas, coffee, and pineapples that were grown for cash exports on large plantations. **Why couldn't Ivorian planters compete with French planters?** All Ivorians over the age of 10 had to pay a head tax. If they did not have the cash, they were forced into unpaid labor. French plantation owners could use this labor, but Ivorian plantation owners could not. In fact, it was common for Ivorian plantation owners to be forced to work unpaid on French plantations.

August 7 is Ivory Coast's Independence Day, but it is not celebrated until December 7. Why? (Hint: think agriculture.) Crops are usually not ready to be harvested until September in Ivory Coast, and then it takes a month or so before farmers are paid. People want to celebrate when they have more food and money, and so Independence Day is celebrated in December. **Are there any holidays in your country that are celebrated on different days from when they originally occurred?** (Perhaps someone's birthday celebration has been moved to a Monday.)

Despite many families not sending all of their children to school (boys are often sent rather than girls), many schools are overcrowded and cannot accept all the students who want to attend. Cost is also a factor—most village families cannot afford to send a child away to the larger towns where the secondary schools are. There are public and private schools in Ivory Coast. Typically, private schools are Catholic in the southeast and Muslim in the north. The government funds public schools. It also pays a percentage of a teacher's salary at a private school as long as the school follows the same program as a public one and does not require a student to learn about a religion. Many Catholic schools receive funding under this policy, but few Qur'anic or Islamic schools have because they emphasize religious instruction. **What is the policy in your country about government funding for private schools? If a school receives government support, should the government be allowed to have a say in the curriculum?**

Africa

The elusive Pygmy people make their homes in the forests here in Africa's third largest country, where ants are a delicacy. Unfortunately, there is poverty and widespread starvation because of political strife, civil war, and a legacy of colonialism. King Leopold II of Belgium was recognized as the leader of this country during the Berlin conference of 1884–1885 when European powers divided Africa; but he was not a good leader. People were horribly mistreated. There was an international outcry when reports of the atrocities were made public. As a result, in 1908 the governing of the country was turned over to the Belgium government. Today, if children are lucky enough to go to school, they often sit on a dirt floor and have no books or paper. *Where on Earth are you? Can you find your place?*

Democratic Republic of the Congo

Previously known as the Belgium Congo and Zaire, the Democratic Republic of the Congo has a turbulent history. First, the slave trade shattered society, and second, the colonial years depleted the country further. Soon after independence was gained in 1960, a civil war ensued, and a dictator named Mobutu took control. Mobutu brutally suppressed human rights, stole humanitarian aid money, and spent extravagantly on himself. In addition, his soldiers looted extensively. Mobutu fled the country in 1997 when the rebel leader Kabila captured nearly half of the country. When Kabila was assassinated, his son came into power.

Is the Congo (also called the Zaire) the longest river in Africa, and what hemisphere does it flow through? The second longest river in Africa (the Nile is the first), the Congo crosses the equator twice, flowing through both the northern and southern hemispheres. The river is 10 miles (16 km) wide at times, and there are over 4,000 islands in the river, many inhabited by fishermen.

Different Pygmy groups live in the undergrowth of the Ituri forest region and were most probably the earliest people to inhabit the Congo basin. **What do you think the average height of a Pygmy is?** Typically, a Pygmy is little more than four feet (1.2 m) tall. A nomadic people, they live by hunting and gathering. Except for weapons, most possessions are communally owned. **How tall would a Pygmy be compared to you?**

Disease is rampant in this nation, and the medical facilities are appalling. Many health clinics have closed because supplies have been stolen and sold on the black market.

Both Lowland and Mountain gorillas live in the Democratic Republic of the Congo. **Using the name as a hint, can you guess which one is bigger, darker, and has longer hair?** The rare Mountain gorilla is the largest and has the darkest and longest hair. It gets very cold high in the mountains; and the dark, thick hair absorbs heat from the sun and keeps body heat from escaping.

Africa

You are in a desert with a river—the longest in the world—running through it. Cats were first domesticated here, and oddly enough, you may go back and forth between Asia and Africa and never leave your home country. *Where on Earth are you? Can you find your place?*

Egypt

Most of Egypt lies on the African continent, but Egypt's Sinai Peninsula lies in Asia. **What is the dividing mark between the two continents?** The world's first inter-ocean shipping canal, the Suez Canal, is the dividing mark between Africa and Asia. Built by the French (1859–1869), it was acquired by Great Britain in 1875. Egypt's President Gamal Abdel Nasser nationalized the Canal in 1956.

Although Egypt is 96% desert, some of the earliest civilizations on Earth developed here because of the richness of the Nile River. **What direction does the Nile flow?** Generally flowing north, the Nile is about 4,160 miles (6693 km) long from its most remote headstream, the Luvironza River. Its trunk stream is formed in Khartoum, Sudan, by the convergence of the Blue Nile and the White Nile.

There were Seven Wonders of the Ancient World. Many of you know Egypt's Great Pyramid of Khufu (or all the pyramids) as one of them. In 1995, an archaeologist dredged up massive chunks of granite from the murky waters of Alexandria Bay that turned out to be pieces of yet another of the Seven Wonders. **What could it be?** The Pharos Lighthouse of Alexandria was built in the third century B.C. It stood over 400 feet (122 m) high in Alexandria's harbor and was able to be seen by ships as far as 70 miles (113 km) away because of the ingenuous use of a mirror that reflected the light of a continuous flame. The lighthouse collapsed in 1375 when an earthquake struck.

In the famous story of Oedipus, a classical tale from Greek mythology, there is a Sphinx who stops travelers on their way to Thebes and kills them if they cannot answer this riddle: "What creatures walk on four legs in the morning, on two legs at noon, and on three legs in the evening?" **Can you answer this riddle, and how can one correctly identify the Greek sphinxes from those in Egypt?** Human beings are the creatures who go on all fours as an infant, two legs during the middle of their life, and then three (two legs and a cane) when they are old. All sphinxes have the body of a lion, but the Greek ones have female heads, while the Egyptian ones have male heads. The most famous sphinx is the Great Sphinx in Egypt. Carved out of stone, its massive head is six stories high while its body is four-fifths as long as a football field. Time, wind, sandstorms, rain, and pollution have damaged the Sphinx. Workers have had to restore crumbling stones.

Scattered around the countryside in Egypt are structures that look like towers and often are only accessible by ladders. Traditionally made of mud and clay, they are tall, rounded, and full of holes. **What could they be?** The structures are built to house pigeons, a bird that returns to nest in the same place that it hatches. Pigeons are bred for their meat, and their droppings make excellent fertilizer.

Africa

You are in a country so young that you might be older than it is. There isn't much to eat—in fact, this country doesn't produce enough food yet to feed all of its population. Due to chronic drought, many families living in the rural areas face famine every day. But when they do sit down to eat, children usually sit apart from the adults. Why? Children are considered to have no table manners. Families eat communal-style, meaning they share food from a tray. Eat only with your right hand—not your left! (That's considered rude!) *Where on Earth are you? Can you find your place?*

Eritrea

Lining the top edge of the Horn of Africa, Eritrea is one of the smallest and youngest countries in Africa. Eritrea was declared an independent nation on May 24, 1993. **Despite its small size and poverty, Eritrea has always attracted the envy of neighboring nations. Why?** (Hint: is Eritrea landlocked like its large neighbor Ethiopia?) Eritrea's northeast border runs 715 miles (1,151 km) along the Red Sea, placing it on an international trade route.

Locusts are a pest in Eritrea. **Are locusts grasshoppers?** Locusts are a species of short-horned grasshoppers. They can eat their own weight in food everyday, decimating crops and eating every bit of green on trees. Once a locust plague has developed, they are almost impossible to control. One swarm that flew across the Red Sea in 1889 was estimated at about 2,000 square miles in size.

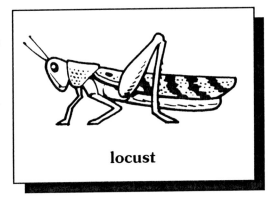

locust

Eritrea has been an Italian colony and a British Protectorate. In 1962, it became Ethiopia's 14th province. During the 30-year liberation war against Ethiopia, many people died and many others fled. Some returned after the war was over and others decided to stay at their new homes, sending money back to family remaining. **If your parents were refugees, but you were born in a new country, would you feel Eritrean? Would you want to return to a country you had never seen?**

Many tribes in Eritrea lead lifestyles that have not changed for centuries. Some people are nomads. The majority of the people live in the countryside or rural areas. Most homes are huts built of stones, clay, and palm leaves. There is no indoor plumbing or electricity. Women and girls sometimes walk more than two hours a day to bring water home from a well.

The Denakil Depression is the hottest place in Eritrea. It is one of the lowest places on Earth not covered by water. At maximum depth, it reaches 380 feet (116 m) below sea level. **Do you think this is a good place for agriculture?** It is not a good place; it is too hot and barren. **Which do you think is lower: The Denakil Depression or the point with the lowest elevation in the United States, Death Valley?** The lowest point in Death Valley measures 282 feet (86 m) below sea level.

Africa

One of the most mountainous countries on the continent, this nation is unique in that it remained, for the most part, independent during the era of European colonization of the continent beginning in the late 19th century. Italian forces were repelled in a decisive victory in 1896, and though they returned 39 years later, marching into the capital of Addis Ababa, they were forced to surrender five years later. The 3,000-year-old monarchy remained intact. It didn't come to an end until 1974 when the emperor was deposed in a military coup. *Where on Earth are you? Can you find your place?*

Ethiopia

Why is Ethiopia often described as being located on a horn? The part of the African continent that juts out into the Indian Ocean just south of the Arabian Peninsula is often referred to as the "Horn of Africa" because of its shape. The other side of Africa is often referred to as the "Hump of Africa."

Over the years, Ethiopia has been beset by drought and famine. Ethiopia has been deforested to make room for farmland, but overgrazing has led to a loss of ground cover and erosion. In addition, the encroaching desert has shrunk the amount of land suitable to farming. In 1985 alone, over 300,000 Ethiopians died of hunger, in part because the government hindered international aid relief by blocking food deliveries to regions it considered politically hostile. **Is it right to deny someone aid, even if one disagrees with the religion or beliefs of those in need?**

What is the difference between the Tropic of Cancer and the Tropic of Capricorn? Ethiopia lies between the equator and the Tropic of Cancer, an imaginary line located at a latitude of 23°27' north of the equator. It forms the northern boundary of the tropics and is the farthest point north at which the sun can be seen directly overhead at noon. The Tropic of Capricorn is the parallel of latitude 23°27' south of the equator. The southern border of the tropics, it is the farthest point south that the sun can be seen directly overhead at noon. Because land in the tropical zone receives the sun's rays more directly than areas in higher latitudes, average annual temperature is higher and seasonal changes in temperature are less.

Ethiopia is home to an extraordinarily wide range of mammals, including hyenas. **Are hyenas members of the dog family?** Hyenas are not members of the dog family, but they are dog-like carnivores. **What is the difference between a *carnivore*, *omnivore*, and *herbivore*?** It helps to know the Latin roots of each word. In Latin, *carn* means "flesh," and carnivores eat flesh. *Herb* refers to "plants," and herbivores eat plants. *Omni* means "all," and omnivores eat both plants and animals. With their incredibly strong jaws and teeth, hyenas are capable of crushing large bones; and when food is scarce, they have been known to attack sleeping people and carry off children.

Spices are important to Ethiopians, and when author Laurens van der Post was offered raw meat, he wrote, "If one must eat meat raw, it is surely best done in this way, for the sauce gives the impression of being hot enough to cook the meat right on the tongue." **Have you ever "burned" your tongue with spice, rather than by heat?**

Africa

There is not yet a university or a railroad in this tiny sliver of a country that runs along the banks of a single river. A low and flat country, its main cash crop is peanuts. Despite its cultivation, rice is imported because there is not yet enough grown to feed the population. English is the official language in this nation where the dry season frequently brings wind that carries fine sand from the Sahara. At times these winds, known as the *harmattan*, are so powerful that dust blizzards occur. Visibility is limited to a few feet, and the sun looks like nothing more than a weak light bulb. *Where on Earth are you? Can you find your place?*

Gambia

Little more than a river basin in the middle of Senegal, Gambia—or "The Gambia" as it is more often called—is a strip of land that starts at the Atlantic coast on the hump of western Africa and runs about 200 miles (322 km) inland. It extends about 6 miles (10 km) on both sides of the Gambia River. The Gambia became an independent country in 1965, but it wasn't until 1970 that it became a republic and voted to leave the British Commonwealth. **What is the British Commonwealth?** An association of sovereign (independent) states, the British Commonwealth consists of the United Kingdom and a number of its former dependencies.

The mouth of the Gambia River—a wide, deep, flooded river valley—is the most important feature of The Gambia's coast. It is an estuary. **What defining quality gives it this distinction?** An estuary is almost like an arm of the sea; tides flow in. Upstream, the Gambia River is freshwater. Salt water, however, flows 56 miles (90 km) in from the Atlantic, so that the next 99 miles (159km) of the river is a mixture of salt and fresh water.

One of The Gambia's major health problems is malaria. **How is malaria spread, and what are its symptoms?** Malaria is caused by various species of the Protozoa (one-cell animal organisms) and is one of the most ancient infections known. Carried to man by the bite of a certain kind of mosquito, malarial symptoms include chills and fever, anemia, enlargement of the spleen, and often fatal complications. Today, malaria is worldwide. **Why do you think it is more prevalent in the tropics?** Malaria is common in the tropics because the conditions for mosquitoes are favorable all year. Hippocrates (c.460 B.C.–c.370 B.C.), a Greek physician, described malarial fevers. Malaria was probably a post-Columbian importation to the Americas.

Do you think most people in The Gambia live by the Gambia River? People live parallel to the river, but because of flooding and the importance of peanut production, they do not live alongside it. Instead, they live outside of the floodplain or farther away on the uplands.

Many people from The Gambia were taken as slaves to the United States. Alex Haley, an American, traced his roots back to a young man who lived in a Gambian village. He describes his journey in the book *Roots*, published in 1976. **How far can you trace your history?** Haley used words that had been orally passed down through generations to help him. **Are there any oral traditions in your family?**

Africa

You are in the very first black nation in Africa to break free of European rule. It was in 1957 on March 6 that this important event took place. The colonial rulers no longer had a say in the way lives should be run, how the economy should be managed, or on the use of natural resources. Kwame Nkrumah, this nation's first president, led his country by not going to war. Instead, he followed the principals of Gandhi, the leader of India's independence movement. Nkrumah urged people to peacefully refuse to obey unjust laws. The British imprisoned Nkrumah for civil disobedience, but even when Nkrumah was in prison his message was heard. At rallies, people would say, "Nkrumah's body is in jail but his spirit is going on." *Where on Earth are you? Can you find your place?*

Ghana

Ruled by the British since 1874, Ghana was known as the "Gold Coast" before it gained independence in 1957. Ghana forged the way for other African nations to also become independent. Just five years after Ghana, 25 African nations gained independence. **Do you think Ghana's independence helped the other countries gain theirs?** (One might want to consider how Gandhi and India's independence influenced Nkrumah.)

There are several ethnic groups in Ghana, and some of them were organized into well-developed and powerful empires. Gold was a symbol of the powerful Asante kingdom before European contact, and it remains so today. Before the Portuguese arrived in 1471, with other Europeans following, gold from Ghana was already being traded to Europeans. **How?** It was carried in caravans across the Sahara and shipped to Europe.

A center for the slave trade, it is estimated that at least a half million of the strongest African men and women were sold and shipped from Ghana alone. Slavery was a part of Ghanaian society before the arrival of the Europeans, but the demand for slaves rose enormously when laborers were wanted for the plantations in the New World. **What would happen to your city or state if all the strongest people were taken away?**

Prices are not fixed in Ghanaian markets; one bargains. **If you had to bargain, do you think you would pay more or less than other people? Do you think people shop almost every day in Ghana because they enjoy bargaining?** There is little refrigeration in Ghana, so foods like meat and fish must be bought daily.

Son of a Fante chief, Kofi Annan is secretary-general of the United Nations. Annan speaks several African languages as well as English and French and went back to school to earn a master's degree from the Massachusetts Institute of Technology at the age of 33. **Is it ever too late to return to school? How would someone know that Kofi Annan was a male and born on Friday?** Many Ghanaians name their children according to the day of the week on which they were born on. Kofi is the name given to Fante male children born on Friday. **How many would have the same name in your class using this naming method?**

Africa

In many village schools, shoes and socks are not part of the uniform because parents can't afford them. Some schools may be located at the equator, but that doesn't mean the weather is warm. It all depends on the elevation. After all, there is snow year round on the top of this nation's highest mountain—the second highest on the continent—and it is almost on the equator. Every year an amazing migration of more than a million hoofed animals thunders across the savannah, moving north in May, south in November. *Where on Earth are you? Can you find your place?*

Kenya

Zebras, wildebeests, giraffes, antelopes, and African buffalo don't think about the border between Kenya and Tanzania when they migrate. They simply follow their instinct that keeps them in fresh grass. The carnivores that follow close behind—like the lions, leopards, cheetahs, hyenas, and wild dogs—don't care about borders either. They simply remain ready to feast on any animal that stumbles or strays from the herd. This vast Kenyan/Tanzanian savannah holds the world's greatest concentration of wild animals. Kenyans know their worth: tourists from all over the world come to view them. The animals are protected in Kenya's national parks and game reserves that cover almost 10% of the country. **Would you rather visit a game reserve park or an amusement park?**

Arab traders dominated Kenya's coast until the arrival of the Portuguese in the 16th century, who were in turn expelled by the Omanis. The British took control in 1895, until Kenya's independence in 1963. The British built roads and hospitals, but the Kenyans were forced to labor as servants or in the fields of plantations. **How would you feel if you were forced to help build a beautiful house or hotel but were only allowed to enter as a servant?**

One of Kenya's nomadic tribes is the Masai. Until recently, to demonstrate their bravery, young Masai men were required to hunt a lion alone, armed with nothing but a shield and a spear. **How do lions hunt, and what separates lions from all other cats?** Lions are the only cats in the world that live in family groups (called prides). Prides are very important, for it affects how lions obtain food. First, if lions can take food from other animals—usually hyenas—they do. Second, when lions do hunt, the females of the pride usually do the work, though there are times where the extra strength of a male is needed to bring down larger prey. In any case, the male lion eats first. Typically, the pride's hunting team divides into two groups, with one group circling around to get ahead of the prey. The second group scares the prey to stampede or run to where the first group is waiting. A lion misses more prey than it catches, and it is common for lions to go for days without eating.

Over three-quarters of Kenyans live in the rural areas. **What is the difference between *rural* and *urban*?** Rural is country; urban means city.

Africa

Negotiations started in 1816 with local rulers, and by 1821 land was purchased. In 1822 the first settlers arrived—emancipated slaves and freeborn African-Americans from the United States. By 1824 this country's name became what it is today. *Where on Earth are you? Can you find your place?*

Liberia

Located on the west coast of Africa, Liberia's name is derived from the Latin word *liber*, which means "free." After slavery was abolished in the United States, the American Colonization Society and some other like-minded philanthropic organizations thought that freed slaves would be best off if they were returned to Africa. Land was purchased, and the territory expanded as more people came. By 1847 Liberia had announced its independence from the American Colonization Society. Until recently, Liberia was one of the most stable countries in Africa. Now that the civil war—finally ended after seven years in 1997—is over, perhaps once again Liberia can flourish and make economic gains. Liberia is a fascinating mixture of Western and African culture. **If you were forcibly taken from your country, would you want to return and start over in the unknown?**

The rare pygmy hippopotamus is found in Liberia. Its eyes are on the sides of its head, whereas the eyes of the common hippo are on top. **What does this tell one about their behavior?** Pygmy hippos spend more time on land. Common hippos spend more time in the water. Their ears, eyes, and nostrils are all on top of their huge heads so that they can hear, see, and breathe while remaining safely hidden underwater. A pygmy hippo only lives in West Africa and can grow 3 feet (91 cm) tall and weigh 400 pounds (180kg). Compare that to the common hippo, which can be twice as tall and three times as long as a pygmy hippo and weigh 4,000 to 8,000 pounds (1,800–3,600 kg)! Pygmy hippos are secretive. They hide in forests and swamps and are camouflaged by a greenish sheen on their black backs.

pygmy hippopotamus

Because both types of rice—wet and dry—can be grown in Liberia without having to set up complex irrigation systems, it is no surprise that every rural every household grows rice to eat and sell. Cassava, an edible starchy root, thrives in the damp Liberian climate, and it too, is grown for home consumption and sale. Cassava is poor in nutrients, but there is something about it that makes it well worth growing. **What could it be?** Cassava can be left in the ground until it is needed. Think how important this can be where there are pests aplenty and little refrigeration.

Africa

The U.S. Marine Corps Hymn starts with, "From the halls of Montezuma to the shores of Tripoli . . ." Tripoli is where the Barbary Pirates sailed from to raid ships. These pirates attacked ships sailing on Mediterranean shipping lines, stealing goods and taking crew members as slaves. At one point, they held over 25,000 people for ransom along the Mediterranean coast, the U.S. paid tribute—yearly fees of over 2 million dollars. Starting in 1795, to the pirate leaders to keep them from attacking U.S. ships. In 1801 an even higher tribute was demanded. Instead of paying, the U.S. started fighting. There are no Barbary Pirates raiding today, but the riches are aplenty in Tripoli and the entire country—despite 90% of it being part of the Sahara. *Where on Earth are you? Can you find your place?*

Libya

Oil was discovered in Libya in 1959, and its discovery changed Libya from a poor country, where most people made their living by farming or hunting and gathering as they wandered across the desert, to a country of unheard of wealth. Searching for oil was dangerous. **Can you think why?** There are risks at any job that include machinery, but in Libya there was the added risk of heat, sandstorms, and land mines. Millions of land mines from WWII had been left buried in the desert. Wars end, but the land mines remain. Civilians, including little children, are killed or maimed when they accidentally step on these land mines. There are some people who are working for the banning of land mines. **How do you feel about this subject?**

Water evaporates quickly in the desert, both from the land and from the people. People need to drink water every day to stay hydrated. **How long can a camel go?** With camels, a little water goes a long way. In really hot conditions, they can go one week, and in the cooler times, they can last six months. But when camels do drink, watch out! They can drink as much as 35 gallons (135 L) at one time, guzzling it all in less than six minutes! When a camel is really thirsty, it can drink 50 gallons (200 L) in one day.

Libya also has another great resource underground. **What could it be?** Water, as unbelievable as it seems. When the glaciers of the last ice age melted, water slowly sifted down through the earth. Now, these aquifers, large reserves of water trapped between layers or rock and sand, are being tapped. Since 1984, the Libyans have been constructing a great manmade river. Already over 2,000 miles (3219 km) of pipe have been laid, and water is flowing through the system. The plan is for the river to flow across the nation, extending over 3,000 miles (4,828 km). Some scientists are worried that the water will be depleted within a century. The water does not evaporate right now because it is protected by the thick sand dunes on top of it. It doesn't rain enough in Libya to replace what is taken.

There is no freedom of speech in Libya today. The government cannot be criticized, and it decides on what books can be read. **Is this a wise policy?**

Africa

When astronauts from space look down, they say that it looks as if this island is bleeding to death. When the supercontinent Gondwana broke up, creating the continents of Africa, Asia, and South America, this island broke off on its own. A "mini" continent, plants and animals developed without any outside influence. More than 90% of this island's natural environment is unique—plants and animals that are found nowhere else on Earth. You hear something in the trees around you. Is it a lemur? You have to turn your head to look, but the chameleon next to you doesn't move—a chameleon's eyes swivel independently so it can look forward and backward at the same time. *Where on Earth are you? Can you find your place?*

Madagascar

Lying in the Indian Ocean, Madagascar's western coastline would fit like a jigsaw puzzle piece into the eastern coastline of Africa's Mozambique and Tanzania. It is the fourth largest island in the world. 90% of all the world's lemurs are in Madagascar, and two-thirds of the world's species of chameleons. The soil on Madagascar is a deep red. Madagascar has a serious problem with erosion because too many trees have been cut. When it rains, the soil runoff is so great that, when viewed from space, Madagascar does indeed look as if it is bleeding to death. **Which three islands are bigger than Madagascar?** Greenland, New Guinea, and Borneo are the big three.

Madagascar may have been one of the last places on Earth to be settled by humans. The first people arrived from Indonesia and Malaysia about 2,000 years ago. Africans were brought to the island during the Slave Trade. The French made Madagascar a colony in 1896, and it became independent on June 26, 1960. Today, the entire country of Madagascar is an endangered environment. **Why?** Most Malagasy are farmers. Forests are cut down and burned so that crops can be planted. As the population increases, more forests are being cut down. There is a Malagasy saying, "Without the forest, there will be no more water, without water, there will be no more rice." Yet the slash and burn method of agriculture is the only way most people know. **What would you do?**

Six of the world's eight species of the baobab tree are found only in Madagascar. Baobab trees can live for a long time. In fact, there are some baobab trees growing on Madagascar that are over one thousand years old. A baobab has a huge trunk, and because its spindly root-like branches only grow from the trunk top, it is often called the "upside-down tree." It is called the "bottle tree," too, because of how it looks and its ability to store water in the trunk for times of drought. **How much water do you think a baobab tree can store?** The Bontona baobab has a trunk that can reach 49 feet (15 m) in diameter and store up to 30,000 gallons (113,562 liters) of water. Think for a moment what this says about the climate where these trees grow.

baobab tree

24

Africa

The famous city of Timbuktu (now known as Tombouctou) lies within the borders of this landlocked country. Once known as the "Pearl of Africa," Timbuktu was a thriving metropolis 400 years ago when caravans of up to 50,000 camels came through. At its peak, Timbuktu had over 100,000 inhabitants, two universities, 180 schools, and more than 20,000 scholars. About 20,000 people live in Tombouctou today, in two-story mud brick houses that crowd narrow streets ankle-deep in sand. There wasn't even room for cars until the middle of the century, and that was when the French tore down houses to widen some of the streets. *Where on Earth are you? Can you find your place?*

Mali

The largest country in West Africa, Mali is a landlocked nation of mostly flat savanna in the south and rugged hills in the northeast. The great Sahara desert lies in the north, and the Sahel crosses the south. Mali was the site of several medieval empires, with the last one falling to Morocco in the 16th century. Mali came under French control in the 19th century, and it gained its independence in 1960.

What was the primary trade? Gold for salt. The gold fields were in the vicinity of Ghana and Guinea. The salt was found in stratified beds in the Sahara, and prisoners or slaves carved it out in huge tombstone-like slabs. From Tombouctou, the salt was loaded onto wooden canoes and floated down the Niger River to the city of Djenne.

It was common for boys to take on the responsibility of herding and caring for camels at a young age. They learned to recognize brands and tracks, becoming so skilled that often they could tell the camel's sex as well as the age of the tracks. Over time, they could recognize their camels among thousands of others, just as you can recognize your friends. **How does a camel save water in the desert?** We sweat, as camels do, to cool our bodies, but we lose water when we sweat. Camels sweat less though because they have the ability to let their body temperature rise 6°F (3.65°C) without hurting itself. Also, think how much warmer you get when hot sunlight hits your body directly. Camels turn their bodies to affect how much of the direct sun hits them. On hot days they turn the front of their body toward the sun, and on cooler days, to warm themselves, they turn the side of their body toward the sun, making more body surface available to direct sunlight.

The streets in Tombouctou are often higher than the floors of the houses. **Why?** When powerful sandstorms occur, the streets are filled with sand. Over time, the streets became higher than the floors of the houses.

One of the oldest mosques in West Africa is the Djinguereber mosque, built in Tombouctou in the 1300s. The same man who had this mosque built—Mansa Musa—traveled to Mecca in 1324 with thousands of escorts. When he reached Cairo, Egypt, he disrupted prices for over a decade. **How could one man do this?** He gave away so much gold that it lost its rarity.

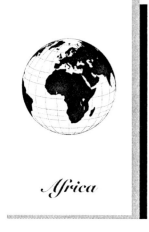

Looking across the Strait of Gibraltar, you see Europe. You can also see the Atlantic Ocean on one side of the Strait and the Mediterranean Sea on the other. In a way, you feel as if you are on an island because although there is not a body of water behind you, there is a desert as vast as an ocean in back of you. Is that really a goat in a tree? *Where on Earth are you? Can you find your place?*

Morocco

Located in North Africa, Morocco is so close to Europe that one can stand on the shore at Tangier and see Spain just 8.5 miles (13.6 km) away across the Strait of Gibraltar. Ferries travel back and forth between the countries, but there is talk of building a bridge. There are indeed tree climbing goats in Morocco, and unless one is used to it, it is a very odd sight to see a goat calmly chewing leaves while standing on a tree branch high above the ground. Moroccon goats relish the leaves of the argan tree. The leaves are too high up for the goats to reach from the ground, so the goats scramble up the tree trunks and stand on branches. This tree species is unique to Morocco, so don't expect the goats around you to suddenly start climbing.

The Romans brought camels to Morocco almost 2,000 years ago. Camels were used in the caravans that traveled from Marrakesh in Morocco to Timbuktu (now known as Tombouctou) in Mali. **Why would people make this dangerous journey through an inhospitable desert?** Salt! Before refrigeration, salt was needed to preserve food.

What is it about a camel's feet and head that help it to survive in a desert? A camel has huge roundish feet, often as large as a dinner plate. The shape and size make it harder for the foot to sink into the sand, thus making it easier for the camel to walk. The small size of the eyes and ears make it less likely that sand can get in them, and the skull bone is shaped so that there are broad ridges of bone above each eye. These ridges shield the eye from the sun, even when it is directly overheard. Think of how a sun visor helps you!

Morocco became an independent country in 1956 and is a constitutional monarchy. **What is a constitutional monarchy?** Morocco has a monarch, or king, as well as a constitution and parliament. The king inherits the throne, so he is not elected, but the parliament is elected.

Morocco is an Arab country with the population divided into two main language groups, the Arabic speakers and the Berbers. The Berbers came about 4,000 years ago from Europe or Asia. They traded with the Phoenicians over 3,000 years ago, and about 1,000 years later with the Carthaginians. The majority of Moroccans—both those of Arab and Berber descent—are Muslims; and Morocco is an Islamic state. One of the religious duties of a Muslim is to observe the specific requirements of the holy month of Ramadan. **What does this entail?** During Ramadan, Muslims are not allowed to eat, drink, or smoke from sunrise to sunset. The Muslim calendar is based on the lunar cycle, so Ramadan takes place in different seasons from year to year. This is extremely difficult during the hot summer.

Africa

Like the Arab traders that once came here and established trading posts, you are being extremely careful exploring on the Zambezi River. In the water, you see lumps that look like little more than floating logs. But you are cautious, for you are wary of startling a hippopotamus. The ears, eyes, and nostrils of the common hippo are all on the top of its head so that it can hear, see, and breathe while the rest of its body is safely hidden underwater. Startle a hippo, and you may be in grave danger. Like a sledgehammer, a hippo can swing its massive head and knock over a boat. Their two-foot wide (½ meter) lips may not scare you, but you don't want to get in the way of their razor sharp teeth. *Where on Earth are you? Can you find your place?*

Mozambique

Located along the southeastern coast of Africa, Mozambique faces the Indian Ocean. Effectively separating the nation into halves, the Zambezi River forms a natural barrier to travel from southern to northern Mozambique. **Is there a natural barrier in your country or town?** (A barrier does not have to be natural, like a river or a mountain range. It can be manmade, like a freeway that a pedestrian cannot cross.)

There are forts in Mozambique built in the 1500s. **Many of the stones used in these forts came from Portugal. Why and how?** Vasco de Gama was a Portuguese explorer who first landed in Mozambique in 1498. The Portuguese recognized the riches developed from the Arab traders and wanted it. By 1510, the Portuguese controlled coastal trade between Sofala in Mozambique and Mogadishu in Somalia. They built forts to protect their trade. **When the Portuguese sailed from Portugal, they filled their ships with stones for ballast. Why?** The stones made their ships heavier, providing stability. When the Portuguese returned to Portugal, they did not need the stones for ballast because their ships were heavily filled with trade goods. The stones were not thrown away; they became part of the forts.

One of the biggest economic activities for the Portuguese in Africa was involvement in the slave trade. Even after Portugal outlawed slavery in 1878, some captains still smuggled shipments of slaves. **Why would slavery severely disrupt and alter the development of African cultures?** Thousands of slaves were taken from Mozambique each year. The most desirable were young and strong. The least able to take care of themselves were left.

In 1975, when Mozambique became independent, no longer under Portuguese control, almost 90% of the people were illiterate. **What does this mean, and how would this affect daily life?** When one is illiterate, one cannot read or write. A country wants a high literacy rate. **How can one be a doctor, nurse, or teacher if one can't read or write?**

Africa

Thousands of camel caravans once snaked across the burning sands of this nation's desert, carrying spices, salt, gold, tea, and dates. Despite the passage of time and the growth of modern transportation, Tuareg salt traders still lead caravans over ancient routes in this country so desperately poor that even by this nation's standards, two-thirds of its inhabitants live below the poverty level. The Tuareg people sell their salt in Nigeria, but today this country is known more for its uranium—it's one of the world's top suppliers. *Where on Earth are you? Can you find your place?*

Niger

Descendents of North African Berbers, the semi-nomadic Tuaregs have long been known as fierce warriors and powerful merchants. They are Muslims, but because they are a matrilineal society (ancestors and descendents are figured through the line of the mothers), Tuareg women hold freedoms not allowed in other Muslim cultures. For example, the women are unveiled, but the men are veiled. Women can own property, and even if they marry someone of a lower caste, they retain their social class. The salt trade has long been the realm of the Tuareg, and even today it is a Tuareg sultan that arranges for protection from bandits. **Why do some outsiders know the Tuareg as the Blue Men of the Desert?** The indigo dye from their clothes stains their skin.

Niger became a French possession when European countries got together at the Berlin Conference of 1884–1885 and divided up Africa. Niger did not become a full-fledged colony until 1922 because of the Tuareg—the Nigerian Sahara had practically belonged to them for over 1,000 years. They resisted coming under the rule of anyone. Despite its independence in 1960, Niger has gone through political turmoil, with coups and assassinations. People from Niger often define themselves as an ethnic group (for example, a Hausa, Songhai, Djerma, Fulani, or Tuareg) rather than a nation. **If someone came and arbitrarily drew a dividing line in your community, perhaps even separating family members, with each half belonging to a different country and under different governments, would you consider yourself part of the "old" community or part of the newly created state?**

In Djerma villages, millet is stored in huge, round, mud-walled structures. A small opening that can be covered and needs a ladder to access is left at the top. **What is millet, and why are the granaries raised up on rocks or stilts?** Millet is the common name for several plants of the grass family and is similar to wheat. It is cultivated mainly for cereals in the Old World, and for forage and hay in North America. The granaries are raised to guard against moisture.

There are over 7,000 species of dung beetles world wide, with more species on the African continent than any other. **What do dung beetles eat?** Dung beetles live on the food material they find in dung—animal excrement. Some Niger dung beetles fashion a chunk of dung into a ball that can weigh up to 50 times as much as the beetle. **How do they get it to their nests?** They roll it by running backward with their front legs on the ground and their back legs up high on the ball.

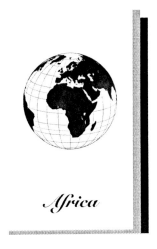

Africa

Despite the population being mostly rural, you are in the most densely populated country on the entire continent. The country is also one of the wealthiest—oil, tin, and rubber are exported. In pre-colonial times, a bride spent time in a "fattening room." She gained a lot of surplus fat, thereby indicating that she was in a healthy state. One of your early states was so powerful that at its height, it could send 50,000 soldiers into battle.

Your name comes from the large river that runs through this country (hint: the Niger River.) *Where on Earth are you? Can you find your place?*

Nigeria

Before colonial times, there were empires, kingdoms, and city-states in what is today Nigeria. One empire, the Kanem-Borno, had an elaborate government and dominated the eastern trade route across the Sahara. Other states became famous for bronze casting, blacksmithing, and glass manufacturing. Some Yoruba kingdoms developed models of administration that are still admired today. The British claimed Nigeria at the Berlin Conference in 1885 when the European powers divided up Africa among themselves. **With space exploration, should we or how will we divide space?**

Europeans sailed to West Africa starting in the 1400s to trade metal tools, cooking utensils, cloth, and glassware for African gold, ivory, and spices. By 1480, trading began for slaves. Many of the slaves bought in West Africa and Nigeria were used to work on the plantations in the Americas. Africans sold slaves to the Europeans because to them, they were not—as the Europeans saw them—all "Africans." They were Ibos, Yorubas, Hausas, or Fulanis. In Nigeria alone, there are 250 different ethnic groups. **Do Germans see themselves as Pacific Islanders? Do Italians see themselves as Russians? Should there be universal human rights laws?**

Nigeria became an independent republic on October 1, 1963. A civil war soon followed. **What is a civil war, and what might be one reason it would occur in Nigeria?** A civil war takes place within a country, as opposed to a war that is against another country. It was the Europeans who divided up the continent of Africa into countries. When the lines were drawn, no accounting took place for ethnic differences. The Ibos formed the bulk of the administrative classes during the time of British rule and held many governmental posts. Massacres of Ibos occurred soon after independence, and a general exodus of Ibos back to their own region began. They wanted to become an independent Republic of Biafra. From 1967–70, a civil war ensued. Few African states recognized Biafra. **Why?** Their own countries were made up of different ethnic groups. If they supported Biafra, they ran the risk of every economically powerful area seceding.

Would you like to be born a twin? If you were of the Yoruba tribe, being a twin would be considered sacred. You would always be given the same names, Taiwo and Kehinde. The Ibos, on the other extreme, consider twins an abomination (a hateful and disgusting thing). The mother is often driven from the village. **How is it possible to change people's attitudes? Whose attitudes are right?**

Africa

Your coastline juts out further into the Atlantic Ocean than any other point on this continent. Your capital is on the tip of this peninsula, and the notorious Goree Island, the main departure point for slave ships of the past, is close by. The Sahara is encroaching to the north, and the Sahel, the southern semi-desert fringe of the Sahara, is expanding as well. You would like to see a lion in one the national parks, but you won't mind if you miss out on a green mamba. *Where on Earth are you? Can you find your place?*

Senegal

Located on the hump of Africa, Senegal almost completely surrounds the country of Gambia. Most of Senegal is flat and low-lying, with little seasonal variation in its climate because it is close to the equator. During the day it's hot inland, but it's milder at the coast. Once the administrative hub of French West Africa, Dakar, Senegal's capital, is one of the leading cities of West Africa. Its port is one of the most important seaports in all of Africa, and it can accommodate 40–50 oceangoing vessels at one time. Once a French colony, Senegal became an independent country in 1960.

A green mamba is arboreal. **What is a green mamba?** A green mamba is a slender, agile snake with large scales and long front teeth. Belonging to the cobra family, the green mamba grows to about 9 feet (2.7 m) long. Poisonous, a mamba bite is usually fatal without antivenom treatment. The green mamba hunts small animals in trees. It is *arboreal,* which means "inhabiting or frequenting trees."

Throughout most of Africa's history, Africans have held and traded slaves. **A big change came in the 16th century. Why?** The large plantations in the New World required massive numbers of laborers. Clearing land, planting, and harvesting crops was backbreaking toil. No free person would do it. It has been estimated that more than 12 million slaves were taken from Africa between 1500 and 1850. It was not until 1848 that France abolished slavery. Part of Senegal, Goree Island was held by Portugal, then Holland, France, England, and back to France during colonial times. It was always a center of the slave trade, no matter which European power was in control. Before being shipped across the Atlantic, tens of thousands of men, women, and children, were imprisoned in the island's slave warehouses. The conditions, as the slave trade itself, can never be justified. Goree Island was declared a historical site in 1951, and its buildings preserved. **Would you visit the site if you could? Should it be preserved?**

The fishing industry has grown dramatically in Senegal, and today fish products are one of Senegal's leading exports. Fish are an important part of the Senegalese diet—Senegalese consume about twice as much fish as people in other parts of the worlds. **What made the fishing industry grow?** The introduction of modern fishing vessels.

The majority of the major ethnic groups of Senegal traditionally followed a caste system—a rigid system of social stratification determined at birth. There were three main strata: free people, artisans, and slaves. Even today, despite the fact that it is illegal, the caste system may determine how one is treated, and lying about one's caste can be grounds for divorce. **Should people change their attitudes about class? Can you make them?**

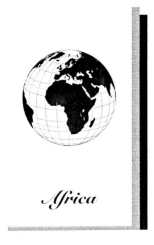

Africa

Poetry and storytellers are important, as are names. But when one discovers that for centuries, people have lived as nomads it begins to make sense. As a matter of fact, even today well over half of the people still live in their traditional manner of pastoral nomads. The indispensable camel carries their home as they follow their goats. Tall and thin, they share a language they have spoken for centuries and a religion. Rhinoceroses—desired for their horns—have all been killed, but there is one "horn" still around—the one they live on. *Where on Earth are you? Can you find your place?*

Somalia

Located on the eastern coast of Africa, on the continent's "horn," Somalia is a land of deserts, coastal plains, and mountains. Separated from Arabia only by the Gulf of Aden, Arab influence has had a major impact on the country. Nearly all Somalis are Muslims, and religion is one of the most important aspects of their lives. Somalia became an independent country in 1960, but drought, famine, and civil war have hindered Somalia's progress. The Somali system of writing wasn't even established until 1972, and the country still has a high illiteracy rate.

Somali names are long. Each child receives a personal name from his parents, but then come the names that explain his heritage. There is the father's personal name, the personal name of the father's father, and so on up to the name of the founder of the sub-clan, and then the clan family. There are six clans in Somalia. Somalis can tell how closely related they are to someone simply by their name. Go to a strange town, and one can find clan family by asking where a certain name can be found. There is a strong loyalty between clans, and so family members are always welcome, even if they have never met before. **Do you feel any kinship toward anyone who shares your last name?**

Although the rhinos and most of the elephants have been killed in Somalia, there are still cheetahs. **What is it about a cheetah's foot that makes it different from all other cats and helps it run fast?** (Hint: think of track shoes.) The cheetah is the only cat whose claws are always pushed out. Like cleats on a track shoe, the claws dig into the ground as the cheetah pushes off, helping it to build up speed fast.

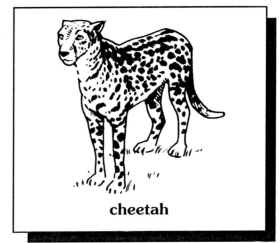

cheetah

Verbal poetry has been a rich tradition. When village leaders make a decision, they go to the local poet. The decision is announced in a poem. Then special poetry reciters have the honored job of repeating the poem to other people and villages. While the poems were being recited, these reciters were not allowed to show facial expression or emphasize words. The poems would contain decisions, but also local history, current affairs, and customs. It is feared the art of verbal poetry is dying away. **Do you think it is worth writing down these poems? Do you think they might become classical Somali literature?**

Africa

In 1990, a man was released from prison. He had been incarcerated for 27 years. A son of a tribal chief and a lawyer, this man spent many of his years in jail on a barren limestone rock called Robben Island where he pounded boulders into gravel. He was not permitted to receive mail, and if he was allowed a rare visit, the warden listened to every word. Yet this man never lost his dignity, and his beliefs remained the same: all people, no matter their color, should be treated equally. No color was inferior to another. Just four years after his release, this man—Nelson Mandela—was elected president. *Where on Earth are you? Can you find your place?*

South Africa

It was a Portuguese explorer who was the first European to visit South Africa in 1488, but it was the Dutch who established the first settlement in 1652. The Dutch were joined soon after by Huguenots who had left France to find religious freedom. These people became known as Africaners or Boers, the Dutch word for farmers. In 1795, the British took over the cape. Conflicts followed, with fighting between the British, the Boers, and the Zulu and the Xhosa. The Union of South Africa was proclaimed in 1910. The Boers had lost to the British, but the real losers were the Zulu and the Xhosa and the other African peoples. It had been their homeland, but they no longer had rights. When the Afrikaners' National Party won the national election in 1948, a series of laws were enacted that became known as "apartheid." **What is *apartheid*?** Apartheid forced absolute segregation between the races. Black people could only live in certain areas and go to certain schools. People could not use the same restrooms or go to the same hospitals. Living conditions for the black inhabitants were terrible, and if they did go to a city or town to work, they had to carry special passes.

During apartheid, many countries refused to trade with South Africa. In addition, South Africa was banned from participating in most international sports competitions. Although it wasn't expelled from the Olympics until 1970, South Africa hadn't participated in the Olympics since 1960 because so many other countries threatened to boycott the Games. **What is a boycott?** A boycott is when one refuses to have dealings with a person, store, organization, or country to express disapproval or force acceptance of certain conditions. The Olympic committee readmitted South Africa in 1991.

South Africa lies at the junction of two oceans. Which two? The Indian and the Atlantic Oceans.

Not one of South Africa's languages is spoken by a majority of the population. **Should a nation have a national language?** Today, the South African government recognizes 11 languages. Today, students are taught in English and one of the other 10 languages dominant in the area.

A special program has been started in South Africa's wildlife parks to help White Rhinos breed and to protect them from poachers who kill them for their horns. **What do rhinos have that compensates for their bad eyesight?** A wonderful sense of smell. Upwind, they could smell you from hundreds of feet away.

Africa

You are in the largest country on the continent. Not only is the country large, but so is the Sudd, a vast swamp that for thousands of years stood as a physical barrier between the north and the south. The remains of an ornately decorated swimming pool with a complex set of water channels bringing water into it from a nearby well just north of Khartoum and dating back to the fourth century B.C. can be found in this nation. Perhaps the royal family felt that swimming in the Nile—that runs the entire length of the country—was too common or unsafe. *Where on Earth are you? Can you find your place?*

Sudan

Sudan is a country whose landscape changes dramatically as one travels its length. The north is chiefly desert or semi-desert. In central Sudan, there are semiarid grasslands and low hills. The Sudd swamp lies in the south, with rainforests in the extreme south. Just as its topography is different in the north and south, so too are its people. Unfortunately, this has contributed to civil wars and strife. **From its location on the continent, can you surmise some of the cultural and religious differences?** In the north, the Arab culture dominates, with the majority of the people being Muslims. In the south, there is a diversity of black African tribes who wish to keep their cultures and religions intact.

After WWII, Sudan was jointly controlled by Britain and Egypt, but it formally became a republic in 1956. Decades of civil war have undermined the stability of the country, and although today the northern Islamic groups wield the most power, there are southern rebels who are fighting for independence. Human rights abuses are rampant, and millions of people have been driven from their homes. One example: the Nuba people. Made up of 50 different tribes, the Nuba lived peacefully for centuries. Recently, the government began a campaign to force the Nuba to wear clothes and follow traditional Islamic rules. As a response to the government persecution, the Nuba declared support for the SPLA, the Southern People's Liberation Army. In return, the government changed their policy of "civilizing" the Nuba to eradicating them. Carrying out a scorched earth policy, government troops pillaged the countryside, burning even crops and animals. **Is it right to force religious rules on everyone? Does your government have a state religion?**

Many people in Sudan practice the ancient tradition of scarring. Some scars are for beauty, and others mark the initiation rites of manhood. **Does a government have the right to decide what is disfigurement rather than beautifying? Does a government have the right to punish parents who allow the scarring of their children?**

What palm flourishes across the Sudd and has been used for fuel, food, paper, boxes, shoes, and even boats? Answer: the papyrus palm. A member of the sedge family, papyrus grows to about 10 feet (3 m) in height. It has long, woody roots that spread under the surface of the water and help to anchor the plant. It was these roots that were used for fuel by ancient civilizations of Sudan and Egypt. They also made paper from the pith (the inside of the stem). When the pith is boiled, it can be eaten. Boiled pith is still used as a food source today.

Africa

Small and landlocked, you are in a country that has only two neighbors, one of which almost encircles this nation entirely. This country is unique in that it has one culture. Most countries on this continent have more. Unity came about because King Mswati II (who assumed the throne in 1840) adopted the practice of "age regiments." Ties of region and kinships were ignored, and instead young men of the same age were brought together to form "armies." These age-related men became known for their military skill and discipline, and King Mswati was able to unite many different clans into one nation during his reign. *Where on Earth are you? Can you find your place?*

Swaziland

Because of its proximity to South Africa, events in Swaziland were often a result of what happened there. For example, because some Europeans saw the Swazis as nothing but a labor force for the vast gold mines discovered in South Africa in 1886, every Swazi adult man and woman had to pay a tax—in cash. Mine work was the only work that paid cash, and so Swazis were forced to work in mines to pay to live on their own land. **If all the adult male members of your community left for extended periods of time, how would it affect your family and culture?** In Swaziland, so many people went to the mines that the country lost its ability to feed itself, thereby becoming even more dependent on South Africa.

King Sobhuza II ruled from 1921 until his death in 1982, guiding his country with a remarkable blend of tradition and adaptation through its journey to independence from the British in 1968 and after. The king's mother felt that it was "their money and books" that gave whites power. With a special tax paid by every Swazi, she financed King Sobhuza's education, as well as that of a number of other boys from all levels of Swazi life so that, despite his superior education, the king would never lose touch with his people. **Do "money and books" wield power? Did educating others along with the king help unify the country?**

At the beginning of the 20th century, even the vultures left Swaziland. What does that tell you about the number of animals in Swaziland? Vultures eat carrion (dead flesh). They have an important role in the ecological cycle, for the disposal of dead animals is vital. A departure of vultures signifies an extreme lack of wildlife. Indeed, because of over hunting, both legal and illegal, and several epidemics of a terrible disease, Swaziland's large mammals virtually disappeared. Small game parks have been started, and animals like the elephant, which were entirely hunted out by the 1950s, were reintroduced. Yet animals today are still not safe. Take the rhinoceros. One man started acquiring rhinos in 1987, paying $250,000 for a breeding group

vulture

of five, so that he could reestablish the animals in Swaziland. But between 1988 and 1992, poachers with automatic weapons came and killed almost all of the rhinos reintroduced in Swaziland. They cut off the horns and left the carcasses to rot. The horn is of high value because many people believe that it has great medicinal properties.

Africa

You are in the country that contains both the highest point and the lowest point on the entire continent. This country also has the world's longest freshwater lake—a lake so deep that it contains seven times the amount of water in Lake Victoria. Lake Victoria is the largest lake on the continent, third in the world; and part of it lies within this country's boundaries. Several islands make up part of this country, two of which were primary producers of cloves, an aromatic spice used in preserving and flavoring meat in the days before refrigeration. *Where on Earth are you? Can you find your place?*

Tanzania

Tanganyika became a fully independent nation on December 9, 1961. In 1964 when it joined with the islands of Zanzibar and Pemba, it changed its name to Tanzania. If the president is from the mainland, the vice-president must be from Zanzibar, or the other way round. Over the centuries, Tanzania has been raided by Arab and Portuguese traders and slavers. It was a German protectorate in 1891. During WWI the Germans were pushed out by the British, and it became a British mandate.

What language do you teach in schools when the student body comes from over 120 different cultures, with as many different languages? Kiswahili is the official language, despite it being the second language for 90% of the population. Having one common language meant that textbooks could be developed. Children speak their tribal language at home, but in school, the army, government institutions, etc., Kiswahili is used. Kiswahili was the best choice because use of the language was already widespread. It spread from the coast by the traders who brought it inland. English is widely used in business, and it is usually taught at the secondary level.

Tanzanians know that many tourists are interested in coming to view wildlife in its natural habitat. Large animal reserves have been established for this reason, but preserving land for animals has created some new problems. People who live around the animal reserves have been deprived of their hunting grounds, and because of the money to be made from elephant ivory and rhinoceros horns, poachers enter the park illegally to hunt these animals. **What part of the elephant has the ivory that the poachers covet?** Elephant tusks are made of ivory. **What do elephants use their tusks for?** Plowing up the ground to find roots to eat, prying open tree trunks to get to the soft wood inside, and drilling into dry riverbeds to dig up water when water is scarce. To stop poaching, some people feel that there should be an international ban on all ivory imports. Others feel that a ban only makes the ivory more valuable. **How would you stop poaching?**

Are there 4, 40, 400, 4,000, 40,000, or 400,000 muscles and tendons in an elephant's trunk? There are 40,000. This makes the trunk strong and flexible. An elephant can pick up a huge log or a single flower.

In the mid-1990s, Tanzania had just one doctor for 20,511 people. **Do you think this is part of the reason life expectancy for a newborn is only 42 years?**

Africa

The famed ancient Phoenician city of Carthage was located in this country. Perhaps one of Carthage's most famous sons is Hannibal. Hannibal was a brilliant general who, back in the Second Punic War (218–201 B.C.), led his 26,000-man army across the Pyrenees and the Alps during his campaign against Rome. There are nomads in this country who carry their tented homes with them on the backs of camels, as well as others who live in troglodyte homes. While the desert makes up nearly half of this African nation's total land area, nearly half of its total boundary is coastline. *Where on Earth are you? Can you find your place?*

Tunisia

Located on the northernmost tip of North Africa, Tunisia fits like a tiny wedge between Algeria and Libya. Tunisia became a French protectorate in 1883, but in 1956 it became a fully independent nation. The Punic Wars took place long before Tunisia was a part of Arab and Turkish North African empires or its independence. **What were the Punic Wars?** Three distinct conflicts between Carthage and Rome, the Punic Wars spanned a total of 112 years. At the time of the First Punic War (264–241 B.C.), Carthage controlled Northwest Africa, as well as the islands and trade of the western Mediterranean. By the end of the Third Punic War, (149–146 B.C.), Carthage was burned, and Rome had become the greatest power west of China.

What are *troglodyte* homes? Troglodyte homes are underground dwellings. Living underground may seem unusual to many, but for centuries this type of home has safeguarded Tunisians from weather extremes, as well as sand, wind, and wild animals. Typically, there are rooms for eating, sleeping, stabling, and storage off an open courtyard. Animals can be brought in through the gently inclined entrance tunnel, while their food can be restocked via a pipe from the ceiling leading to the outside. People can move from room to room through smaller connecting tunnels. Have you ever seen a troglodyte home? (Perhaps you have seen the movie *Star Wars*. Scenes were filmed in Tunisian troglodyte homes.) **Would a troglodyte home be suitable for where you live?** (Consider weather conditions like snow.)

Tunisia has a rich collection of mosaics. There is a mosaic in one Tunisian museum dating back to the 5th or 4th century B.C. **What is a mosaic?** A mosaic is an art form where small pieces of different colored tiles or other materials are inlaid on a flat surface, forming pictures or patterns.

When many people think of a camel, they think of nomads and transportation. But some camels work with the press. **What kind of press could it be?** Tunisia exports olive oil, and it is one of its largest agricultural exports. Olives are crushed to extract oil, and camels are used to turn the press wheel. In some parts of Tunisia, camels are also used to pull plows.

If one had to guess Tunisia's national language, what would one guess? Was location or colonialism a factor in your answer? Tunisia's national language is Arabic, but French is still used in some areas.

Africa

You are where the world's largest river originates. You are fascinated by the water, but despite your interest, you keep a keen eye out for the dreaded tsetse fly. This bloodsucking fly looks very much like our common housefly, but with crossed wings. Though the tsetse fly bite can be quite painful, that is not what concerns you. What you do not want to contract (become ill with) is sleeping sickness, a disease that could result from a tsetse fly's bite. *Where on Earth are you? Can you find your place?*

Uganda

Uganda is located in East Africa. The Nile, the world's largest river, originates in Uganda's southeastern corner at Lake Victoria. Known as "The Cradle of the Nile," Uganda is a landlocked country with water and swamps covering one-sixth of the land. The famous Ruwenzori Mountains are in Uganda. This range is also known as "The Mountains of the Moon."

In Uganda, one can work in one hemisphere and live in another. **How is this possible?** The equator runs through Uganda. The equator is an imaginary line that circles Earth. This line, equally distant from both the north and south poles, divides Earth's surface into the northern and southern hemispheres. **What hemisphere do you live in?**

When one hears the word antelope, about what size animal do you think of? Did you think of an animal about the size of a deer? There are many varieties of antelope that live in Uganda. One of them is the dik-dik. This antelope weighs only eight to 10 pounds (3.6 to 4.5 kilograms)!

Many people think of termites as wood-eating pests, but have you ever considered them as a valuable source of protein? Termites in Uganda nest in large colonies. Many of these colonies easily number 10,000 insects. Composed of earth and partially digested wood, the nests, on the exterior, look like large sun baked hills. The hills take about six months to construct, and many of them are larger than a grown man. The nests are actually quite sophisticated, and inside there are tunnels and even little ducts that provide a natural cooling system. The termites even grow some of their own food in their nest—a particular type of fungus. Humans, in turn, can then eat the termites. Fried, they provide a valuable protein supplement.

Uganda gained its independence from England in 1962, but years of political turmoil and military rule have followed. Several coup d'etats have taken place. **What is a *coup d'etat*?** A *coup d'etat* is a French phrase that literally means "blow against the state." When a *coup d'etat* occurs, the government is toppled or taken over, usually with sudden violence and armed forces.

Can there be snow at the equator? Yes! Margherita Peak, 16,762 feet (5113 meters), although near the equator, has permanent snow cover and glaciers at the top. On the lower slopes, there are dense forests. It is the third highest peak in Africa.

Africa

Although a poor country, there are riches when it comes to wildlife. For example, there is a sitatunga antelope here that has webbed feet. It swims, dives, and often feeds in the water. If it wants to hide, it simply submerges. Because this country lies between 8 degrees and 18 degrees south of the equator, it is a tropical land. But the climate is largely mild because of the elevation of the high plateau that makes up this interior nation. The copper mining industry helped to propel this society into the modern world, but much of it remains as it has for years—with subsistence farmers eking out a living in inaccessible places. *Where on Earth are you? Can you find your place?*

Zambia

When Zambia gained independence from the British in 1964, only 120 Zambians held university degrees and 1,000 Zambians had completed secondary education. The numbers are higher today, but much remains to be done. **How will you use your education? Will it help your country progress?**

Zambia was one of the world's top producers of refined copper by the end of WWII. Despite the output, a "color bar" kept Zambian miners in unskilled positions. **What is meant by the term "color bar"?** This term refers to racial discrimination—no matter how smart or industrious a black Zambian miner was before independence, he could not advance beyond a certain level. His color barred him from going further. **Have you ever come across a color, gender, or age bar?**

Zambia has established 18 national parks to conserve different ecologies and their wildlife, including one park that is half the size of Taiwan! Long-necked giraffes are some of the animals one can see in their natural habitat. A human being has seven neck bones. **How many neck bones do you think a giraffe has: 7, 24, 46, or 135?** A giraffe has only seven neck bones, the same as humans, but there is a difference. Each individual neck bone can be over 10 inches (25 cm) high!

Before independence, Zambians engaged in a heated debate as to what language should be chosen as the official language. The two main contenders were English and Swahili. Some felt that English was tainted by colonialism, and they preferred Swahili because it was closely related to Zambian languages. By choosing Swahili, a language spoken in other parts of East Africa, they could help unite Africa while not showing preference for one Zambian language over another. Others felt that it was irrelevant that English had been the language of the colonizers, pointing out that Swahili had been the language of the Zanzibari slave traders who had wreaked havoc in the country before the British. English was chosen, in part because it was the most widely used international language. There are seven local languages that have semi-official status, but all government offices and police and defense forces use English. **If you had to choose a national language for a country today, what factors would you consider and what language would you choose? Would the speakers of the language you choose have an instant head start?**

You're not ever invited to someone's home. **Did you unknowingly insult someone?** It is not the custom in Zambia to invite someone over. Instead, friendly people just show up!

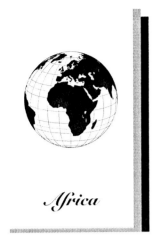

Africa

In 1965, the leader of this British colony signed a Unilateral Declaration of Independence and announced that it was an independent country. The only other colony that had declared its independence illegally, or without British consent, was the United States of America, almost two hundred years before. Britain refused to recognize this country as an independent state, and economic sanctions were set in place, not only by Britain, but by other world nations, too. It wasn't until after a long and terrible civil war that this country became legally and unquestionably independent in 1980. Millions of dollars had been wasted, and over 27,000 lives were lost. Unfortunately, this nation is still witness to violence because of land inequities and the manner in which land reform is being implemented. *Where on Earth are you? Can you find your place?*

Zimbabwe

Landlocked Zimbabwe (then known as Rhodesia, along with some other territory) was declared a British protectorate in 1891. This protectorate was divided in 1896, and annexed as a colony by Great Britain in 1923. Despite blacks being the majority of the population, they had no say in how the country was run. When Ian Smith declared Rhodesia an independent country in 1965, it was to keep intact the system of white rule. Black nationalist activity and guerrilla fighting increased, and violence and fear was rampant. With British help, a new constitution was written, and in 1980, Zimbabwe became legally independent, with Robert Mugabe as its leader. Today, there are power struggles between Zimbabweans from different tribal groups, food shortages, and problems with land division. **How do you view yourself: as a member of a group or a citizen of a country?** For example, Irish, Irish-American, or an American of Irish descent? **Does language help unite you?**

While observing animals from your jeep in one of Zimbabwe's wildlife sanctuaries, you might notice that when two zebras stand side by side, they usually face in opposite directions. **Why? Is it because they have bad breath?** The zebra's line of defense is to detect enemies—like lions, leopards, hyenas, and wild dogs—before they attack. With its eyes set high on the sides of its head, the zebra has a wide range of vision, and it can see over the tops of grasses while its bending down to graze. If a zebra stands in the opposite direction of another, between the two of them, they can spot predators in all directions.

The water tumbling over Victoria Falls, located on the Zambezi River, can be heard up to 10 miles (16 km) away, while the spray can be seen up to 40 miles (64 km) away! In 1855, David Livingston was the first European to see Victoria Falls. **Can it be presumed that you know who Livingston was?** Livingston (1813–1873) was a Scottish missionary medical doctor who had gone to work in South Africa and had become famous because of his exploring. He was the first European to travel the Zambezi River and cross the Kalahari Desert. When he went to find the source of the Nile, people assumed he had died or was lost. A man named Henry Stanley was hired by a newspaper to find him. When the two met up beside Lake Tanganyika, it is said that Stanley uttered this now famous phrase, "Dr. Livingston, I presume."

Welcome to Antarctica!

Map of Antarctica

Antarctica
(page 42)

Antarctica

You are in the driest place in the world. In fact, there is a valley where it has not rained for over two million years. Yet the world's largest, deepest freshwater lake lays hidden near by. As you pull your coat around you, you agree that you are in the world's coldest and windiest place. You are on both an island and a continent. *Where on Earth are you? Can you find your place?*

Antarctica

Despite the snow and ice, Antarctica is the driest continent on Earth. On the polar ice cap, only one to two inches (2.5 to 5 centimeters) of snow falls a year. Only about 2% of Antarctica's land mass is exposed. Dry valleys, where it has not rained for over two million years, are places scientists believe most resemble the planet Mars. Falling snow evaporates before it hits the ground, and the air is so dry that nothing decomposes. There are seal carcasses over 1,000 years old scattered throughout the valleys. **Why is Antarctica considered to be both an island and a continent?** Antarctica is an island because it is surrounded by water on all sides. It is considered a continent because of its size—two times as large as Australia! It is believed that Antarctica was once part of the super continent Gondwana.

More than 90% of Earth's permanent ice is found in Antarctica. Built over countless years by falling snow that never melted, the continent is covered in a colossal ice sheet that contains 68% of the world's fresh water. **How can there be the world's largest freshwater lake if everywhere you look there are glaciers and ice shelves, and icebergs?** Discovered in the 1970s and hidden under 2.5 miles (4 km) of ice, Lake Vostok is 1,764 feet (510 meters) deep. Using radar from a satellite in 1996, scientists calculated that the lake covers more than 5,400 square miles (14,000 square km). Scientists want to drill into the ice and see if there are any living microbes in the water, but they have agreed not to drill until they can find a way to be sure not to contaminate the lake.

All penguins live south of the Equator. **Why are penguins black and white?** The black and white of a penguin is more than a tuxedo. It is a camouflage suit. When a penguin swims nears the surface in the ocean, the white underside blends with the bright light coming from above. This makes the penguin hard to see by leopard seals and other predators swimming below the surface, ready to attack. **How do baby Emperor penguins survive since their parents can't build nests—there is nothing but snow and ice—and they hatch during the coldest months of the Antarctic winter?** Emperor penguins don't need nests because the females lay their eggs on the feet of the males. For six weeks, while winds up to 120 m.p.h. may blow and the temperature may drop to -80°F (-26°C), the males huddle together for warmth and balance the eggs on their feet.

Why is Antarctica colder than the Arctic? The Arctic region is an ocean surrounded by continents; Antarctica is a vast continent surrounded by water. The Arctic Ocean is a source of stored heat, whereas Antarctica's ice reflects more than 80% of the sun's radiation.

Welcome to
Asia!

Map of Asia

Tab

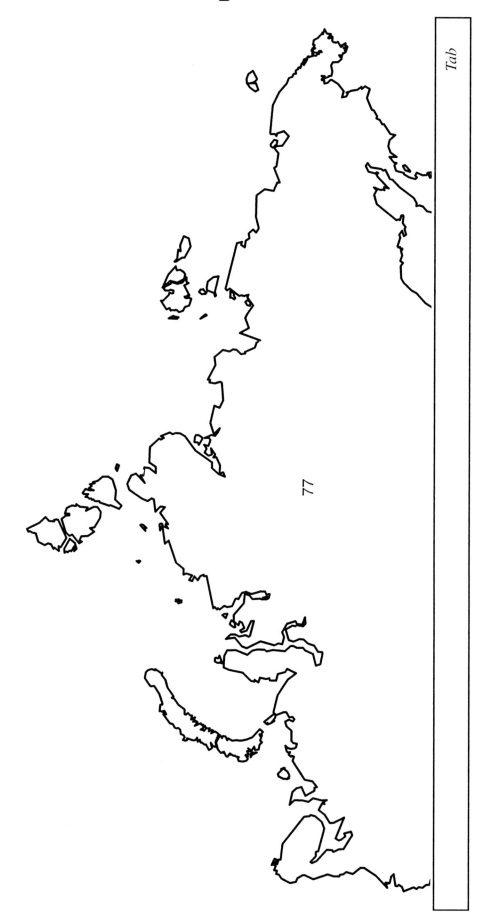

77

Map of Asia *(cont.)*

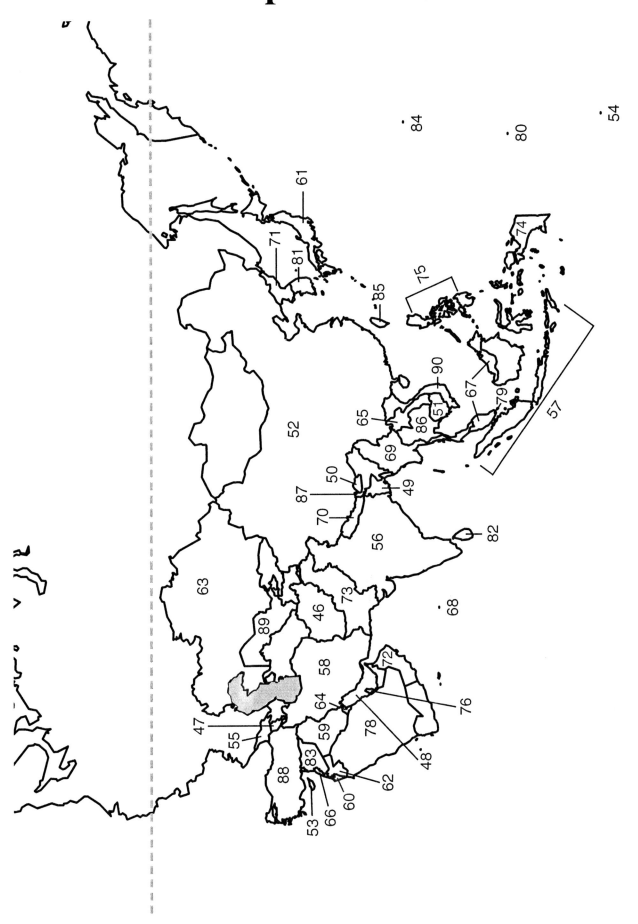

Asia

You are in a country located on ancient trade routes, both north-south and east-west. This country is known for its fierce fighters, but perhaps its people had no choice. There is a long history of warfare and conquest because of its strategic location at the crossroads of ancient Asian trade routes. Over the years, the Persians, Greeks, Mongols, British, and Russians have participated at various times in invasions and strife. Genghis Khan and Alexander the Great have been among the invaders. Recently, even U.S. forces have been deployed there. *Where on Earth are you? Can you find your place?*

Afghanistan

Located in south central Asia, Afghanistan is landlocked, with over half of its area consisting of high plateaus and mountains. Mountains separate the rich, fertile northern provinces from the deserts and plains of the south. Afghanistan has very cold winters and hot, dry summers. **If Afghanistan were not landlocked, do you think its climate would be more moderate?** Yes. Proximity to an ocean or other large body of water helps make the climate less extreme. The water can have both a cooling and a warming effect.

Two of Afghanistan's domesticated animals are favorites in the pet world. They are the Afghan hound and the Persian cat. Many people think that the Persian cat comes from Persia because of its name, but it actually originated in Afghanistan.

There have long been rumors that there are hoards of ancient gold hidden in Afghanistan. When Soviet archeologists found gold at the site of the Tillya-Tepe dig in 1978, the archeologist in charge was said to have told members of his team that he wished they were dealing with pieces of clay pots. **Why?** Pottery or clay tablets with writing often tell more about the past than gold. In addition, gold is stolen more often than broken pieces of pottery. Guards had to be placed around the excavation site, and every day each piece had to be counted.

Islam is the state religion in Afghanistan, and the majority of the people living in Afghanistan are Muslims. All Muslims follow the prophet Muhammad. There are two major groups of Muslims. **Can you name them and the name of the holy book of the Muslims?** The two major groups of Muslims are the Sunnis and the Shiites. Each group has different customs because they interpret Islamic law differently. The majority of the Afghans are Sunni. The holy book of the Muslims, where the revelations from God to Muhammad are compiled, is the Koran.

Many Afghans are refugees. From 1979 to 1993, during the 10-year Soviet invasion and the civil war that followed, more than a million people died and more than 5 million fled the country and became refugees in Pakistan and Iran. In 1996, the UN said that Kabul, the capital city, contained more landmines than any other city in the world. Fighting is still going on in Kabul today. Buildings have been destroyed, and it is very dangerous. **At what point should refugees go back? Should they be forced to return? What if the host country doesn't want them? What if they will be killed if they return?** There are no easy answers to these questions.

Asia

This nation seems like an island, but it is not surrounded by water. Instead, it is rock-bound, rising out of the surrounding lowlands, steppes, and plains. The smallest of the 15 former Soviet Republics, it contains snow-capped mountains, countless ravines and canyons, and one great lake. Only a little over one-third of the land is fit for settled habitation, and nomads follow their herds in the more desolate areas. The handmade rug you are looking at may have been made to go on the floor, but its colors are so vibrant and its design so beautiful that it is more like a piece of art. Anyone up for a game of chess? It's practically a national sport here. *Where on Earth are you? Can you find your place?*

Armenia

Located in southwestern Asia, Armenia became part of the Soviet Union after WWI in 1922. Armenia declared itself an independent nation in 1990, and it withdrew from the Soviet Union in 1991. In 1995, it adopted a constitution that, among other things, provides legal guarantees of civil rights. **What are civil rights?** Civil rights are the nonpolitical rights of a citizen. They are fundamental freedoms guaranteed to every person, regardless of color, religion, or sex. For example, the freedom to live, travel, and use public facilities wherever one chooses are civil rights, as is the right to free expression and action, and the right to enter into contracts, own property, and initiate law suits. **If one cannot buy a house in a particular neighborhood or sit in the front of the bus, is that a violation of one's civil rights? How about if one cannot attend the church of one's choice?**

Both chess and backgammon are popular in Armenia. Armenia has produced many grand masters of chess. Although national champion Gary Kasparov was born in 1963 in Azerbaijan, his mother was Armenian. Kasparov speaks 15 languages, and he was young—only 22—when he won his first World Chess Championship. **What game is younger: chess or backgammon?** Chess can be traced back to India and the 6th century. Backgammon is much older, believed to have originated in Mesopotamia. It may be the oldest game in recorded history.

chess pieces

A terrible thing happened in Armenia's past. In the late 1800s, when most Armenians still lived under harsh Turkish rule, the Turks massacred thousands of Armenians. During WWI, it only got worse. The Turkish government tried to eliminate its entire Armenian population. Nearly one and a half million Armenians were killed in massacres and forced deportations to the Syrian Desert where they were left without food or water. These murders have been called the "first genocide of modern times." **What is *genocide*?** Genocide is the deliberate and systematic destruction of a racial, political, or cultural group. **If you somehow managed to survive, do you think you would ever be able to trust someone outside of your group again?**

Asia

You are very thirsty, so you ask for a drink. You are told to grab your jar and walk out into the ocean. You're not sure you heard correctly because you know the ocean is saltwater. But not wanting to insult your hosts, you do as you are told. Much to your surprise, the water you fill your jar with is indeed fresh. This country has been known for its water for years. Ancient Phoenicians stopped here, as did Alexander the Great in the third century. Even today it is a major port, with huge oil tankers coming to be serviced as well as for supplies. You may be in the first place in the world where a credit card was used! *Where on Earth are you? Can you find your place?*

Bahrain

A small archipelago, Bahrain is located in the Persian (or Arabian) Gulf between Saudi Arabia and the Qatar Peninsula. A 14-mile (23 km) causeway, completed in 1986, connects Bahrain to Saudi Arabia. Although a desert, Bahrain has a number of artesian wells. These are deep wells with water bubbling up to the surface because of underground pressure. The submarine springs are the most remarkable of these, and they are marked by iron bars pounded into the seabed. Fresh water bubbles up so forcefully there that one can indeed wade out and fill up jars with fresh water.

Artifacts have been found in Bahrain that are believed to be the world's first credit cards. Carved from shell or stone, each had its own individual seal that acted as its owner's signature. Seals were guarded and handed down from one family member to another. They were imprinted into wet clay attached to shipments. These seals were respected from India to the Mediterranean from 2,000 B.C.

Bahrain is a monarchy where strict rules of primogeniture are enforced. **What does *primogeniture* mean?** Primogeniture is when the first son inherits everything after the death of his father. **Why might some agree with this method?** Primogeniture keeps large estates in one family; they are not divided up between children. One might not like this system if one was a second child or a female.

pearl

Though not important today, pearling was an important source of revenue for Bahrain for years. Dangers were extreme for pearl divers: they risked sharks, sea snakes, rays, and jellyfish. But in 1929, one gulf pearl sold for $100,000! **Pearl divers used leather thimbles and beeswax. Can you think why?** Leather thimbles protected the divers from sharp coral, and a wad of beeswax was used to plug each ear. Nose clips were made from bone or tortoiseshell. Fifty dives a day were common, and divers worked in water anywhere from 30 to 120 feet (9–36 meters) deep.

Bahrain's first oil well was drilled in 1931. Bahrain's "black gold" is just a drop compared to other Middle East oil producers, but Bahrain has spent its oil money wisely. In preparation of its fields drying up, Bahrain has developed other sources of income, like shipbuilding and repair yards, a first-rate airport, manufacturing, and banking.

You are in a country that has been born twice. First there was the fight for independence to protect its religion, and then the fight for independence to protect its language. Everywhere you look you see water, but that is not surprising. A large portion of the country is permanently flooded because the land is flat and monsoons bring heavy rain. There is also an extensive and intricate web of rivers, providing the principal means of transportation and bringing rich alluvial soil to form the Ganges Delta. Did you hear a tiger roar? *Where on Earth are you? Can you find your place?*

Bangladesh

In 1947, under the provisions of the Indian Independence Act, India was given independence from Britain, and Pakistan became a separate nation. It was hoped that the idea of a separate Muslim state (Pakistan) would stop Hindu and Muslim conflicts. Bangladesh (then called East Bengal and later renamed East Pakistan) became an eastern province of Pakistan. But there was a strong feeling in East Pakistan that their leaders, mainly from West Pakistan, were not representing all of the people. For example, Urdu was declared the national language, when only 3% of the people spoke Urdu and 56% spoke Bengali. A civil war erupted in 1971 when the president of Pakistan (from West Pakistan) did not like the election results and postponed the opening of the National Assembly. With the help of Indian troops, Bangladesh became an independent country in 1972.

The Bengal tiger, the national animal, lives in protected parks in Bangladesh. **How is a tiger's face like your thumb?** No two tigers have the same stripe pattern, just as no two people have the same thumbprint. A tiger's stripes make it easier for it to hide: the stripes blend perfectly with the grass. In the jungle, they look like streaks of shadow and sunlight.

What is the acceptable way of sitting in Bangladesh? Men may sit cross-legged. Women may sit with their legs tucked beneath them and to one side on the floor or cushions. But neither men nor women may sit so that the soles of their feet show (think of how westerners often cross one leg over and rest it on the other.) Exposing the soles of one's feet to someone is a big insult. **Is it important for a visitor to learn the social customs and body language of the country one visits?**

Bangladesh is one of the poorest countries in the world. Malnutrition and poor sanitation cause hundreds of deaths every year. There are not enough schools or hospitals. **Despite free primary school education in Bangladesh, many children do not attend; and there is a high illiteracy rate. Why?** When there are more immediate needs, such as food, to be met, there is little incentive for a parent to send a child to school. If a child does go, it is more likely to be a boy than a girl. Girls are kept at home to help with the household chores.

Most marriages are arranged—the bride's father or another male guardian sets it up. **How do you expect to meet your future wife or husband?**

Asia

Before the first roads were built in 1960, even royalty had to travel by foot and muleback in this tiny landlocked nation located on the "Roof of the World." No one grovels in the mud when the king visits, for everyone—even the king—is equal under the law. There is one way though to tell who the king is, even if he is sitting among schoolchildren or farmers on the floor. It is by the color of the scarf he wears over his left shoulder and draped across his body. Scarves are worn not for warmth, but to show status. Only the king and the chief abbot are allowed to wear saffron-colored (orange-yellow) scarves. *Where on Earth are you? Can you find your place?*

Bhutan

One of the most ruggedly mountainous countries in the world, Bhutan is bordered by China and India. Much of the country lies in the Himalayas, the "Roof of the World." From south to north, the country rises from a narrow semitropical strip to an elevation of over 24,615 feet (7,500 m). Over the years, Bhutan has had dealings with the British and was forced to guarantee Britain's trade interests. Bhutan was recognized as an independent country when India received its independence from Britain. In 1949 the two countries signed a treaty in which land was returned and Bhutan agreed to be guided in its foreign affairs by India. Bhutan is controlled by a hereditary monarchy, and the recent king ascended to the throne in 1974, when he was only 17 years old. It is this king who is credited as the architect of modern education. He also set up a system of free national health care. Not only has he built roads and initiated conservation programs, but he has broadened diplomatic representation and introduced democratic reforms that grant power to the legislature and reduce the power of the monarch. **Do you think you will have the maturity at the age of 17 take on the reign of a country?**

An isolated country, Bhutan has limited the number of tourists allowed to enter the country. (Tourists were not allowed in until after 1974, and at that time, only 200 were allowed in per year.) Each tourist has to pay a set amount of money per day to remain in the country. **Do you think this kept tourists away?** No, it only made the country more desirable. **What does this tell you about supply and demand?** When supply is limited, the demand goes up.

Almost 90% of the Bhutanese still live as their ancestors did centuries ago. The government is working on getting electricity into homes and schools, and many development projects are being introduced. **Why do you think an attempt to expand its domestic silk industry did not work?** Presently, the Bhutanese allow silkworms to eat their way out of their silk cocoons. In order for the industry to expand, long threads of silk would be needed, and for that, one has to throw living silkworm cocoons into hot water, thus killing the worms before they damage their cocoons. The national religion of Bhutan is Tantric Buddhism; and because Tantric Buddhists believe in reincarnation, they believe that killing the worms prevents them from fulfilling their destiny.

Asia

You are at the largest religious building in the world. This beautiful temple, built in the twelfth century, extends for over half a mile long on either side. What makes it even more unique is that it is the only structure of that time period built facing west rather than east. The longest day of the year in the Northern Hemisphere is June 21, and on this day, the sun rises directly behind the temple's central tower. Because of this, it is believed that ancient astronomers used the temple as a base for studying the movements of the planets and stars. *Where on Earth are you? Can you find your place?*

Cambodia

Located in Southeast Asia, Cambodia is a country that has recently suffered great political strife and hard times. Yet Cambodia has a rich artistic heritage that can be seen in its many stone monuments and temples. Angkor Wat, the largest religious building in the world, is in Cambodia. The ancient city of Angkor Thom, with over 50 towers and over 11,000 wall carvings depicting everyday life, is also there.

Some of the carvings on the walls of Angkor Thom show people riding on elephants. **How do the elephants found in Cambodia differ from those found in Africa?** Asiatic (or Indian) elephants have smaller ears. Only the males have tusks, and the back bends up in the middle. In African elephants, both the male and female have tusks, and their back bends down in the middle. Asiatic elephants are easier to train than African elephants. They are still used today to do heavy work in some parts of southern Asia.

Many houses in Cambodia are built on stilts. **Do you think there is a connection with the weather?** Cambodia has a monsoonal climate. Monsoons are winds that change directions twice a year. When the monsoon winds blow across the land to the ocean from November to April, the days are sunny, clear, and dry. But when the monsoon winds change direction, blowing across the ocean toward the land, they carry water. Thus, from May to October, it rains every day, usually for an hour or so in the afternoon. By the end of the rainy season, the soil is saturated. Most of the country, roads and rice fields included, is covered with a foot (.3 m) of water.

Is it cold in Cambodia with all that rain? Cambodia is warm because it lies close to the equator in the tropics. Daytime temperatures are about 80°F (27°C), and at night it only falls to 60°F (15°C).

Cambodia's national language is Khmer. One just can't say "you" in Khmer. Pronouns are used to signify a person's social status, and so the "you" one uses depends on whether one is speaking to a child, a parent, a Buddhist monk, or a member of the royal family. **How does your choice of words reflect familiarity or deference (respect)?**

Livestock production is important in Cambodia because a supply of draft animals is needed. **What are draft animals?** Draft animals are animals that are used for pulling or hauling loads, as well as transportation. Getting around in ox-carts is common in Cambodia. **Can you think of another meaning for *draft*?**

Asia

You are on a wall. A wall may sound like a simple structure, but the one you are standing on is one of the largest engineering and building projects ever carried out by mankind. It starts to rain, so you put up your umbrella and wipe off your glasses. You look at the piece of paper that has directions printed on it. After checking the direction with a compass, you set off. You may not know it, but you are in the country where umbrellas, eyeglasses, paper, printing, and compasses were invented. *Where on Earth are you? Can you find your place?*

China

The Great Wall of China is truly one of the world's greatest engineering and building projects ever carried out. Started in the third century B.C. when the Chinese emperor joined a series of walls built by previous warring states, The Great Wall is about 1,500 miles (2,414 km) long. The walls were used to keep out invaders and to launch attacks. Prisoners and criminals were used to link the walls, as well as ordinary men and women. Often, they were hungry and cold. When the workers died, their bodies were sometimes thrown into the structure and covered by bricks. The wall has been rebuilt several times.

There are four inventions from China that are often referred to as "The Four Great Inventions of Ancient China." Paper, printing, and the compass make the list. Paper money, kites, the mechanical clock, gunpowder, and the washboard are also Chinese inventions. **Which one of these inventions makes the "Four Greatest" list?** Gunpowder. It was accidentally discovered when alchemists were trying to make immortality pills!

China is known for its Great Wall, but there is something else that stands as a magnificent achievement of ancient China. It was constructed with forced labor, including female workers, and it took 1,779 years to build. **What is it?** It's the Great Canal, which was started in 486 B.C. and finished in A.D. 1293. It is 1,115 miles (1,794 km) long. It begins in Beijing and ends in Hangzhou, linking the Hai, Yellow, Yangze, and Qiantang Rivers. Today, China is constructing what will be the world's largest dam.

Pandas are known as China's ambassadors because people like them so much. **What do pandas mainly eat, and how does this affect their chances of survival?** A panda's diet consists mainly of bamboo. There are hundreds of different kinds of bamboo, but pandas are limited to only about 20 types. In one year alone, a panda can eat more than 10,000 pounds (4,500 kg) of bamboo, spending up to 16 hours a day eating. Eating a specialized diet makes it difficult for the panda to survive in today's world because there has to be enough land reserved for the type of bamboo that a panda likes to eat. As China's population increases, this becomes more and more difficult.

China is the most populous country in the world and there are hundreds of dialects. Yet the first emperor did something back in 221 B.C. that made it possible for everyone to understand each other. **What did he do?** He standardized written characters. This written link from the past to the present is unique in the world.

Asia

You are on the third largest island in this sea. Starting from the 14th century B.C., this country has been a prize for, among others, the Mycenaeans, Ionians, Phoenicians, Assyrians, Persians, and the Romans. It's been captured by Arabs as well as by Richard I of England during the Third Crusade in 1191. It's been attacked by the Republic of Venice, and it was made part of the Ottoman (or Turkish) Empire in 1572. It finally gained independence from the British in 1960, but armed strife between Greek and Turkish sectors of the population necessitated United Nations Peacekeeping forces. Since 1974 Turkish troops have occupied the northern third of the island. *Where on Earth are you? Can you find your place?*

Cyprus

Located in the eastern corner of the Mediterranean Sea, Cyprus is easily accessible from Europe, Asia Minor, and the Middle East. **What territory makes up Asia Minor, and what two islands in the Mediterranean are larger than Cyprus?** Asia Minor is the peninsula forming the western extremity of Asia, between the Black Sea on the north, the Mediterranean Sea on the south, and the Aegean Sea on the west. The greater part of Turkey lies in Asia Minor. Sicily and Sardinia are larger than Cyprus.

What was it that archaeologists found that told them that even the earliest inhabitants of the island from the Neolithic Era (New Stone Age) had contact with the outside world? (Hint: do you know your rocks?) Archaeologists found tools made of obsidian, a glossy black stone not native to Cyprus. The obsidian probably came from Turkey and Mylos, an island in the Aegean Sea.

Houses in the rural areas of Cyprus have stayed virtually unchanged since early times. **In the lowland areas, roofs are often flat. Why?** Constructed from earth that rests on reeds or a wattle of woven sticks, flat roofs provide a safe place to dry agricultural produce and a sleeping area during the hot summer months. Because of its warm Mediterranean climate, which is dry except for some winter rainfall, Cyprus has six months of summer with an average of 11 1/2 hours each day of cloudless weather.

A "Green Line" runs through Cyprus. **What is the "Green Line?"** The "Green Line" is the line patrolled by United Nations peacekeeping forces that separates the Turkish Cypriots (the minority population) in the north from the Greek Cypriots in the south. Turkish troops remain to this day in Northern Cyprus, and they occupy some of the best farmlands. In 1983, the north declared itself the Turkish Republic of Northern Cyprus, but only Turkey recognizes its sovereignty. For 3,000 years, Greek and Turkish Cypriots were able to intermingle and live together, but today many Greek Cypriots have become refugees in their own country. **How can the United Nations help resolve this conflict? Did you know that the UN had peacekeeping forces?**

Some of the most important art forms in Cyprus are music and dance, with certain melodies retaining an ancient Greek style. Some dances can be traced back to ancient origins. **Would you rather watch a dance or visit an art museum? Which art form do you think would be easier to keep intact or save as part of your heritage?**

Asia

This country was once known notoriously as the "Cannibal Isles." Due to the belief that all shipwrecked voyagers had been cursed and abandoned by the gods, a most horrible fated waited those unlucky enough to wash up on shore. Cannibalism, of course, is no longer practiced and today is only part of history. The first European to see these islands was Dutch navigator Abel Tasman in 1643, and Captain James Robert Cook was the first English explorer to land there in 1774. As early as 1804, escaped convicts from Australia were making their way to these tropical shores. *Where on Earth are you? Can you find your place?*

Fiji

Located in the southwest Pacific Ocean, Fiji gained its independence from Britain in 1970. About 100 of Fiji's 800 islands and islets are inhabited. The eastern sides of Fiji's main islands are covered in dense tropical forests while the western sides are covered in dry grasslands and patches of scrub. **What do you think is the cause?** The amount of rainfall. The windward or southeastern sides receive up to 120 inches (3,050 mm), while the leeward or northwestern sides receive only 70 inches (1,780 mm).

One of the animals in Fiji that one needs to watch out for is the centipede. Fijian centipedes, which are nocturnal creatures, can grow up to 7 inches (18 cm) long and may inflict a painful sting through its front legs. Centipedes are often confused with millipedes. **What separates centipedes from millipedes?** Although centipedes in Fiji can have anywhere between 15 to 180 pairs of legs, they have only one pair of legs per body section, whereas millipedes have two.

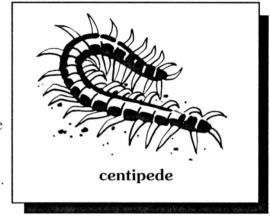

centipede

The ocean surrounding its islands is very important to Fijians. Tourists come to enjoy its blue waters and reefs, and fishing is one of Fiji's chief occupations. **If one happens to be stung or injured by a marine animal, why is it advised (if a hospital or clinic is unavailable) to soak both the injured part and a noninjured part in very hot water for 30 minutes?** Venom from marine animals is usually destroyed by heat. The afflicted area often goes numb as a result of the poison, and therefore one may not realize if the water is too hot. An uninjured hand or foot in the water insures that one can accurately feel the water temperature, thereby decreasing the risk of scalding.

Chief Cakobau was a brilliant strategist who ruled Fiji with iron-fisted power for half a century. During his reign, Fiji became politically consolidated and ceded to Britain. Cakobau was known for warring, but there was one thing he brought back from a visit to Australia in 1875 that killed one-third of the entire Fijian population without Cakobau raising a weapon. **What was it?** When Cakobau returned with two of his sons from a visit to Australia, they were infected with the measles. They survived, but one-third of the population did not. Today, immunization and vaccination programs have greatly eliminated the danger of this disease. **Many people feel immunizations should be mandatory for all, while others feel it should be up to individuals. What do you think?**

Although there is an American state with this same name, you are not in the United States. You are separated from Russia by mountains higher than the Alps—the magnificent Caucasus Mountains. Your capital has been destroyed an estimated 29 times, all by different conquerors. Speaking of conquerors, this country is the birthplace of one of the world's cruelest and most ruthless dictators. The country may not be very old—independence was declared only in 1991, but there are plenty of centenarians around to make up for it. *Where on Earth are you? Can you find your place?*

Asia

Georgia

Georgia used to be part of the Union of Soviet Socialist Republics, also known as the U.S.S.R. The U.S.S.R. was a large Eastern European and Northern Asian nation that consisted of 15 member-republics from 1922 to 1991. Georgia was included in the U.S.S.R. in 1936, and it became a fully independent state in 1991 and a member of the United Nations since 1992. The U.S.S.R. supported communism. **What is *communism*?** Communism is an economic system in which the government owns all the farmland and the means of producing goods in factories.

What is a *centenarian*? A centenarian is someone who is over 100 years old. **Do you see the similarity between the words *century* and *centenarian*? What do you think a *centennial* is?** It's a 100th anniversary celebration. Georgians are famous for their longevity, with the republic claiming 51 centenarians for every 100,000 inhabitants. Some people think Georgian's longevity is partly due to their healthy diet that includes vast amounts of yogurt and fresh vegetables.

Joseph Stalin (1879–1953) was born in Georgia. He was anti-tsarist, but he did not believe in independence for Georgia. He felt Georgia's salvation lay in becoming part of a greater political structure. It is estimated that as many as 20 million Russians died as a result of his policies of forced collectivization and political purges. Many more were imprisoned. Yet during WWII, because he led the Soviet Union to victory over the Germans, Stalin gained a reputation of being a great war leader. **What does it mean to be *anti-tsarist*?** A tsar or a czar is the name given to Russian emperors. If one is anti-tsarist, one is against the tsars. The Russian Revolution occurred in 1917, and led by Lenin, the tsarist army was defeated by the Bolsheviks. In 1921, the Bolshevik Red Army marched into Georgia and took control. Stalin replaced Lenin.

Georgia is ranked in the top 10 countries in the world for this sport. It involves a board and playing pieces that include a king, queen, knights, bishops and castles. **What is the game?** Chess. Georgian women have done especially well in chess, and one Georgian woman was the women's world champion from 1962–1978, only to be ousted by a fellow Georgian (a 17 year old!) who then held the title for 13 years. **What words does one speak when one has won?** One says "check" when an opponent's king is in immediate danger and "checkmate" when there is no safe move for the king to make.

Asia

Chess began in this country more than 1,000 years ago in the sixth century. Princes played games on huge fields, with servants acting out the parts of horsemen, archers, chariots, and elephants. Polo, a game played on horseback, was also played by princes and noblemen in this country, the seventh largest in the world. Polo began as a training exercise for the army and was brought to the country by the Moguls (a Muslim people of central Asia, who conquered and ruled this country for centuries, starting in 1526). In turn, when the British took control, they were so enamored by the action, that they played it too, and today it has become a worldwide sport. *Where on Earth are you? Can you find your place?*

India

Today, India is a democratic republic. In 1947 independence was gained from the British (who conquered all of India in 1857). The British had been involved in India since the 1600s, making huge sums of money from trading in spices, silk, cloth, and later tea; and it behooved them to control the country entirely. Feeling that they were being discriminated against in their own land, Indians fought for independence. They ultimately won the battle through civil disobedience. **What is *civil disobedience*?** Civil disobedience is when one peacefully protests, without violence. One refuses to obey unfair laws by using nonviolent methods, perhaps by marching or striking (refusing to work). **Can you name the famous lawyer who was instrumental in successfully leading India to independence by use of this method?** Mohandes Gandhi (1869–1948) is regarded as the father of independent India. He was arrested several times by the British, but Gandhi was always released when he threatened to fast until death. The British knew that he would, and they were afraid of what his many followers would do if he died.

What Indian entertainment industry is the largest in the world? The movie industry. People outside India may think that the movie industry would be larger in the United States, but Indians love movies. Having the second largest population in the world, second only to China, there are plenty of people to watch movies.

The Taj Mahal is one of the most famous sights in all of the world. **What is the Taj Mahal?** The Taj Mahal is a beautiful mausoleum that holds the tomb of Mumtaz, the favorite wife of Shah Jahan who was one of the last of the Mogul rulers. Mumtaz in 1629 died while giving birth to her fourteenth child. It took almost 20 years to build, and it has been said that more than 20,000 workers and 1,000 elephants were used.

India is a diverse population. There are more than 200 languages and 1,600 dialects, with about one-third of the people speaking Hindi. More than three-quarters of Indians are Hindus, with the second-largest religion being Islam. The caste system is part of the Hindu religion, and though it is illegal, there are still many people that others consider "untouchables," those of the lowest caste. The "untouchables" work with "unclean" objects, like garbage or sewage. **Do you think someone's place in life should be determined by birth?**

Asia

Someone is talking to you, and because you do not want to seem as if you are challenging them, you do not make eye contact. You look down, and you see a little child. You know that it is a grave insult to pat this child, or any child, on the head so you refrain from doing so. You see what you think is an orangutan in a tree. You point to the creature, asking what it is. When you point, you point only with your thumb. If you used any other finger it would be considered rude. Could it be an orange man? *Where on Earth are you? Can you find your place?*

Indonesia

A nation of over 17,500 islands, Indonesia stretches 3,200 miles between the Indian and Pacific Oceans and covers an area two and a half times that of Australia. Sounds enormous, but 80% of Indonesia is water. The islands vary in size and climate, with the biggest being Sumatra, Java, Kalimantan (on Borneo, the world's third largest island), Sulawesi, and Irian Jaya (on New Guinea, the world's second largest island). Indonesia is the fourth most populated country in the world, and more Muslims live in Indonesia than any other country on Earth.

In Indonesia, smiling does not necessarily mean one is happy. Indonesians may smile when they are sad or giving bad news. **Why would it be important to know this?**

The only place orangutans live in the world is on the islands of Borneo and Sumatra. The word *orangutan* literally means "man of the jungle." Orangutans are the largest animals in the world that live on fruit. Orangutans inhabit trees. **Which one goes the highest in a tree: the youngest orangutan or the oldest?** The youngest. It's lighter; the branches don't have to be as sturdy.

Indonesia is one of the world's largest producers of oil. It also produces many of the world's spices. The Moluccas are a group of islands in Indonesia that were known to the ancient world, and today, as the Spice Islands. Spices were needed to cover up the taste of not so fresh food! Indonesia gained independence on August 17, 1945. Until the Japanese invaded during WWII, Indonesia had been ruled by the Dutch, who wanted the spices. Indonesia's motto became "Unity Through Diversity." **Why do you think this motto was chosen?** With so many islands and different peoples, it was necessary to view differences as an asset, not a liability. A national language, Bahasa Indonesian, was chosen so that everyone could communicate, no matter a person's local dialect.

A dragon is found in Indonesia. What type? The fierce Komodo dragon has survived for millions of years in Indonesia on the island of Komodo. These giant lizards eat meat, using razor-sharp teeth to rip apart goats, deer, and wild pigs. They can grow up to 10 feet (3 m) and weigh 300 pounds (136 kg).

The world's largest flower, the rafflesia, grows in Indonesia. Its petals can grow to 39 inches (1 m), and it can weigh 20 pounds (9 kg).

komodo dragon

Asia

Though now grown throughout the world, it was in this country where the pistachio tree first grew. The oldest equestrian sport also originated here. Oil rich and with plenty of natural gas, this nation has just one volcano, but it stands out: it's the tallest mountain in all of western Asia. While sitting on your beautiful carpet, colorful and handmade, you open a book, making sure that you read the proper way: from right to left. *Where on Earth are you? Can you find your place?*

Iran

A nation of plateaus and mountains, Iran has plenty of neighbors: seven countries and three bodies of water. Those countries include Turkmenistan, Afghanistan, Pakistan, Iraq, Turkey, Azerbaijan, and Armenia, while the water includes the Caspian Sea, the Persian Gulf, and the Gulf of Oman. Before 1935, Iran was known by another name. **Do you know what that name was?** Persia. Around 500 B.C., Cyrus the Great founded the Persian Empire when he started conquering surrounding lands. At one point, the Persian Empire extended from the Indus River to the Mediterranean and from the Caucasus Mountains to the Indian Ocean. At a later point, it even included Egypt. This magnificent empire lost territory to Greece during the Persian Wars, to Egypt when it revolted, and later to Alexander the Great. It then flourished again, but finally came to an end in 642 when Muslim Arabs successfully invaded. It was at this time that many people were converted to Islam. Despite other invaders over the years, Iran has remained an Islamic country.

What is the oldest equestrian sport? Polo. Polo is a game played on horseback where two teams use mallets (wooden hammers) with long flexible handles to drive a wooden ball between two goal posts. Today, there are only four players per team, but when the game started in Iran (dates have been given from the 6th century B.C. to the 1st century A.D.), polo was a training game for elite (the finest or the best) troops. Sometimes, there would be over 100 tribesmen on each side!

In 1979, the shah (king) of Iran was forced to leave, and the Islamic religious leader Ayatollah Khomeini, returning from 15 years of exile, took over. Khomeini engaged the country in an Islamic Revolution where western ideas and clothes were thrown out. A strict code of religious laws was enforced, and women were forced to cover themselves from head to toe. **Should one be forced to follow religious laws? Should a religious law take precedence over a civil law?**

Would you expect to find pork in an Iranian market? No, the Islamic religion prohibits the consumption of pork, as well as wine and other alcoholic drinks.

Why are towns in Iran often located a short distance from the foot of a mountain? Water is scarce in Iran, and most towns are supplied by an irrigation system in which water from an underground mountain source is tapped and channeled down through a series of tunnels to the town level. Some of these tunnels measure 50 miles (80 km) in length.

Asia

You are in what has been called "the cradle of civilization." The ancient Sumerians lived here sometime between 3500 and 3000 B.C. You look down at your watch, and you remember that it was the Sumerians who, with their mathematical system based on the number 60, devised the 60-minute hour. Looking at the cultivated fields, you think how the invention of the plow—another Sumerian invention—has changed the world. Some say the single invention that changed the world more than anything else was the wheel, and once again, credit goes to the Sumerians. How different it is today! The Sumerians are long gone, and today oil is the country's most valuable natural resource. *Where on Earth are you? Can you find your place?*

Iraq

Ancient Iraq was known as Mesopotamia. In 1921, after WWI, a kingdom was established from Turkish territory. It became a British mandate until its independence in 1932. Saddam Hussein became president in 1979. He invaded Iran and Kuwait, provoking the eight-year Iran-Iraq War (1980–88) and the Persian Gulf War (1991). It is sad to think that a country once known for its contributions to civilization is now known for a leader who used banned chemical weapons on Iranians and his own citizens, the non-Arab minority Kurds. The Kurds who live in northeastern Iraq, have sought autonomy since independence. There is no excuse for the evil of Hussein, but some feel that guilt for chemical weapons extends to those companies in other countries who sold Iraq the materials. **What do you think?**

The development and use of the number zero is credited to Muhammad Ibn Musa al-Khwarizmi. Al-Khwarizmi was born around 780 in Baghdad, the capital of Iraq. He introduced Hindu-Arabic numbers (what we use) and the concepts of algebra into European mathematics. Al-Khwarizmi was the first to use the zero as a placeholder in positional base notation. The Mayans had a zero symbol, but it didn't work with calculations because of their inconsistencies in base notation. The Egyptians sporadically used a zero, but it was never at the end of a number. It was only used between two numbers to indicate an empty position.

Someone comes to you and wants to sell you a vase with a finely detailed picture of a boy watching over his animals on it. "It's worth a million," you are told. "It's an authentic Islamic Iraqi piece of art." "No," you say, "This is a fake. I'm calling the authorities." **How did you know?** Islamic art forbids the portrayal of human or animal forms. Not only is the artist not from Iraq, he or she isn't from any Muslim country. Islamic art is filled with intricate designs and magnificent colors.

The airport in Iraq has been shut down, and you can't land. You are told there is no visibility. **What could be the cause?** A dry wind from the south called a *sharqi*. A *sharqi* can carry dust high into the air and gust up to 50 miles (80 km) an hour.

Asia

You are in the holy land for three of the world's great religions: Judaism, Islam, and Christianity. The "Wailing Wall," all that remains of the Western Wall after the Romans destroyed the Temple in Jerusalem in A.D. 70, is one of the holiest cites for Jews. There is the mosque where the Muslim prophet Muhammad is said to have ascended to heaven, and there is the city of Bethlehem, believed to be the birthplace of Jesus Christ. What an intersection of ancient and modern cultures and beliefs! *Where on Earth are you? Can you find your place?*

Israel

Israel declared itself an independent state on May 14, 1948. After WWI, the newly formed League of Nations granted authority over Palestine (modern day Israel and Jordan) to Britain. The British divided Palestine in 1922, and Jordan became a separate kingdom. More Jews began to immigrate to Palestine because they were persecuted in other parts of the world. Immigration was restricted to keep the number of Jews down, and the restriction remained in place during WWII, even as 6 million Jews were murdered in Europe. The British renounced their mandate to govern Palestine in 1947, and the United Nations then recommended separate Jewish and Arab states, with Jerusalem having special international status.

Despite the Arab rejection of this proposal, Israel declared its independence. Iraq, Syria, Egypt, Jordan, and Lebanon immediately attacked Israel, but Israel survived. There were more wars, one in the Sinai Desert in 1956 and another in 1967. One of the results of the 1967 "Six-Day War," as it has become known, was the reunification of Jerusalem; the take over of the Gaza Strip, the Sinai, and the Golan Heights; and the occupation of the West Bank. Today, some land has been returned, like the Sinai, but there are still violent and passionate disputes about territory. **What decides ownership: history? defense? might? Do you think it is possible to have a city with international jurisdiction?**

Why is it that everyone can float—even non-swimmers—in the Dead Sea, and does the answer have anything to do with the fact that wooden boats are used to cross it? The Dead Sea is really an inland lake. At 1,312 feet (400 m) below sea level, the Dead Sea is lower than any other inland sea in the world. Because the mineral content of the water is so high, even non-swimmers float. (To see how this works on a smaller scale, put an egg in a cup of water and begin to add salt. At some point, there will be so much salt in the water that the egg will begin to float.) Wooden boats are used because they withstand the high salt and mineral content best. Just so you know, it's not completely dead! There are at least 11 types of bacteria found in the Dead Sea.

What does the word *zealot* mean? A zealot is someone who is very passionate or enthusiastic about something. Back in A.D. 70, when Jerusalem fell to the Romans, freedom fighters known as the Zealots took refuge in a fortress known as Masada. It took 15,000 Romans and almost two years to defeat the fewer than 1,000 Zealots. The Zealots zealously defended their freedom.

Asia

It's Saturday, but you are in school because classes meet 5½ days a week. You are wearing a uniform like everyone else, and you and your schoolmates are responsible for cleaning your own school. Competition is very tough, beginning as early as kindergarten, and many of you go to juku or cram schools for several hours every day after your normal seven-hour school day to get extra tutoring for the examinations you must take to get to the next level. This doesn't leave much time to play. Good thing the train you commute to school on goes so fast. As a matter of fact, the bullet train you ride is the fastest in the world. It goes at speeds of more than 180 miles (290 km) an hour. *Where on Earth are you? Can you find your place?*

Japan

Known as the "Land of the Rising Sun," Japan is made up of over 3,900 mountainous islands, all in a bow-shaped cluster. Japan is an archipelago. **What is an *archipelago*?** An archipelago is a group or chain of many islands in the sea. **Can you think of some other archipelagos?** Examples include Hawaii, the Galapagos Islands, and the Samoa Islands.

Japan is part of Asia, but it is also part of the Pacific Rim, a great circle of lands bordering the Pacific Ocean. **Can you think of some other countries besides Japan that make up the Pacific Rim?** The Philippines, Indonesia, Australia, Chile, and two U.S. states: California and Alaska. Pacific Rim countries share many geographical features as well as trade ties.

Earthquakes shake Japan thousands of time a year. Tsunamis, often called tidal waves, also strike. **Why is Japan afflicted with so many natural disasters?** Japan rests on top of four tectonic plates. These plates still meet and continue to move against each other, resulting in earthquakes and volcanic eruptions. Japan has over 250 volcanoes, 67 of which are "live" (meaning they are active or potentially active.). Tsunamis are waves that are started by underwater volcanoes or offshore earthquakes. By the time the waves crash against the shore, they may be moving at over 100 miles (161 km) an hour and may reach 100 feet (30.3 m) high. Tokyo today is one of the greatest cities in the world and its buildings have been constructed under tight earthquake building codes. But in 1923, Tokyo was destroyed by an earthquake. In the earthquake and the fires that resulted, over 100,000 people died.

One of the world's largest markets is in Japan. It starts early and is usually done by 8:00 A.M. **What do you think is sold?** The world's largest fish market is in Tsukji, on Tokyo Bay. Fresh catches are delivered early in the morning. Over 2,500 tons of fish are sold per day with over 400 species to choose from. There is a separate auction for tuna alone, and on the average, one tuna is sold every four seconds.

There is a special name for the art of paper folding. One can fold paper into cranes, frogs, birds, masks, and many other things. **What is this art form called?** The answer is *origami*.

Asia

There is a special police branch in this country that patrols on camels. With the decline of the traditional Bedouin lifestyle, they aren't really needed any longer to keep peace among warring tribes, but they continue to assist any desert traveler who needs help. Although Bedouins who still live a traditional nomadic lifestyle account for less than 1% of the population, they are guaranteed legislative representation, as are other minorities. This ensures that even minority groups are represented and their rights protected. This country was once part of Greater Syria before it was divided by the European powers after WWI. *Where on Earth are you? Can you find your place?*

Jordan

Before Jordan was known as Jordan (it was renamed in 1946), it was known as Transjordan, a name given by the Ottoman Turks who took over the area in the mid-16th century. **Would this name make sense if you were told that the Ottomans used Transjordan primarily as a land corridor—a passage from the northern area to the holy cities of Mecca and Medina?** The root *trans* means "across," and Transjordan was simply a place to cross. **How does knowing the meaning of the root** *trans* **help one to decipher the meaning of** *transportation, transform, transcribe, translate, transfusion, transient,* **and** *transpacific?*

oryx

The Arabian oryx is a large and beautiful antelope that is able to live in harsh desert environments. It was near extinction because of indiscriminate hunting by man, but when the Arabian Oryx World Herd Trustees was established in 1962, 14 oryxes were shipped from Oman, Germany, Switzerland, Saudi Arabia, Qatar, and the United States to three special American zoos for breeding. In 1983, eight oryxes from these special zoos were sent to Jordan so that a viable population could once again establish itself. **How much effort should we put into saving a species? Do you think oryxes for the breeding program were solicited from different zoos to insure genetic variety? Is it important for zoos to keep extensive genealogical records of all their animals?**

There is an extraordinarily forbidding black wasteland in Jordan's northeastern desert. **What makes it black?** Volcanic mountains, small cinder cones, and vast fields of sharp, rough, black lava rocks compose this bleak moonscape.

An Arab people called the Nabataeans built a great city called Petra in the 4th century. A true hidden city, Petra is carved into Jordan's sandstone cliffs hundreds of feet high in a network of canyons. Its main entrance is through a narrow winding gorge between 65-foot cliffs, accessible only on foot or by camel and horse. Conquering Romans in the 2nd century found the city's only weakness and succeeded in overcoming the Nabataeans. **What do you think Petra's weakness was?** The Romans found Petra's water source. When they dammed it, they were able to defeat the Nabataeans.

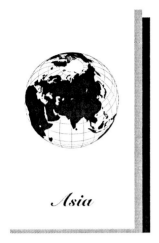

Asia

Independence was declared on December 16, 1991, by this ninth largest country in the world. No longer part of the U.S.S.R. (Union of Soviet Socialist Republics), this country, along with 10 other of the 15 previous republics that made up the U.S.S.R., became a member of CIS, the Commonwealth of Independent States. The CIS members share a common policy for foreign affairs and defense, but are independent nations. You can't touch an ocean in this country, but you can touch the Aral Sea and the Caspian Sea. As you take a bite of expensive caviar, you hope that it was legitimately harvested. You would hate to think you were supporting poaching. *Where on Earth are you? Can you find your place?*

Kazakhstan

Sturgeons are large freshwater fish in the Caspian Sea whose eggs are worth more than their flesh. The eggs are processed into caviar. The Soviet government used to regulate the caviar industry, ensuring that only a limited amount of fish could be caught. But with the breakup of the U.S.S.R. and the independence of Kazakhstan, Russia, Azerbaijan, and Turkmenistan (they all border the Caspian Sea), there is no longer a single authority monitoring how many fish are being caught. Poachers are illegal hunters who have been taking unlimited amounts of fish and depleting the stocks. The fate of the sturgeons became even more fragile when the area where the fish could lay their eggs was reduced: the hydroelectric dams built on the inflowing Volga River caused a

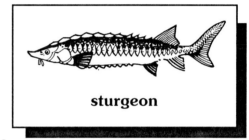

sturgeon

drop in sea water level. Pollution and oil spills only compounded the problem. Fish farms have been established by environmentalists in Kazakhstan, and citizens have formed rescue committees.

Is it possible for a sea to disappear? The saltwater Aral Sea crosses the border between Kazakhstan and Uzbekistan. Fertilizer, chemicals, and irrigation waste dumping have caused the lake and the surrounding area to become seriously polluted. Many people living near the sea have become ill from the pollution. Combine the pollution problem with the fact that the Aral's main sources of inflowing water have been rerouted to irrigate farmland and with the natural process of evaporation; and yes, a sea can disappear. Fishing fleets were stranded, villages abandoned, and finally Aral's fishing industry went out of business in 1992. Some experts predict that the Aral Sea will cease to exist in about 30 years.

Steppes, deserts, plains, and mountain ranges are all parts of Kazakhstan's territory. **What is a *steppe*?** Steppes are open and level grasslands that are suitable for herding livestock or growing crops (depending on rainfall and irrigation). After the Russian Revolution in 1917, the Soviet government established the Kazakh Soviet Socialist Republic and began to cultivate Kazakhstan's extensive steppes. Wheat and corn were grown.

Today, some people want to make Kazakhstan an Islamic state. **Should a country have a state religion? What if you agreed with the religion?**

Asia

Invaded and annexed by its neighbor in August 1990, this country was liberated early the next year by international coalition forces led by the United States. In his farewell speech to U.S. troops, U.S. General Schwarzkopf said, "Don't ever forget to say in your story there were Kuwaitis, Omanis, French Foreign Legion protecting our right flank, with Egyptian forces involved, because you were part of the great coalition—the great coalition of forces determined . . . to show a petty dictator that they just can't get away with bullying neighbors and taking what they want because they think they are so tough." In all, 29 countries were involved in the coalition forces. *Where on Earth are you? Can you find your place?*

Kuwait

A small but oil rich country with perhaps the hottest and most air-conditioned capital, Kuwait lies on the northwestern shore of the Persian Gulf (also known as the Arabian Gulf). In 1914, Kuwait was independent under British protection, and finally in 1961, Kuwait became fully independent. Oil was discovered in 1938.

Preliminary results of the 1995 census showed that Kuwaiti nationals made up a mere 41.6% of the population. **Why do you think there are so many foreigners in Kuwait?** Income from oil has made the government of Kuwait very wealthy. Kuwait's wealth has allowed it to import goods and services, along with the labor to run them. **Would you clean your own house if you had an excess of money? How does a society change if it is made up of a class of people who do not have to work?**

What are the requirements for Kuwaiti citizenship? Can a foreigner ever gain citizenship?
Foreign workers can never gain citizenship or resident status, but even some Kuwaitis don't have citizenship! When Kuwait gained independence, citizenship was (and still is) not granted unless one can prove Kuwaiti ancestry, with family residence from at least 1920. This proved difficult for nomadic tribes, and though many tribespeople were entitled to citizenship, they did not understand its importance or register their children. Kuwait has three levels of citizens, with first-class going to one-third of the native population, second-class or partial citizenship going to a third, and potential citizenship going to the last third. Only citizens receive government payments from oil revenues. **What are the requirements for citizenship in your country?**

When Iraq invaded, many Kuwaitis fled the country, mainly to Saudi Arabia. In fact, approximately 400,000–600,000 of Kuwait's 700,000 citizens were abroad. **Would you leave your country if it were at war? How do you think those who stayed felt about those who left? If you were a parent and felt you had to stay, but you had a chance to send your children away, would you?**

What would happen to Kuwait and other oil rich nations if an alternative fuel source were discovered? Should they be saving a percentage of their profits or investing in other ventures?
Kuwait does have a Reserve Fund for Future Generations (RFFG). By law, 10% of all petroleum profits are to be put in this fund. RFFG funds were used to rebuild the country after the war. **Do you have an RFFG in your country?**

Asia

The longest stretch of the Mekong River flows through this landlocked country in Southeast Asia. Considered one of the 12 great rivers in the world, the Mekong and its tributaries are a defining feature, for their annual flooding during the monsoon season makes wet-rice cultivation possible. It doesn't matter that only a little over half of this river is navigable all year by flat-bottomed boats. What's important is that an important source of protein—fish—comes from its waters. *Where on Earth are you? Can you find your place?*

Laos

Before its independence in 1954, Laos was part of French Indochina. **What three colonies of France made up French Indochina?** Laos, Vietnam, and Cambodia.

What continent has the greatest number of types of deer? Asia. **What do all deer have in common?** They are plant eaters; they have hooves, slender bodies, and long thin legs; and most males have antlers. The barking deer is found in Laos. **Does it really bark, and do you think it has antlers?** (Hint: consider that it lives in dense forests.) Also known as the *muntjac*, this little deer does bark—to protect itself! When a barking deer sees a predator, it starts to make a noise that sounds like a dog barking, and the deer can keep it up for an hour! The barking deer has tiny antlers. If the antlers were big, they would hinder the deer's movement through the dense foliage. **What are male, female, and baby deer called?** Males are bucks, females are does, and babies are fawns, except in the case of moose, elk, and caribou. For the biggest members of the deer family, males are bulls, females are cows, and the young are calves.

If an image of Buddha breaks, what do you do? It is forbidden to destroy any image of Buddha, so broken Buddhas are piled up in caves, temples, and other holy places. Buddhism was practiced as early as the 11th and 12th century in Laos, and this makes for some pretty impressive piles of discarded Buddhas. **If you didn't know the custom, how would you feel if you discovered one of these caves?**

A *conundrum* is like a riddle that cannot be answered; it is a problem with no clear answer. The Plain of Jars in Laos is a conundrum. About 300 stone jars are scattered over this plain. Roughly 2,000 years old and made before written records were kept, these jars weigh an impressive 4,000–6,000 pounds (1,800–2,700 kg) and are between 1–8 feet (.3–2.4 m) tall and 3 feet (.9 m) in diameter. Archeologists find the jars a conundrum. They still do not know what the jars were used for: rice or wine storage? burial urns? **What do you think?**

Why is the Plain of Jars covered in bomb craters? During the Vietnam War (1954–1975), over three quarters of a million Laotians were forced to flee their homes when U.S. planes carpet-bombed the vicinity of the Ho Chi Minh Trail, North Vietnam's main supply route running along Laos' border, and the Plain of Jars. The U.S. bombed this region because it was a stronghold of the Pathet Lao, a left-wing resistance movement strongly affiliated with the North Vietnamese communists. The U.S. also backed a "secret army" made up of U.S.-trained mercenaries. **What is a *mercenary*?** A mercenary is a soldier hired for foreign service.

Asia

Olives were cultivated as early as the 3rd century B.C., here in this country where one can take a morning swim in the warm waters of the Mediterranean Sea before taking off for an afternoon of snowskiing. The snow is important: it melts and provides water for irrigation in the fertile Bekaa Valley. Cedars once covered vast areas of this land; and though few groves stand today, it remains this country's national emblem and is prominent on its flag. This nation has suffered through a terrible and recent civil war where schools were forced to close down regularly and over half of the country had their homes completely destroyed. *Where on Earth are you? Can you find your place?*

Lebanon

Located at the eastern end of the Mediterranean Sea, Lebanon is a largely mountainous strip of land. Lebanon gained its independence from France in 1943. In 1948, Lebanon took in over 100,000 refugees. The resettlement of these refugees—and the thousands more that continued to cross the border—has affected almost every event in Lebanon's recent history. **Where did the refugees come from?** During the Arab-Israeli War (1948–49) when Arabs attacked Israel, Palestinian refugees fled across the border to Lebanon. More refugees arrived over the years as Arab-Israeli conflicts continued, including members of the Palestinian Liberation Organization (PLO). The PLO used Lebanon as a base for attacking Israel after being expelled by Jordan in 1970.

Lebanon's civil war lasted from 1975–1990. **What happened to the capital Beirut during the war?** It became a violently divided city, with Christians occupying the eastern half and Muslims in control of the west. Rebuilding and reconciliation has started, but it will be a long process. **How would you feel if you lived in a city divided by religion? How can one ensure religious protection for all?**

Canaanites, who became known as Phoenicians, occupied what is now Lebanon around 3,000 B.C. Great traders, the Phoenicians built sailing ships out of Lebanese cedar wood and navigated the seas by using the stars to guide them. **How did the Phoenicians waterproof their boats?** With pitch, a black, viscous (sticky) substance. Pitch can be found in certain evergreen trees (like the Lebanese cedar) or as a residue from the distillation of tars or other organic materials. **What happens when something is distilled?** When a substance is distilled, it is heated up so that it vaporizes. The vapor is then cooled, and the result is a purer substance because the impurities are left behind (they didn't vaporize). When salt water is distilled, it can become drinkable for humans.

hyrax

Hyraxes—small, rodent-like mammals about the size of house cats—are found in Lebanon and are native to Africa and extreme southwestern Asia. They are classified as primitive ungulates. **What is an *ungulate*?** (Hint: elephants, horses, swine, tapirs, and rhinoceroses are all ungulates.) Ungulates are hoofed mammals. Hyraxes have small hoofs on the first and third digits of their hind feet. The middle digit is clawed. Hyraxes also have curved, continuously growing upper incisors.

This country is made up of two pieces of territory, separated by 400 miles. A prosperous nation, its capital holds the world's tallest building. This country's economy once focused on rubber, palm oil, lumber, and tin. Petroleum products became profitable in the late 1970s, and today, more than two-thirds of its exports are manufactured goods, including high tech items like equipment for computers and cars. *Where on Earth are you? Can you find your place?*

Asia

Malaysia

Located in Southeast Asia, Malaysia lies on both the end of the long Malay Peninsula and on the northern coast of Borneo, the third largest island in the world. The South China Sea lies between the two land areas. A former colony of Great Britain, Malaysia gained its independence in 1963.

Batik is a traditional art in Malaysia. **What is *batik*?** Batik is the process in which an artist covers parts of a piece of cloth with hot wax. The artist then soaks the cloth in dye, with the wax-covered cloth remaining color free. The artist will repeat this process several times, scraping off wax and reapplying it, depending on how intricate the design is and how he or she chooses to blend colors.

The Petronas Towers in the capital city of Kuala Lumpar are each about 1,482 feet (452 m) high, but because 241 feet (73.5 m) of this height comes from nonfunctional stainless pinnacles placed on the top, some claim that the Sears Tower in Chicago, Illinois, should be considered the world's tallest office building. In the Guinness World Record book, the Petronas Towers are listed as the world's tallest office buildings, but it states that the Sears Tower can still boast that it has the highest occupied story. **Which do you think should be considered the tallest?**

Just north of the equator, Malaysia is a hot and tropical country. Humidity is typically 85%. **What is humidity?** Humidity is the moisture content of the air. In weather reports, the term humidity usually refers to relative humidity, the ratio of the actual water vapor content of the air to its total capacity at a given temperature. **Are you more comfortable in a hot dry climate or a hot humid one? In which one would mold and fungus be more likely to grow?** The humid one.

Why is there typically sparse vegetation at ground level in the tropical forests of Malaysia? The leaves of the tallest trees create a canopy that allows little light to filter through to smaller species. Many vines take root on the floor and then "climb" on trees up to the sunlight while other plants find rootholds on upper tree branches.

What are *tapirs*? Found in the tropical forests of Malaysia and the New World, tapirs are shy, hoofed, plant-eating mammals that can grow up to 8 feet (2.5 m) long. All tapirs take refuge in the water to escape their enemies and are able to stay underwater for long periods. Enemies of tapirs include man, jaguars, and tigers.

Asia

You are in the flattest country in the world. There are no hills. There are no rivers. As a matter of fact, the highest elevation is a whopping 7 feet (2 m) above sea level. This presents a problem because of global warming. Global warming results in polar ice caps melting and sea levels rising. Here, in the middle of the Indian Ocean, even a slight rise could be catastrophic. As it is, the official number of islands in this archipelago changes daily. Are you counting at low tide or high tide? Then there is the added problem of erosion. Some islands vanish into the ocean completely! But on the other hand, after a storm, some islands seem to appear out of nowhere! *Where on Earth are you? Can you find your place?*

Maldives

A chain of small coral islands in the Indian Ocean, the Maldives is south of India and east of Sri Lanka. Typically, there are about 1,190 islands in the archipelago, 200 of which are inhabited. The islands are spread over 34,750 square miles (90,003 square km), but land mass only adds up to 115 square miles (298 square km.) What this means is that 99.669% of the Maldivian territory is seawater! Seawater isn't drinking water. **Maldivians get their drinking water three ways. Can you think of them?** 1. <u>Rainwater</u>. Large reservoirs are built on the roofs of schools and mosques so villagers can collect the fresh water from a tap. 2. <u>Wells</u>. Rainwater collects at about 6 feet (2 m) underground, but if more water is drawn than is supplied by rains, saltwater infiltrates the ground and mixes with the fresh water. As it is, people (women and children) sometimes have to stand in long lines to fill their pails. 3. <u>Desalination plants</u>. Right now, the Coca-cola plant in the Maldives is the only plant in the world where seawater (desalinated, of course!) is used in its product.

The Maldives became an independent nation on July 26, 1965. Its official religion is Islam. As early as 2,000 B.C., the islands were known to sailors and were an important stop on trading routes between the east and the west. The Portuguese occupied the islands for 15 years, but with the help of India, the islands were freed. In 1887 the Maldives became a British protectorate in return for an annual tribute. This was a strategic move for the Maldives because it meant that the British could not colonize the islands. The Maldives became independent when the British lifted the protectorate.

Throughout all these years, and even today, an all-purpose tree has grown on the Maldives. What is it? The coconut palm. The coconut palm provides food and oil with its milk, flesh, and sap. The husk is turned into rope. The fronds are used for roofs, mats, and walls. The trunks are used for boats, houses, and furniture. Any leftovers are burned for fuel.

Maldivian fish exports are certified as dolphin-safe. **What method do you think Maldivian fishermen use?** In Maldives, fishing is still done in the traditional manner, with rod or lines and hooks. When large nets are dropped into the ocean, all types of animals are caught in them and the result can be ecological damage.

Asia

Despite having changed its name in 1989 from Burma, this country is still known as "The Land of Pagodas." This largely Buddhist nation has over 135 ethnic groups, including the Padaung tribe. Though small in number, the Padaung are known because of their neck rings. Copper rings are placed around the necks of young girls, and they are increased every year until they total about 20 pounds (9 kg)! Take the rings off, and one has to substitute a neck brace because the neck has been weakened and there is a danger of suffocation. The majority of the people here are employed in agriculture. Teak is exported, as are rubies. Is that really a fruit that weighs 80 pounds (36 kg)? *Where on Earth are you? Can you find your place?*

Myanmar

Myanmar, located in Southeast Asia, gained its independence from the British in 1948. Since 1989 Myanmar has been locked in a struggle between democratic and military elements. Aung San Suu Kyi won the 1991 Nobel Peace Prize for her opposition to Myanmar's military regime. Kyi is the daughter of Aung San, a revered hero who is considered to be the father of independent Myanmar. Aung San was assassinated less than six months before independence.

What is a *pagoda*? Solid conical structures with a central treasure vault below, pagodas contain holy relics and are usually elevated since they are not supposed to be lower than houses. Often there is a terrace around the pagoda where pilgrims can pray, meditate, or give offerings. Pagodas are different from temples in that temples are built with a hollow chamber so pilgrims can enter them.

Can the human neck really be stretched? No, though when one looks at a female Padaung, it certainly seems that it has been. The neck looks unusually long because the rings depress the collarbones and ribs. This deliberate deformation is supposed to prevent female tribe members from being taken by other tribes.

What is *teak*? Teak is a hardwood tree that makes up about one-tenth of Myanmar's forests. A valuable export, the wood is coveted because it is hard and durable. Teak forests have been owned by the state since 1948. Many opposed to the logging feel that the forests are being cut—for profit—at a rate that is fast depleting the supply and causing irreparable harm to the forests. Others point out that there are politics involved. Some hill minorities want independence, and by building roads into the forests for logging, the government can better penetrate rebel areas.

Rice is on the list of Myanmar's main exports, along with teak, minerals, and gems. Though big, the jackfruit is not exported. With its yellow, fibrous, sweet flesh, jackfruit can weigh up to 80 pounds (36 kg) and measure up to 3 feet (1 m) in length! The olive-green spiky durian is another large fruit that grows in Myanmar, but it only gets as big as a soccer ball. If one is asked, "Want a piece of fruit for lunch?" should one first ask, "What size?"

Asia

You see this country's flag, and you are not sure it is the real flag. Instead of being rectangular, like the flags you are used to, it is two adjoining triangles. The flag is crimson (the national color of this country) and outlined in blue. There is a moon on the upper triangle and a sun on the lower triangle. You ask a "Tiger of the Snow" about the flag, and you are told that the flag is the only nonrectangular flag representing a country in the world. The "Tiger in the Snow" also informs you that the sun and the moon represent this country's hope that it will last as long as the sun and the moon. *Where on Earth are you? Can you find your place?*

Nepal

Located in Southeast Asia and completely surrounded by land, Nepal has some of the highest and most rugged mountains in the world. Eight of the world's highest peaks are in Nepal. **Can you name the highest?** Mt. Everest is 29,028 ft. (8,848 m). The air is so thin at the top (oxygen decreases with elevation) that man cannot survive there for any extended length of time.

Why do people climb mountains? It has been said that George Mallory, who led the first expedition to climb Everest and died in the attempt, answered, "Because it is there." Edmund Hillary and Tenzing Norgay were the first men to reach Everest's summit in 1953. Hillary was a New Zealand beekeeper, and Norgay was his guide.

Who are the "Tigers of the Snow"? Nepal consists of about 35 separate ethnic groups. The Sherpas, a tribe from the north, are considered to be the best guides and porters in the Himalayan region and are nicknamed "Tigers of the Snow." Norgay was a Sherpa.

What do you think the staple food of Nepal is? For the majority of the Nepalese, rice is the staple food. The Sherpa tribe is the exception, with their staple food being the potato. **Why do you think this is so?** The Sherpas live in the hill region, and potatoes grow better there than rice does.

Could it be that hyenas and bears live in Nepal? Yes, they do! Forests cover about ⅓ of Nepal, and Nepal also has swamps and jungles. The snow leopard and the Indian rhinoceros are found in Nepal, but they are on the endangered species list. Rhesus monkeys, deer, wild oxen, goats, and tigers also live in Nepal.

Nepal is the only official Hindu kingdom in the world. **What is Hinduism?** Hinduism is a religion. About 85% of Nepalese are Hindus, about 10% Buddhists, and about 5% Muslims or members of the animist religions.

Is there really a *yeti*? The yeti is also known as the Abominable Snowman. It is supposed to be a huge, white, shaggy beast that lives high on the Himalayan slopes. People claim to have seen it and its footprints. Edmund Hillary set out on an expedition in 1960 to solve the mystery of the yeti. He and his team of scientists concluded that the yeti does not exist. Evidence was fabricated as a hoax, or it came from other animals.

Asia

You can't go south. Your family may be in the south, but it doesn't matter. The border is closed. You can't cross the D.M.Z. (Demilitarized Zone). You hope one day you will be able to visit your relatives, but time is running out. Meanwhile, being in the mountainous north (80% of the country is mountainous), you concentrate on staying warm. Your house is built to keep out the cold: the rooms are small and there are few windows and doors. The floor is warm, though: a system of pipes that are connected to the kitchen stove pass under the floor, spreading the warm air. Whatever the temperature, you know the rule: always take off your shoes before entering the house. *Where on Earth are you? Can you find your place?*

North Korea

Korea was once one country. There was no North Korea or South Korea. The old problem of Japanese control ended when Japan was defeated and expelled by the Allies in WWII, but then came a new problem. The Soviet Union wanted Korea to be a communist government, and the U.S. wanted Korea to be a capitalist democracy. An agreement was made to accept the 38th parallel, where Japanese troops surrendered, as a dividing line until the country could be reunited. The United Nations decided there should be an election, but only the south voted. The Soviet Union wouldn't allow entry to the U.N. commission that was to oversee the election. Instead, the Soviet Union formed North Korea with Kim Il Sung, a Korean Communist general, as leader. North Korea attacked South Korea, now a democratic capitalist country, in 1950. The U.S. sent soldiers, and the U.N. sent a force of soldiers from 16 nations. China entered the conflict to help the communists. Although a ceasefire agreement was signed in 1953, no permanent peace treaty has been signed. Kim Il Sung held the highest ranking position in his government until his death in 1994. Power then passed to his son Kim Jong Il. Many countries have term limits, meaning that one can only be elected to an office for a certain number of terms or years. **Which system is better? In the United States, who has term limits: the president or a senator?** (Answer: the president)

North Korea is bordered on two sides by seas: the Sea of Japan lies to the east and the Yellow Sea is to the west. Much of the land consists of hills and low mountains, and very little of it is suitable for cultivation. Because of this, water and soil conservation are important for North Korea's future.

What does the Japanese word *kamikaze* have to do with Korea? In 1281, The Mongrel Emperor of China Kublai Khan enlisted thousands of Korean men and ships to invade Japan. A typhoon destroyed the ships. The word *kamikaze* means "divine wind." In WWII, this word was used for the name of any of the pilots who made deliberate suicide attacks into enemy targets. The pilots wanted to destroy their enemy, just as the divine wind had destroyed theirs.

What martial art originated in Korea more than 2,000 years ago? *Tae kwon do* is a form of karate that has developed from a method of self-defense to a national sport.

Asia

No permanent rivers or freshwater lakes lie in this country where some of the channels used for irrigation are over a thousand years old. Long involved in trade, this country is known for its frankincense. Its ancient walled city of Ubar, located on a major east-west caravan route, served as a water stop for caravans transporting frankincense across the desert. Despite its oil reserves being small compared to other oil-producing nations, it is oil, first commercially produced in 1967, that fuels the economic development of this country today. It was not until after a son ousted a father in 1970 that movies were allowed in the capital city, as well as radio stations, sunglasses, and bicycles. *Where on Earth are you? Can you find your place?*

Oman

Located on the eastern part of the Arabian Peninsula, Omar has coastlines on both the Gulf of Oman and the Arabian Sea, enabling access to the Indian Ocean.

What is *frankincense*? A fragrant aromatic gum resin, frankincense is collected from trees bearing the same name. Cuts are made in the trunks; and a milk-like liquid, or gum, flows out. This gum hardens when it is exposed to air. The hardened gum is then stripped off and sold. In earlier times frankincense was used in worship and medicine, and its incense was thought to counteract poison. Frankincense provided important income for Oman, up into the sixth century. Frankincense trees grew only in Oman, Yemen, and Somalia at that time, facilitating control of the trade. Today, Oman earns most of its money from oil, but frankincense is still sold as an ingredient for incense, perfumes, and fumigants.

In ancient times, Oman dominated the world of maritime trade. **What is maritime trade?** (Hint: do you think the resemblance between the words *marine* and *maritime* are a coincidence?) *Maritime* is related to navigation or commerce on the sea. The Omanis sailed the seas in *dhows*, traditional Arab boats. When the 15th century Portuguese explorer Vasco da Gama sailed to India, he hired Ahmad bin Madjid, an Omani sailor, to pilot his ship from Africa across the Indian Ocean to Calicut, on India's west coast. To replicate one of the routes that the Omanis made famous, a traditional dhow was built in 1980 and sailed successfully to Guangzhou China. There were no nails used in the construction of the 87-foot (27 m) long dhow. **How was it held together?** The planks were sewn.

Education is not compulsory, but it is free in Oman. **What does *compulsory* mean?** *Compulsory* means mandatory and enforced. **Would you go to school if you didn't have to?**

Four species of giant turtles come ashore in Oman each year to lay their eggs. Many turtles are endangered, but to help protect them, the government of Oman has set aside protected preserves. **Have you ever seen a turtle's skeleton?** A turtle's shell is part of its skeleton, for its ribs and backbone are attached to the shell's flat, bony plates. **How do sea turtles get fresh water?** Sea turtles drink ocean water, but like you, if they take in too much salt, they could die. By shedding big, salty tears, turtles are able to rid their bodies of excess salt.

Asia

Two-hundred and fifty of the world's highest peaks are in this country, as well as the elusive and endangered snow leopard. Created from another country as a home for Muslims, this new nation, too, had a piece of it become yet another country. The first woman ever elected prime minister of a modern Islamic state came to power here in 1988. *Where on Earth are you? Can you find your place?*

Pakistan

In 1947, at the same time that India received independence from Britain, a partition took place in which India was divided into two sections. Pakistan, one section, was created as a homeland for India's Muslims. Its birth resulted in a great exodus. Some 7.5 million Muslims fled to Pakistan, and about 10 million Hindus left Pakistan for the new India. It was a terrible and violent time. There were instances where trains carrying Hindus out of Pakistan were stopped by Muslims, and every passenger was murdered, and vice versa. In total, over one million people died. When Pakistan was created, it consisted of two parts, with 1,000 miles of India in between. **In 1971, East Pakistan, with the backing of India's army, became what country?** East Pakistan became Bangladesh. This war cost one million lives, and Pakistan lost half its population and a seventh of its area.

The Indus Plain is the most prosperous agricultural region of Pakistan, in part due to the tributaries of the Indus River that run through it. Because of this water, Pakistan has been able to create one of the largest artificial irrigation systems in the world. Yet successful irrigation has created excessive salinity. Because the rate of evaporation is greater than the rate of rainfall, mineral salts accumulate in the water and ultimately into the soil. Scientists are working on ways to neutralize the salinity, as well as developing new plants that aren't affected by saline soils.

K2 is the second highest mountain in the world. Professional mountaineers consider this mountain in Pakistan to be much more difficult and dangerous to climb than Mt. Everest. K2 (so named because it was the second mountain measured in the Karakorams) may be more difficult, but attention goes to Everest because of its height. Most people want to climb the highest and gain the fame that comes with it. **Which one would you climb?**

Some women in Pakistan live in purdah. **What is *purdah*?** *Purdah* is a form of apartheid in which women are kept separated from men. In extreme forms, a woman may not leave the house unless completely covered, including the face, by a *burquah*. A woman's husband or another close relative must accompany her. **Would the rule about females having to be accompanied by males change or restrict the way you live?** Different levels of purdah are practiced throughout the Islamic world.

On December 2, 1988, Benazir Bhutto was sworn in as prime minister of Pakistan, becoming the first woman to head the government of an Islamic state. She has worked hard to try to end gender inequality in Pakistani society. She has also promoted health and education reform.

Asia

You just spotted a moth with an unbelievable wingspan of over 38 square inches (250 sq. cm). You're a little uncomfortable with the giant millipedes and the stick insect over 12 inches (30 cm) in length, but you smile at your host as he looks for something inside the sago palm. The sago palm is an important source of food because it grows in areas where cultivated crops won't grow due to flooding. You think your host is going to harvest the starch inside the palm's trunk because you know this starch is a food staple. Whoops—you were mistaken. Your host was actually looking for the large maggot-like grubs that live inside the palm. You get to feast on a valuable source of protein! *Where on Earth are you? Can you find your place?*

Papua New Guinea

Just north of Australia, over 600 small islands and archipelagos make up the country of Papua New Guinea. The main area of Papua New Guinea is on the eastern half of the island of New Guinea, with Indonesia's Irian Jaya on the west. A United Nations mandate under Australian administration after WWII, Papua New Guinea gained independence in 1975. Previously, parts of it were German and British colonies. With over 700 different linguistic and ethnic groups, Papua New Guinea is an amazing array of peoples and cultures. Some people living in the highlands were undetected by the Western world until the 1930s. **Why do you think they were only recently "discovered"?** Inaccessibility: porters could only carry enough food for about 14 days. Relay systems were set up, and though this enabled Europeans to travel further into the mainland, it still had limitations. Explorers weren't able to enter the most remote and inaccessible areas until the use of airplanes and food drops. **Should these stone-age cultures be protected from outsiders?**

In Papua New Guinea, personal adornment is much more than fabric and clothes. Feathers, bones, leaves, seeds, shells, and natural pigments are all used for decoration. Within some tribes, it is traditional for women to tattoo their faces. In other tribes, especially the highlanders, the nose septum—the fleshy wall between the nostrils—is pierced and a variety of objects, including wood, bones, shells, boar tusks, and cassowary quills are placed through the hole. Before saying, "How gross!" think about how fashions change. It was once rare to see people with more than one ear piercing in many countries, and now lots of people have more than one earring. **Is fashion dictated by those around you? What makes something come into fashion?**

Papua New Guinea lies within the "Ring of Fire," the volcanic and seismic belt that circles the Pacific. If people are prepared for volcanic eruptions, the danger can be lessened. In 1994, two volcanoes violently erupted without warning, spewing poisonous gases and ash. Lava poured out. **Were people at risk of being burned by lava?** Lava, hot melted rock, actually flows very slowly. People can outrun it. People were able to return to their homes just seven months later, and the only death that resulted was due to flooding caused by the eruption.

Asia

Some claim that the Banaue rice terraces should be called the eighth wonder of the world. Looking like giant staircases, these terraces cover an area of 4,000 square miles (10,360 sq km) and measure 6,000 feet (1,829 m) up the mountainside. They were built more than 2,000 years ago, and they are still being used today. Over one-fifth of the world's shellfish species are found in this archipelago, located on what scientists like to call the "Ring of Fire." There are over 7,100 islands in this nation, but only about one-third are inhabited, and just 2,773 have names. It was colonized by Spain and was a United States possession from 1901–1946. *Where on Earth are you? Can you find your place?*

The Philippines

An amazing mix of modern and ancient, the Philippines are located in the southwestern Pacific Ocean. Despite the number of islands in the nation archipelago, there are fewer than 150 islands over 5 square miles (13 sq. km), with the two main ones being the largest. The Philippines lie within the tropics, so the climate is hot and humid, with a year-round average temperature of 80°F (27°C). Typhoons can wreak havoc on the nation, and the destruction is even worse when the typhoons hit deforested areas. **What is the difference between a typhoon and a hurricane?** Typhoons are tropical cyclones that form over the Pacific Ocean. Hurricanes are tropical cyclones that form in the Caribbean and Atlantic Ocean. The high winds, coastal flooding, and torrential rains can cause extensive damage. One storm alone in 1991 left over 50,000 people homeless.

Ferdinand Magellan was the first known European to reach the Philippines, landing there in 1521, and claiming it for Spain. Magellan is credited with being the first to captain an expedition that circumnavigated the globe, but Magellan never actually made it. He died in the Philippines, and only one of his five ships made it back and completed the journey. **Should he receive the credit?**

The Ring of Fire is the belt of seismic and volcanic activity that roughly surrounds the Pacific Ocean. Approximately 70% of historically recorded active volcanoes have occurred around this ring. Why? According to the theory of plate tectonics, Earth's crust is divided into contiguous, moving plates that carry the embedded continents. Earthquakes and volcanoes coincide with locations at which crustal-plate subduction is occurring and are believed to be the result of this subduction. Subduction is the action or process of the edge of one crustal plate descending below the edge of another.

Tarsiers live in the rain forests of some of Philippine islands. Tiny primates, their bodies measure only 3.5–6 inches (9–16 cm), with tails twice that length. **What do their large goggling eyes and the expansion of the tips of their digits into disk-like adhesive pads tell you about their behavior?** Tarsiers are nocturnal, preying mainly on insects, and their large eyes help them to see at night. Tarsiers cling vertically to trees, and they can leap from trunk to trunk. Their expanded digits, in combination with elongated hind limbs and their tail, make them well-suited to an arboreal life. (*Arboreal* means inhabiting trees.)

tarsier

Asia

You didn't ride a train here because there are not any trains! When you stepped off the boat onto this country—consisting mainly of a peninsula—you weren't sure everything was exactly right. Why not? Is there really a country whose name begins with the letter *Q*? And even more peculiar—a country that begins with a *Q*, and the second letter is not a *u*! Could you be dreaming? No, it is too hot to even consider sleeping, let alone dreaming! *Where on Earth are you? Can you find your place?*

Qatar

Located on the Persian Gulf and bordering Saudi Arabia and the United Arab Emirates in the south, Qatar is indeed hot! Summer daytime temperatures regularly reach 110–115°F (43–46°C). In the winter, though it is colder, it only gets down to 50–60°F. (10–16°C). Even though the winter temperature may not seem that cold to you, think about the difference between summer and winter. Sometimes there can be a difference of 65°F (18°C). **Regardless of how hot it was to begin with, wouldn't you feel a chill with such an extreme temperature change?**

How many boys are in your class? How many girls? Schools in Qatar follow Islamic Law, and boys and girls are segregated. When something is segregated, it is separated and kept apart. **What are the strengths and weaknesses of single sex schools?** In some countries, people feel that schools that are publicly funded should not be exclusive to one sex, religion, or ethnicity. **How do you feel about this issue?**

How much farming do you think goes on in Qatar? (Hint: consider location and climate) Very little! Composed mostly of sandstone and limestone, Qatar is covered with sand, gravel, and cobblestones. Dust storms and sandstorms are more common than rainstorms, and on the average Qatar receives less than 2 inches (5 cm) of rainfall per year. Less than one percent of Qatar's land is under cultivation, and that land is dependent on irrigation.

What natural resource does Qatar have that can be found underground? Oil. Qatar exports about 90 percent of its oil to other countries. With more than 330 trillion cubic feet of recoverable reserves, Qatar also has the largest single natural gas reservoir in the world. **Can you write the number 330 trillion?** (330,000,000,000,000)

Traditional Qatari life was based on nomadic grazing, fishing, pearling, and off-shore trade. **What "ship of the desert" provided milk, meat, hair (used for making cloth, slippers, and tents) and skin (used for making water bags)?** The camel.

Qatar's most unusual sport is camel racing. **Take a wild guess at how the jockeys (young boys) stay on the saddle.** They wear pants with Velcro bottoms, and the saddles have Velcro on them.

Asia

You are in the largest country in the world. It is so big that one has to combine the second and third largest countries together to get as much land mass. In 1961 this country sent the first man into space and is known for having very cold winters. In fact, there is one place in Siberia where the temperature drops to −160°F (−71°C). When a person goes out, they have to breathe through cloth or fur to protect their lungs from freezing. If a bird leaves its nest, it drops to the ground frozen. *Where on Earth are you? Can you find your place?*

Russia

Russia is a country that has undergone dramatic changes in the last century. After the Russian Revolution in 1917, Russia became a communist nation. It was the largest and most powerful republic in the Union of Soviet Socialist Republics, also known as the Soviet Union or the U.S.S.R. The Soviet Union existed from 1922–1991 and consisted of 15 member-republics.

Can you name at least one of Russia's rulers (present or past)? Russia has had many rulers, including Vladimir Lenin (1870–1924), the founder of the Soviet state and the Communist Party; Joseph Stalin (1879–1953), a ruthless dictator who followed Lenin; and Michail Gorbechev (born in 1931), whose policies of *glasnot* ("openness") and *perestroika* ("restructuring") helped earn him the Nobel Peace Prize in 1990.

What is communism? Communism is a political and economic system in which the government owns all farmland and the means of producing goods in factories. Karl Marx (1818–1883) is considered to be one of the founders of modern communism. After the Russian Revolution in 1917, the Communist Party ruled Russia until the break up of the Soviet Union in 1991.

What is the Kremlin? Located in the middle of Moscow, the Kremlin used to be the headquarters of the Soviet Union. Today it is the seat of the Russian government and the center of the Russian Orthodox Church. Originally a walled wooden fortress to protect traders, the more permanent Kremlin was built by Italian artisans hired between 1475 and 1510 and contains several palaces and three churches. Red Square, a vast public square, lies outside the eastern wall of the Kremlin.

After WWII, the United States was engaged in a "cold war" with the Soviet Union until its breakup. **What is a cold war?** A cold war is the term used to describe the state of permanent hostility that engulfed these two superpowers. There was no actual shooting, but there was a massive military buildup (including nuclear weapons), intensive economic competition, and hostile diplomatic relations.

One of the world's oldest and deepest lakes is Russia's Lake Baikal. Its lowest point measures 5,715 feet (1742 m), and it is estimated that the lake holds one-fifth of Earth's total supply of fresh water. **What contributes to its ability to support over 2,000 species of plants and animals?** Heat from deep within the Earth warms the lake floor, and this causes the water to move and to distribute oxygen.

Asia

Look around, and you will see pilgrims. From all over the world, Muslims come to Mecca. Key responsibilities for Muslims are known as the "Five Pillars of Islam," and they include a declaration of faith, daily prayers, paying a special tax, fasting, and the *hajj*—an annual pilgrimage to Mecca. An estimated 2 million hajj pilgrims come each year, and two-thirds of them arrive by plane. At the busiest time, this means a flight arrives at the rate of one every minute. Mecca and Medina are the two holiest cities in all of Islam. They are both here in this hot desert country, which also happens to contain many of the world's biggest oil fields. *Where on Earth are you? Can you find your place?*

Saudi Arabia

Occupying 80% of the Arabian Peninsula, Saudi Arabia contains many kinds of deserts, including the largest sand desert in the world. France, Belgium, and the Netherlands combined could fit into this desert. At about the same time the Kingdom of Saudi Arabia was created—1932—American prospectors discovered oil in the country. Today, Saudi Arabia is one of the richest countries in the world, using its billions of dollars from oil revenues to build modern cities and provide modern services to its people.

Thirty-five million years ago, when Saudi Arabia began to break away from the African continent, the ocean flooded the northern Great Rift Valley to form what sea? The Red Sea. The Red Sea reaches a depth of 9,350 feet (2,850 m) in contrast to the Persian Gulf (bordering the eastern side of Saudi Arabia) whose average depth is 112 feet (35 m) and deepest point is 332 feet (100 m). Saudi Arabia is still moving away from Africa today, but so slowly it is virtually unnoticeable.

Why are Mecca and Medina so important? Mecca is the birthplace of Islam. The Prophet Muhammad was born in Mecca, and the city contains the Ka'aba shrine, the most sacred place in Islam. Islam was started in the 7th century, and today approximately one-seventh of the world's population is Muslim. This means over 1 billion people from more than 70 different countries face Mecca to pray every day! Medina is the city where the Prophet Muhammad took refuge to escape persecution. The Prophet's tomb is in Medina.

How is oil formed? A mixture of hydrocarbons, oil is a fossil fuel formed over millions of years ago from incompletely decayed plant and animal remains buried under thick layers of rock.

Why were windows in many traditional houses in Saudi Arabia covered with carved wooden screens? It allowed the women the look out without being seen. Women in Saudi Arabia today are still expected to remain covered.

Foreigners who work in Saudi Arabia are not allowed to stay permanently, but they make up about 50% of the workforce. Why? People go where they can earn money. Saudis can afford to hire workers because of their oil.

Asia

With their "greening" program, there is one tree for every four people on this tiny island nation, just 1° north of the equator at the tip of the Asian mainland. With its natural harbor, the country has long been a place of trade, and its port is one of the busiest in the world, with ocean traffic and cargo moving through 24 hours a day. Its strategic location and its people are this nation's greatest resource. Skyscrapers dominate the coastline; they needed buildings to go upward because there is not enough area in for them to go outward! *Where on Earth are you? Can you find your place?*

Singapore

Just south of Thailand and Malaysia, modern Singapore was founded in 1819 by Sir Stamford Raffles when he set up a trading post for the British East India Company. Singapore is made up of the main island (about 224 square miles) and 58 offshore islets. Singapore became independent in 1965.

Singapore is not a world producer of this product, but its refining center is one of the largest in the world and one of the most important in Southeast Asia. What product is it? Oil. Crude oil from places like Malaysia, Brunei, Indonesia, and the Middle East is refined into different grades for varying purposes, and then it is re-exported and sold to Japan, Hong Kong, Malaysia, Australia, Thailand, and other countries. Many of the oil refineries are located on the offshore islets.

Singapore has become an international finance center and is an *entrepot* port. What does this mean? (Hint: Do you see a similarity between the words *entrepot* and *entrepreneur*? An entrepreneur is one who organizes, manages, and assumes the risk of a business or enterprise. Young entrepreneurs may sell lemonade or mow lawns.) An entrepot is an intermediary center of trade and transshipment. Goods like circuits, computer, or communication equipment are imported to Singapore, and they are immediately re-exported to other countries. Singapore also manufactures its own goods (electronics and clothing, for example) for export.

Cottage industries are dying out in Singapore. **What are cottage industries?** With the labor force often being family members or individuals working at home with their own equipment, cottage industries are small and often informally organized business set-ups. The Indian garland maker is an example of a cottage industry in Singapore. The garlands, needed for Hindu ceremonies and temples, are made by hand, and the process cannot be mechanized. **Would you continue with the family tradition of making garlands, or perhaps pottery or joss-stick making?** Every day, you would perform the same repetitive task. **Or would you, like the majority of the young Singaporeans, choose to work in new jobs, in air-conditioned offices with all the modern conveniences?**

Traditionally, food is eaten with chopsticks in Singapore, as opposed to hands or utensils like forks and knives. **Is it proper etiquette to rest one's chopsticks on the rice bowl when finished?** No, for this is a sign that there was not enough food. One should not wave their chopsticks while eating either or leave them stuck in a bowl of rice, for this is considered to be a sign of rudeness. **Are you adept (skillful) at using chopsticks?**

Asia

It was a man from this country who introduced what is known today as the Australian crawl (the freestyle swimming stroke) to the world. Swimming is an important skill for many people of this nation, for it is made up of over 993 islands. Consequently, there is a lot of coast and a lot of fishing. Very few mammals live here, but the sea is rich with fish. The only lizard that can hang by its tail makes it home in island trees. In the capital city of Honiara on the island of Guadalcanal, there are no stands selling snacks like ice cream, chips, or hot dogs. People don't snack as they walk, for here it is considered the height of rudeness to eat in front of others without being willing to share. *Where on Earth are you? Can you find your place?*

Solomon Islands

The Solomon Islands became an independent nation in 1978. "Discovered" by Spain in 1568 and colonized by Europeans and missionaries in the 18th and 19th centuries, the islands came under British protection in 1893–1900. (There were islands under German possession, but some were not ceded to the British until 1900, while others remained under German rule until WWI.) The Japanese occupied the Solomon Islands in 1942 during WWII. As a response, the United States landed on Guadalcanal and fought for its liberation. With many different ethnic groups and languages, the Solomon Islands is a country of diversity where people have had to learn to respect and embrace each other's differences.

So why are mammals the smallest category of animals living on the Solomons? Think about the distance from the Australian or Asian mainland. It's too far for mammals to swim, so unless the mammal evolved naturally or was brought in boats (like the rats), they simply aren't there. Large mammals need large spaces—they eat an awful lot!

What is the Australian crawl or freestyle stroke? Alec Wickham was the son of a British planter and a Solomon Islands woman. When Wickham went to Australia to study, he began to swim competitively. In 1920 he set world records in the 50-yard sprint by using a variation of a stroke used for years on the Solomon island of New Georgia. The Australian crawl is when one lies belly down in the water and alternately swings each arm up over one's head.

Some of the Solomon Islands are called Polynesian outliers. **What is an *outlier*?** An outlier is an item of data with a substantially different value from the rest of the items in the data set. Sometimes outliers are false readings, and other times they are an important part of the data. The Solomon Islands are in the area called Melanesia, but there are some islands within this area—the Polynesian outliers— inhabited by people who speak Polynesian languages and who are not Melanesian. Some scientists think these people came from an island like Fiji and were blown off course and could not find their way home.

About 90% of the working population is involved in subsistence agriculture. **What is *subsistence agriculture*?** Subsistence agriculture is when one grows just enough for their family. Coconuts and sweet potatoes are among the main crops.

Asia

The Japanese were defeated and expelled in WWII, but instead of peace came a divided country. You are below the DMZ, a border stretching 152 miles (245 km) from the Sea of Japan to the Yellow Sea. In contrast to the communistic north, you are democratic; and the teachings of Confucianism influence your way of life. The country you are in follows many customs. When you eat, you mustn't start until the oldest person at the table has taken a bite. Don't forget the chopsticks! They can never touch the table once the meal has begun. And don't wave goodbye the American way when you leave because that motion here means "come." *Where on Earth are you? Can you find your place?*

South Korea

Korea's troubles did not end when the Allies defeated Japan in WWII. The Soviet Union wanted Korea to be communist, and the U.S. wanted Korea to be a democratic capitalist country. An agreement was made to accept the 38th parallel, where Japanese troops surrendered, as a dividing line until the country could be reunited. The United Nations decided there should be an election, but only the south voted. The Soviet Union wouldn't allow entry to the U.N. commission that was to oversee the election. In 1950, the north attacked the south. The U.S. sent soldiers, and then the U.N. sent a force of men from 16 nations. China entered the conflict to help the communists, and although a ceasefire agreement was signed in 1953, no permanent peace treaty has been signed. **The Korean War has been described as a fratricidal war. What does that mean?** (Hint: *frat* is Latin for "brother.") The Korean War divided brothers. Even today, families separated by the DMZ are unable to see their parents, brothers, and sisters. Time is running out.

An eight-hour exam determines whether one is allowed entrance into a university. If one fails, one must wait a full year before taking the examination again. There is no third time. Teenagers spend hours studying, and families often spend hard-earned money for tutors. **Would you like this system? Are the best candidates chosen?**

Many people think that Johann Gutenberg (1397–1468) was the first person to develop moveable type, but Gutenberg was the first European. Two centuries before, in the 11th century, a Korean invented moveable type. This invention had a major impact of the spread of literacy and culture. In a different type of literary feat, a complete set of Buddhist scripture was carved onto 81,259 wooden blocks in the 13th century. The project took 16 years to complete, and the set is still in existence. **Would you own any books if instead of paper, the words were carved on wooden blocks?**

South Korea is the world's leading provider of what root? Ginseng.

Johann Gutenberg

Asia

In 1960, the world's first female prime minister initially came to power in this nation. That's a fairly recent first, but how about this for something fairly old: ancient kings constructed man-made lakes (called tanks) and tamed the rivers, turning arid scrubland into fertile fields. Buddhism was brought to this country in the third century B.C., and there is a living reminder: a sacred tree believed to be over 2,500 years old. It grew from a cutting sent from the Bo Tree, the tree under which Buddha sat as he attained Enlightenment. Some think of this nation as the "Teardrop of India." *Where on Earth are you? Can you find your place?*

Sri Lanka

Sri Lanka lies off the tip of southern India, a mere 30 miles from its gigantic neighbor. Because of its rough pear shape, Sri Lanka has been called the "Teardrop of India." Over the years, Sri Lanka has had different names, with the most recent change occurring in 1972 when it went from being Ceylon to Sri Lanka. Sri Lanka's location made it a strategic position for trading. Consequently, it was a coveted possession. It was colonized by the Portuguese, the Dutch, and the British (in the early 1500s, the middle 1600s, and the early 1800s, respectively). Sri Lanka gained its independence from the British in 1948.

An agriculture-based country, Sri Lanka's chief crop is rice, the staple food of Sri Lankans. Many farmers still plough their rice fields with water buffalos or use handmade hoes. When it comes to exports, the big three are tea, rubber, and coconuts, with tea being the major cash earner.

There are several distinct ethnic groups in Sri Lanka. Sinhalese make up a rough three-quarters of the population and Tamils make up about a fifth. There are also Moors and Burghers. Typically, Sinhalese are Buddhists, while Tamils are Hindus, the Moors Moslem, and the Burghers Christian. Unfortunately, there is ethnic unrest in Sri Lanka. It is a tragedy that while close to three-quarters of the rural population does not have access to safe drinking water, money and energy is diverted to political unrest and terrorism due to racial injustice and religious and language differences. In addition, valuable tourist dollars are being lost because people are choosing to visit safer places. **How can schools help prevent racial injustice? What language should classes be taught in?**

Elephants are a protected species in Sri Lanka, and wild herds can be found migrating through the national parks. **Why do elephants have big ears?** Ears help an elephant stay cool on hot days. Elephant ears have lots of blood vessels, and on hot days, when an elephant flaps its ears, it cools the blood running through the ears' blood vessels. When the cooled blood is carried back into the body, it in turn, cools the body. Bigger ears can cool more blood faster. **Which do you think has the bigger ears: the Asiatic elephants in Sri Lanka or the African elephants in Africa?** African elephants have bigger ears; they live in hotter, drier places and need more cooling.

African elephant

Asia

The largest river in western Asia, the Euphrates, runs through this country where the world's first known alphabet was discovered. This nations' name came from its Assyrian conquerors, but Sumerians, Babylonians, Egyptians, Hittites, Canaanites (or Phoenicians), Persians, Greeks, Romans, Arabs, Ottomans, and the French are also part of its legacy. For the fifth and last time today, you hear the amplified call to prayer coming from thousands of mosque minarets. *Where on Earth are you? Can you find your place?*

Syria

Barren desert makes up two-thirds of Syria, but there is also lush vegetation, a Mediterranean coastline, and several large rivers. It was in the ancient city of Ugarit on the Syrian coast that iron tools were developed and improved and royalty first wore purple robes. The purple dye came from a mollusk unique to Syria's shores. **What is a *mollusk*?** Clams, oysters, and scallops are all mollusks. Mollusks are invertebrates (lacking a spinal column) that typically have soft, unsegmented bodies enclosed in a shell. Ugarit flourished from the 15th to 12th centuries B.C., and archeologists have discovered much about the past there.

The Euphrates River has supported civilization for thousands of years in Syria. A wide and shallow river with constantly shifting sand bars, it is not navigable by ships, but it provides water crucial for irrigation. In 1968, the Euphrates became important for another reason: power. A single damn was built, and today this damn is Syria's major source of electricity. **If Syrians suffer from one of their regular power outages, why do they get frustrated with Turkey?** Only 15% of the Euphrates lies between Syria's borders, whereas 40% lies within Turkey's. Turkey has built several damns, thus blocking water flow to Syria. Reduced water flow results in less power generated. Arguments over water rights are not confined to rivers in arid regions. They are worldwide. **What should be the rules with river water ownership? If the head of the river is in my country, why should I care about the end of the river, perhaps several countries away from me?**

The wondrous remains of arched, bridge-like structures can be found in Syria today. The Romans built them when Syria became part of their empire in 64 B.C. **What could these structures be?** (Hint: water) The remains of aqueducts, these structures are the legacy of the Roman water supply system. The water would run through conduits (channels) on top of the arches.

There are new homes being built in Syria, but there are also houses hundreds of years old. **Why were the houses in the capital of Damascus constructed with high ceilings?** Hot air rises. With high ceilings, the rooms remain cooler.

Syria's diverse cultural heritage and ancestral mix became their own when they gained independence in 1945, and the last of the French troops left in 1946. **From 1958–1961, what country did Syria briefly join with to form the United Arab Republic in an attempt to foster the belief that all Arab people should be part of one nation?** Answer: Egypt. The attempt was short-lived because Egypt completely dominated Syria.

The largest island of French Polynesia, you are in a nation where many people do not care if they have full internal autonomy and French citizenship. They want independence, especially because France tests its nuclear weapons in the nearby Tuamotu Islands, also part of French Polynesia. Over 190 nuclear devices have been exploded so far. There are no plants with thorns in this country, so feel free to walk barefoot. Vanilla, used for flavoring, is harvested here. *Where on Earth are you? Can you find your place?*

Tahiti

Located in the heart of the Pacific Ocean, Tahiti is not only the largest island in French Polynesia, but it is the most populated. **What islands make up French Polynesia, and how could one tell from the French Polynesian name alone that it is made up of islands?** French Polynesia is made up of five archipelagos: the Society Islands, Austral Islands, Tuamotu Islands, Gambier Islands, and the Marquesas Islands. The Society Islands are divided into the Leeward Islands and the Windward Islands, of which Tahiti is part. *Poly* is the Greek word for "many," and *nesos* means "islands." Combined as Polynesia, they mean "many islands." **Can you think of some other words with *poly*?** Here are a few: *polygon* (many sides), *monopoly* (one owns all), and *polyglot* (many languages).

The desire for independence is stronger in some archipelagos than others. What do you think is a major contributing factor? Why would France want to hold on to its territory? Complete independence means added responsibilities. Some Tahitians want self-government without severing all of its ties to France, while other nationalists want complete independence. It is in the Tuamotu Islands and the Marquesas where the nationalist movement is the weakest, and these two archipelagos are the most dependent on French aid. French Polynesia provides a strategic foothold in the Asia-Pacific region for France. One protest sign against France's nuclear testing said, "If it is safe…Test it in Paris/ Store it in Washington." **How does the wording of this sign correspond to the question of independence?**

To prove that people from South America could have colonized Polynesia, Swedish explorer Thor Heyerdahl sailed on a raft called Kon-Tiki all the way from Peru to islands east of Tahiti. **He made it, but how did scientists figure out he was wrong?** (Hint: food) Corn originally comes from South America (as does the potato), and if Peruvians had colonized the islands, they would have brought their staple food along.

Where did the first Polynesians come from? Southeast Asia. Fiji was settled around 1500 B.C., and a few centuries, later Tonga and Samoa were also settled. It was from these islands that the Polynesian settlers came, settling first in the Marquesas. They continued to settle over the next 1,000 years on other islands, including Easter Island, Hawaii, the Society Islands, and New Zealand. Superb navigators, the Polynesians used the movement of the sun and the stars to guide them, as well as swell and wave changes. Once explorers found a suitable island, they would return for their families.

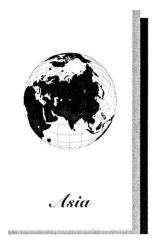

Is this a country exactly? Once, it had a seat in the United Nations, but in 1971 its seat went to another nation that claims this one as its own. The U.S. recognizes the other country, but still it maintains relations with this one through a Special Relations Act passed by Congress in 1979. In fact, the U.S. sent naval forces into the area when the mainland country conducted threatening maneuvers. The Tropic of Cancer (the northern boundary of the tropics) cuts this nation in half. On this island, dragons are a symbol of strength and goodness. *Where on Earth are you? Can you find your place?*

Taiwan

Also known as Formosa, The Republic of China on Taiwan is the seat of the Chinese Nationalist government. Taiwan is separated from the People's Republic of China by the Taiwan Strait, which separates the East China Sea from the South China Sea. During the last Ice Age, over 10,000 years ago, it is believed that Taiwan may have been connected to the mainland by a land bridge. **What gives credence to this theory?** (Hint: depth) Sea levels were lower during the Ice Age, and the sea depths in the Strait are only about 250 feet (73 meters) deep. On the eastern side, where Taiwan meets the Pacific Ocean, the sea depth plummets to thousands of feet.

What is the difference between The Republic of China or Taiwan and the People's Republic of China? China became a republic in 1911 when the last Manchu Ching emperor was deposed in a revolution led by Dr. Sun Yat-sen. General Chiang Kai-Shek became the commander-in-chief of the National Revolutionary Army. There were internal struggles between the nationalists and the communists. In 1949, when the leader of the communists, Mao Zedong, gained power, Chiang Kai-Shek, along with 1.5 million nationalist sympathizers, fled the mainland to Taiwan. Chiang Kai-Shek was the president of the Republic of China on Taiwan until his death in 1975. Mainland China, the People's Republic, continues to claim Taiwan as part of its territory.

When China suffered a crushing defeat in the Sino-Japanese War of 1894, it was forced to hand Taiwan over to the Japanese. The Japanese controlled Taiwan until Japan was defeated in 1945 at the end of WWII. At that point, Taiwan was handed back to China. **During the Japanese occupation, why were some caskets carried to the graveyard under a black umbrella?** Many Taiwanese resented the harsh Japanese rule where language instruction in schools was changed, as well as all business correspondence, to Japanese. By keeping the casket underneath a black umbrella, it was insured that the deceased person was not buried under a Japanese sun.

What was Chiang Kai-Shek saying when he cut off his pigtail? Pigtails, a Manchu tradition, were regarded as a symbol of Manchu rule. When Chiang Kai-Shek cut his off, he was showing his defiance of the Manchus. **Do you sometimes wear your hair a certain way to show defiance? Or are you just following fashion?**

What is *acupuncture*? Acupuncture is a traditional Chinese medical treatment where very fine metal needles are inserted into the skin at specified points. In China, it has long been used for pain relief and for such ailments as arthritis and hypertension.

Asia

You're off to market to buy your food for the day. You do not enter a store—instead, all buying and selling takes place on water. Over 10,000 boats float down the canals, and you can buy vegetables, fruits, dried fish, rice, and flowers. Don't feel like cooking? No problem, just buy from one of the floating kitchen boats. You purchase noodles and other ready to eat foods like fresh coconut milk and fried bananas. A policeman comes by in his boat and tries to straighten out the traffic jam, but you aren't paying attention—you've spotted something, and you're wondering if the world's smallest mammal just darted by your head. *Where on Earth are you? Can you find your place?*

Thailand

Thailand, once known as Siam, is in the heart of Southeast Asia. The capital is Bangkok, and this is where the Floating Market can be found. There are 83 canals in metropolitan Bangkok alone, and all buying and selling takes place on the water.

The world's smallest mammal is the hog-nosed bat. This bat lives only in Thailand, is the size of a bumblebee, and weighs less than a penny. **Bird wings are made of feathers, but what are bat wings made of?** They are made of skin. The wings are so thin that one can almost see through them, but they are strong. A bat's wings, along with its nose and ears, are the only parts of its body that are not covered with fur.

Thailand is united by a common language and a shared religion. **The language is Thai, but what is the religion: Buddhism, Christian, or Islam?** Ninety-five percent of all Thais are Buddhist. Buddhists believe in reincarnation. This means that a person has other lives before and after this one. One is born into a place in society determined by the karma (the effects of thought and deed) of one's past lives. Your actions determine what type of life you will lead next.

What is the Golden Triangle? Thailand, Laos, and Myanmar come together where the Mae Sai and Mekong rivers meet. This area is known as the Golden Triangle.

mulberry leaf

Four out of five Thais live in rural areas, and many grow rice. **There are some farmers (often women) in the northeast who work hard growing a certain kind of tree just to feed to a worm.** **Why?** Mulberry trees are cultivated by the hundreds so that silkworms can feed on their leaves. The silkworms spin silk fiber to make its cocoon, and the fibers are harvested, woven, and dyed into beautiful fabrics that are sold all over the world.

How would you do at *takraw*? Takraw, a favorite game in Thailand, is a little like volleyball, but instead of using your hands to get the ball over the net, you use your feet, and sometimes your head, elbows, and knees! Takraw is played more for the thrill than for the win. **Would you like more sports to be played this way?**

You are on the "Roof of the World." You are isolated, on the highest plateau on Earth, and around you are even higher mountains. You are prepared for any type of weather, for within the same day it can be 100°F (38°C) in the afternoon and below freezing at night. There is an argument as to whether you are an independent country occupied by another country, or a territory rightfully taken back. As you ponder what is right, you sip on yak butter tea. *Where on Earth are you? Can you find your place?*

Tibet

Tibet was an independent nation. In 1950, when the communists and Mao Zedong came to power after China's civil war, one of their first objectives was to "peacefully liberate Tibet." Monasteries were closed, monks were executed, and the centuries-old Tibetan agriculture system was forced to change to a series of collective farms. The Dalai Lama, Tibet's political and spiritual leader, fearing for his life, fled. Today people are still working and hoping for the return of the Dalai Lama. Many Chinese have moved to Tibet, and they now outnumber the Tibetans. They feel Tibet is their home, too.

Still in exile, the Dalai Lama received the Nobel Peace Prize in 1989. **What is the Nobel Prize?** Alfred Nobel was a Swedish chemist and inventor of dynamite. He left money to be awarded every year to people whose work has benefited humanity. Winning a Nobel Prize is a great honor and distinction.

To confirm his position as the spiritual leader of all Tibetans, the Dalai Lama had to pass an oral exam in which Tibet's highest Buddhist scholars tested him on logic, perfection of wisdom, and metaphysics in front of thousands of people. **Would you have been nervous?**

What is different about Tibetans' blood? Oxygen in the atmosphere decreases as the elevation increases. There are only half as many oxygen molecules at 17,000 ft (5,182 m) as there are at sea level. Tibetan nomads have 20% more hemoglobin (produced in the bone marrow and carries oxygen to the body from the lungs) in their blood than people who live at lower elevations. Some athletes have trained at high elevations, extracted and frozen their blood that now contains more hemoglobin, and then reused it before competitions. **Is this fair?**

The summit of Mt. Everest, the world's highest mountain, straddles both the Tibet and Nepal border. **What mountain range is Mt. Everest part of?** The Himalayas. **Do you think it is right or wrong for the Chinese and Nepalese to charge for climbing permits?**

Tibetan nomads make their tents, blankets, ropes, slingshots, boots, and clothes out of yak hair. They burn yak dung for fuel. Yaks carry their goods; and yak milk is used to make butter, cheese, and yogurt. The butter is used for tanning hides, fueling lamps, and making sculptures and candles. It is even smeared over one's face for protection from the wind! Yak meat is dried for food. A yak is ox-like in build with a long, thick coat. **Do you know why yak meat does not spoil for months in Tibet?** Meat does not spoil for months because there is limited oxygen at high altitudes.

Asia

You may be in Europe or Asia: it depends on where exactly you stand. Chances are you are in Asia, because Europe only contains about 3% of the country, but still, you could have one foot on each continent at the same time. The Tigris and Euphrates rivers are familiar, but how about the underground cities of Cappadocia? Believed to be over 2,000 years old, some of these subterranean cities carved out of rock were large enough to house 25,000 people! Even today, the original ventilation system works well enough that one can safely explore 150 feet (46 m) below the ground, visiting stables, wine cellars, and even a room with a large stone-cut table that may have been a school. *Where on Earth are you? Can you find your place?*

Turkey

What is the relationship of the Ottoman Empire to Turkey? The names are often used interchangeably, but modern day Turkey was only a small part of the Ottoman Empire, a vast state founded in the 13th century that was named after the empire's first sultan, Osman I. The Ottoman Empire extended into Asia, Africa, and Europe, reaching its height in the 16th century. Corruption and bribery became rampant as hereditary rulers even killed their own family members. By the early 19th century, Turkey was known as the "Sick Man of Europe." After WWI, peace treaties formally dissolved the Ottoman Empire, and the history of modern Turkey began in 1922, when Kemal Ataturk overthrew the last sultan.

What does a large wooden horse have to do with Turkey? In the ancient Greek epics the *Iliad* and the *Odyssey*, Homer tells the tale of the war between the Trojans and the Greeks. Paris, the son of the King of Troy, stole Helen, the queen of the Greek city of Sparta. Under the leadership of King Agamemnon, Helen's husband Menelaus, and other Greek warriors (including Achilles and Odysseus), sailed off to Troy to do battle. After 10 years of fighting, Odysseus came up with a trick: build a large wooden horse, fill it with soldiers, and temporarily leave. Believing that the Greeks had indeed left, the Trojans brought the horse into their walled city. Later, the encased soldiers made their way out and opened the city gates, allowing the Greeks who had secretly returned to enter. Troy is an ancient Turkish city, and its remains can be visited today.

One of Turkey's most celebrated architects of the Ottoman period was Mimar Sinan (1489–1588). Among other things, Sinan designed the Suleimaniye Mosque, an architectural masterpiece. Atop its square base sits a massive grand central dome, minarets, and balconies. The traditional Turkish art of calligraphy was featured in this mosque. **What is *calligraphy*?** *Kalli* was the Greek work for "beauty," and *graph* means "writing" or "picture," so calligraphy is beautiful picture writing, or the art of penmanship. **Is your penmanship a form of artistic expression, as it has been in Turkey, East Asia, and Arabic-speaking countries for centuries?**

Suleimaniye Mosque

Asia

Part of one of the world's largest deserts lies in this country. With the evaporation of the Aral Sea and desertification, desert land is only increasing. Yet, there is more than desert—there are broad plains, fertile valleys, and snowcapped mountains. Natural gas is one of this nation's resources, and it supplies its neighbors, as well as Russia, through a series of pipelines. A beautiful minaret still stands in the city of Bukhara that dates back to 1127 and is 155 feet (47 meters) tall. When the Mongol commander Genghis Khan arrived in this city in the early 13th century, he ordered the destruction of every structure except for this one. *Where on Earth are you? Can you find your place?*

Uzbekistan

Landlocked in west central Asia, Uzbekistan gained independence from the Soviet Union in 1991 and is the most heavily populated of the former central Asian republics. Uzbekistan has the third largest population when compared to all of the former Republics, trailing Russia and Ukraine respectively. Many Russians emigrated back to Russia after Uzbekistan's independence and the collapse of the Soviet Union, but Russians still make up a large minority group. One reason for their departure was that Uzbekistan refused to grant them dual citizenship. **Do you think countries should allow dual citizenship or do you think a person should have to choose? Should your heritage be taken into account? What requirements does your country have for citizenship?**

Why is the evaporation of the Aral Sea such an ecological disaster? When the Soviet Union decided to grow cotton in the naturally arid and saline Central Asian soil in the 1960s, excessive irrigation was needed. As a result, more than half of the Aral Sea basin is now a dry, salt-encrusted wasteland. As wildlife habitats were destroyed, many plants and animals became extinct. People have gotten quite ill, because windstorms have carried exposed salt, sand, and chemicals, including pesticides, up to 250 miles (400 km) away.

In 1972, the last Turan, or Caspian, tiger was shot and killed in Uzbekistan. It is now extinct. The endangered snow leopard may soon meet the same fate. It lives in Uzbekistan's eastern mountains and is still being hunted illegally for its fur. **What should the fine be for illegal hunting? How can it be enforced?** Some feel the wearing of furs should be banned; others feel that only those furs harvested from the wild should be banned. **How could one distinguish how furs are harvested?**

One of the most famous books in the history of medicine is Iba Sina's (also known as Avicenna) Canon of Medicine. Born in Bukhara in A.D. 980, Iba Sina had a phenomenal memory. By the time he was 10 he had memorized the entire Koran as well as much Arabic poetry. Surpassing even his teachers, he taught himself. By the age of 21, he had mastered law, medicine, metaphysics, and all the other branches of formal learning. He had a wide reputation as an outstanding physician even when he was young, and because he cured a Saminid Prince, Iba Sina was given access to the rich royal library. An avid reader, Iba Sina's access to the library helped his intellectual development. **What does *avid* mean?** Avid means very eager or greedy. **What are you avid about?**

Some say this nation is shaped like "a set of scales balancing two baskets of rice." It is more common to travel this country by bicycle than car, but however one travels, one will see rice. Hill tribes grow dry rice, and wet rice is grown in paddy fields in the delta regions. After its French colonizers were defeated in 1954, this country was divided in two at the Geneva Convention. It was agreed that the people could decide if the divided country would once again become one. The elections never happened, though historians note that the majority of the people—even those in the U.S.-backed south—would have voted to join as one. It wasn't until 1976 that the north and south were reunified. *Where on Earth are you? Can you find your place?*

Vietnam

Located in Southeast Asia, Vietnam has a long indented coastline that follows the Gulf of Tonkin down to the South China Sea, past the Mekong delta, and inward to the Gulf of Thailand. The U.S. engaged in a futile and unpopular war in Vietnam when they decided to support South Vietnam's government against communist insurgents aided by North Vietnam. In 1954, President Eisenhower explained why the U.S. should get involved in Vietnam with an analogy. An analogy is a similar relationship between two unlike things. **Do you know what his analogy was?** (Hint: the domino theory) **Have you ever lined up a row of dominoes and then knocked over the first one, setting up a chain of events so that the next one fell, and then the next one, until they all toppled?** Eisenhower was afraid that if Vietnam became communist, the other countries in the region like Thailand, Laos, Cambodia, Myanmar, and even India and Japan would become communist, too. Eisenhower said, "You knock over the first one, and what will happen to the last one is the certainty that it will go over very quickly." The domino theory was revived in the 1980s when the U.S. became involved in events in Central America.

Who were the Vietcong? Members of the National Liberation Front of the South were known as the Vietcong. The Vietcong were allied to the president of North Vietnam, Ho Chi Minh. It was hard for the U.S. to tell the Vietcong apart from the civilian population, and this contributed to the loss of life and destruction to the land. The Vietnam War ended in 1975 with a communist victory, and the two Vietnams were reunited in 1976.

It is common for schools in Vietnam not to give letter grades but instead rank students from first to last. **Do you think this is a fair system of grading? Do you think it makes students more competitive? Would you prefer it to your own system of grading?**

Someone offers you bird's nest soup. **Should you expect twigs?** Bird's nest soup is a Vietnamese (and Chinese, too!) delicacy believed to have medicinal value. It is made from particular swift's nests that are harvested from high cliffs. The nests are made from sticky secretions from the bird's beaks.

Welcome to Australia!

Map of Australia

New Zealand
(page 94)

Australia
(page 93)

Australia

You have volunteered to help patrol the longest fence in the world; it encloses one-third of the country and protects sheep and cattle stations from dingoes. There's a rabbit fence too, and that fence stretches between the Indian Ocean and the southern shore. Rabbits and foxes were introduced in this country fairly recently and have become huge nuisances, but the dingoes have been around much longer. Speaking of animals, this place has some of the world's most primitive, but doesn't that seem appropriate since this country is considered the oldest continent? *Where on Earth are you? Can you find your place?*

Australia

The country of Australia is an entire continent: the oldest, smallest, flattest, and lowest. Isolated from other continents, Australia's animal life is unique. Dingoes (wild dogs believed to have evolved from the domesticated version of the Asiatic wolf and the Indian wild dog) were brought to the continent by ancestral Aboriginals. There are numerous marsupials that are native, as well as the only two existing monotremes in the world. **Can you name some marsupials and the monotremes and explain what they are?** A marsupial is a mammal that carries its newly born young in a pouch. Kangaroos, koala bears, and wallabies are the most famous marsupials, but there are over 100 different kinds of marsupials in Australia. Monotremes are primitive mammals that lay eggs. The only two monotremes alive today are the duck-billed platypus and the spiny anteater, also known as the echidna.

One of the world's greatest natural wonders is Australia's Great Barrier Reef. **Is this reef on the western side (Indian Ocean) or eastern side (Pacific Ocean) of Australia?** The Great Barrier Reef stretches for more than 1,200 miles (1,931 km), running from just north of Brisbane all the way to New Guinea, along the Pacific coast.

The British first settled Australia in 1788, and it received nation status in 1901. Previously, Britain had sent convicts from their overcrowded prisons to their American colonies, but with the colonies fighting for independence, this was no longer an option. The British began to send convicts to Australia. Many of the people sent to Australia had been imprisoned for very minor infractions—some for merely stealing something to eat! Conditions on the ships were miserable, and life didn't get any easier when they arrived. For 50 years, 90% of all immigrants were convicts. Convicts were used to clear land, build roads, and construct housing. Even today, there are court battles about what rights a prisoner should have. **Do you think a prisoner should have rights? Should stealing a piece of bread merit the same punishment as stealing gold?**

Australia's desert interior is called the Outback. Gold is mined in the Outback, as are the world's highest quality opals. Sheep ranches and farms are thousands of acres in size, and some children are too isolated and far away to go to school. High school students will often go to boarding schools, but some younger children get their lessons by two-way radio and television. Their lessons and examinations are sent by the government through the mail. **Would you do your week's work at once, or would you space it out?**

Australia

There is a large gecko lizard living in this country and it is a very unusual reptile—it does not lay eggs. Instead, it gives live birth to its young, usually twins. The national bird is a large, shy, flightless creature with a long slender bill with nostrils at the tip. It is a good thing this bird only lays one egg because the egg is approximately one-third the female bird's weight. No other bird lays such a large egg relative to body size. The bird is the kiwi, also a popular nickname for the people from this island nation off the coast of Australia. *Where on Earth are you? Can you find your place?*

New Zealand

Consisting of two main islands and several smaller ones, New Zealand has magnificent mountains, volcanoes, glaciers, fjords, rivers, and spectacular coasts. Settled by Polynesians, now known as the Maoris, probably by 1000 A.D., it was sighted by the Dutch navigator Abel Tasman in 1642 and visited by British explorer James Cook in 1769. Whalers and missionaries followed, and in 1840 native leaders ceded sovereignty to the British by signing the Treaty of Waitangi. The English and Maori versions of the treaty carried different meanings, and it wasn't until 1975 that the New Zealand Parliament set up a tribunal to investigate Maori claims, many of which have now been met. New Zealand's colonial status was formally terminated by Britain in 1907.

Before the Maoris arrived, what characteristic did all the mammals of New Zealand share? There were only mammals that could fly. In fact, the only native land mammal is the bat. It was the Maoris who brought with them dogs and rats. Sheep and cattle have been introduced, and today, New Zealand sells 90% of its dairy products for export.

In New Zealand, when water flows down a drain, it swirls counterclockwise. Contrast this to the United States where the water swirls clockwise. **Why?** The water is actually swirling in the same direction—it is all perception. Picture this: you are floating above the North Pole looking down on the Earth. The Earth appears to be turning counterclockwise. Now float over the South Pole, and though the Earth is turning in the same direction, it now appears to be spinning clockwise. Try it with a globe!

Iceland, the United States, and New Zealand are the only three countries in the world with these. **What are they?** Geysers. New Zealand has a thermal region with a belt of geysers, boiling mud pools, and hot-water springs. New Zealand's Frying Pan Lake is the largest hot springs in the world. At its deepest point, the water reaches a temperature of 389°F (200°C). Ready for a swim?

Dame Kiri Te Kanawa (1944) is one of the world's greatest opera singers. **What is an opera?** An opera is a play in which all or most of the speeches are sung. An orchestra usually accompanies the singers.

What did tattoos mean to the Maoris? Tattoos were a ritualized art that was only performed by priestly experts. Each person's tattoo was a form of identification and different from everyone else's.

Welcome to Europe!

Map of Europe

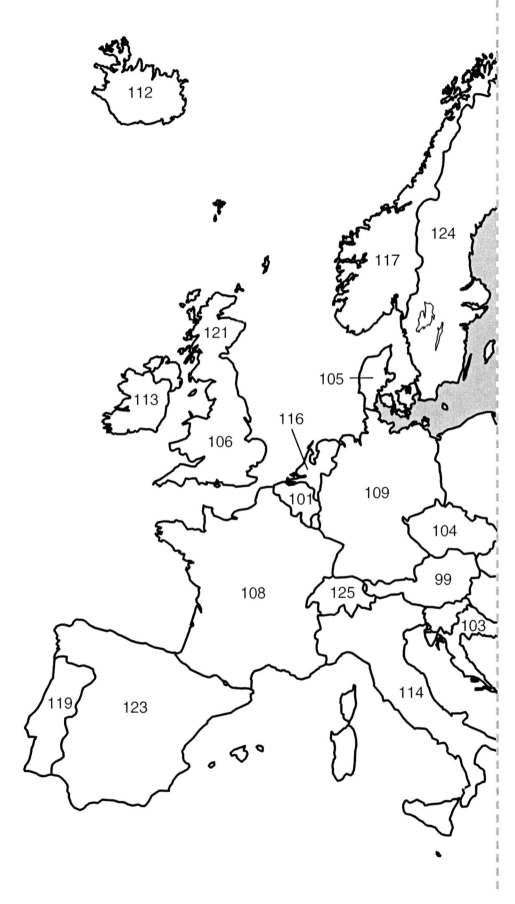

The countries are numbered according to the page number on which you will find them. Not all countries are covered in this book. Use tape or glue to connect page 96 to page 97 at the tab.

Map of Europe *(cont.)*

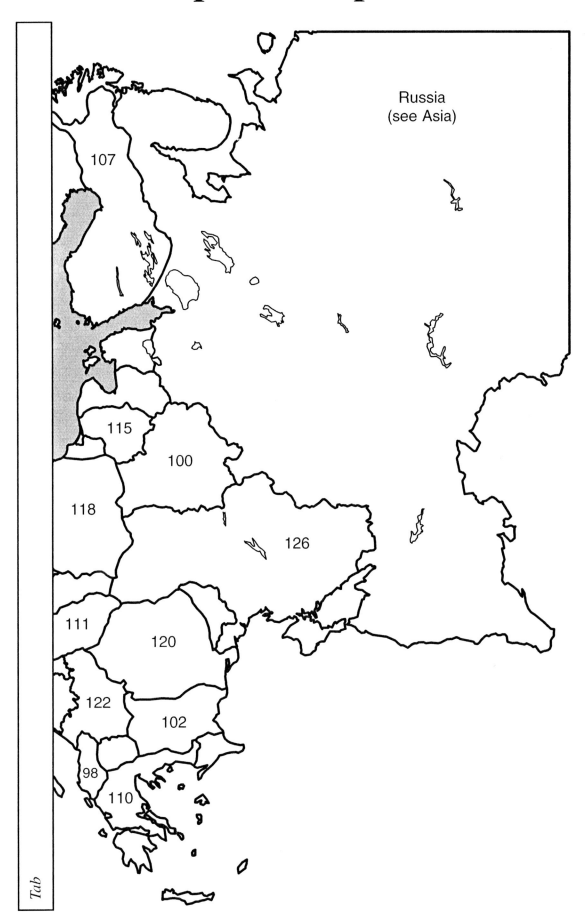

Russia
(see Asia)

107

115

100

118

126

111

120

122

102

98

110

Tab

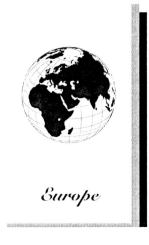

You are in the only European country where Islam is the predominant religion, as well as the last country to reject communism. Nobel Peace Prize-winner Mother Teresa—who worked in some of the worst slums of India—hails from here. *Where on Earth are you? Can you find your place?*

Albania

Located on the Balkan Peninsula, Albania is a mountainous country. Its coast extends along the Adriatic Sea and the Ionian Sea. Communism came to Albania after WWII in 1945, and it did not end until 1990. It wasn't until its collapse that people were allowed to freely leave the country. Many men immediately departed to find work so they could send money back home to their families. **What does it say about a country when it does not allow departures? What rules are there in your country?**

Many Albanians went to bed in one nation—their own—and woke up in another. **Where did they wake up and why?** After being occupied by the Turks and made part of the Ottoman Empire for 500 years, Albania finally proclaimed its independence in 1912. Albania became independent before The First Balkan War, but it was the treaty that ended this war that caused Albanians to be divided. As a result of the new boundaries, nearly half of all Albanians were now in Montenegro, Serbia, or Greece! Kosovo, a province of Serbia, is 90% ethnic Albanian. **How would you feel if you woke up in the same house but a different country?**

Do you think the borders drawn up in 1912 were a factor in the 1913 Second Balkan War? The Second Balkan War erupted soon after the first one, and borders and territory were a primary reason. Bulgaria was forced to cede territory to Serbia, Greece, Romania, and Turkey. In the treaty that ended this war, Albania was recognized as a separate state, but a German Prince was sent to run the country. It wasn't until after WWI (1914–18), in 1920, that Albania was admitted as an independent country to the League of Nations, a now defunct international association created after WWI.

In 1966, there were shortages of even basic foods (like flour) and wage rates were restructured. Almost everyone, no matter the job, was paid about the same. **How would you feel if all of a sudden you received the same wage as every one else, despite having a very different job requiring very different amounts of training and skill? What should determine wage scales?**

A small goatlike deer, the chamois is native to the mountains of Europe and Albania. It lives along the snow line, eating mountain herbs and flowers in the summer and pine shoots in the winter. Hunted for its venison and famous for its soft skin that has been used to make clothing and polishing cloths, the chamois today is a rare and elusive creature. In the 20th century, the chamois was successfully introduced into New Zealand. **Do you think the arbitrary movement of species by man is justifiable? What about if it is a threatened creature like the chamois?**

Europe

You are in a land of musical giants. Mozart was born here, as were Haydn, Strauss, Schubert, and Schönberg. Beethoven, Brahms, and Mahler all came to work here. Everyone seems to be dancing. Elegantly dressed, people are waltzing to Strauss' "The Emperor Waltz," "On the Beautiful Blue Danube," and "Tales from the Vienna Woods." You notice that, even today, gentlemen are keeping the long-standing tradition of only kissing a lady on the hand while at a ball. When you are told that next you will see dancing horses, trained to leap upward with all four legs off the ground and then kick further out with the hind legs while still in the air, you are incredulous. *Where on Earth are you? Can you find your place?*

Austria

The Alps cover more than three-fourths of Austria's landscape. Once a rich empire, Austria is a country alive with history where many tourists come to ski its slopes and view its treasures. The famous dancing horses are the Lipizzaner stallions. Back in the 16th century, the Austrian Spanish Riding School was founded to provide horses for the imperial family. Today, the horses perform a ballet to baroque music. Baroque music is from the period and style of the late 16th century to the beginning of the 18th century. Riding is not a hobby for these equestrians. Many of them apprentice at the age of 17 and spend five years learning how to train a horse and at least ten years perfecting the art of riding. **Would you enjoy a job like this?**

Twice, Europe was struck by a powerful plague. Many people lost their lives. In the 14th century, the Black Death, as the plague was known, killed approximately one-fourth of Europe's population. Later, in the 1600s, almost 100,000 people died of the sickness in the Vienna region alone. **What was one of the causes of the plague?** Bubonic plague constitutes about three-fourths of all plague cases, and this type is not directly infectious from person to person. Instead, the disease is transmitted from rats to people by the bite of a flea. Lack of sanitation leads to these conditions. Our standards of sanitation are fairly current. We can sterilize our dishes and our hands with hot water, and if we find rats or fleas in our homes, we can exterminate them with traps or pesticides.

Wolfgang Amadeus Mozart (1756–1791) was a child prodigy. What does that mean? A child prodigy is a highly talented child. A musical prodigy, Mozart performed in front of the Austrian Empress at the age of six. He was already composing music and playing both the piano and the violin. Mozart composed over 600 works in his lifetime, including operas, symphonies, and chamber music. Despite his talent, Mozart died poor at the age of 35.

Gregor Mendel (1822–1884) was a famous Austrian, though his birthplace is no longer in Austria! Today, it is part of the Czech Republic. A scientist and a monk, Mendel is considered to be the father of genetics. **What is *genetics*?** Genetics is the passing on of characteristics from parents to their offspring. Mendel studied the pea plants in his garden, noting how some traits seemed to be dominant over others. **What do you think Mendel would think of cloning?**

Europe

The unthinkable happened in April 1986. A nuclear reactor at Chernobyl in the Ukraine exploded. The reactor was not in this country, but the clouds of radioactive dust spread northward to cover the entire land. By the time it was over, 70% of the radioactive fallout hit this small and landlocked nation, and one-fifth of the total landmass became a zone of radioactive contamination. Two and a half million people were directly affected by the accident, and thousands of people were evacuated. Today, people continue to suffer health problems, and food grown in the contaminated soil has unsafe levels of radiation. *Where on Earth are you? Can you find your place?*

Belarus

Located in northeastern Europe, Belarus gained its independence from the Union of Soviet Socialist Republics in 1991. **There are those who feel that a country's business is its own, but what if actions in one country affect other countries, as did the explosion at Chernobyl? Should nuclear power be a world issue? If so, who monitors it? Should produce grown in contaminated soil have to be labeled as such? If so, who monitors it?**

One of Belarus' chief products is flax. **What is *flax*?** One of the oldest textile fibers, flax is a plant of the family Linacae. Linen, yarn, and fabric are made from its fibre; and linseed oil is obtained from its seed.

Olga Korbett, an Olympic gold medalist, grew up in Belarus and represented the U.S.S.R. in 1972 and 1976. **She was the first to do what on the uneven parallel bars?** Answer: a backward somersault.

Two of Belarus's famous sons are Marc Chagall and Irving Berlin. Marc Chagall lived in Belarus until his early adulthood. He was born in 1887 in Vitesbsk, when it was part of the Russian Empire. He joined the October Revolution in 1917, but he gradually grew disillusioned and left Russia and Belarus forever. Many of his paintings were of dreamlike subject matter in rich colors. Irving Berlin was born in 1888 in Mogilev, but moved with his family to the United States in 1893. He wrote the score for many famous musicals, including the songs "White Christmas," and "There's No Business Like Show Business." **Would you rather be an artist or a composer?**

Different countries have controlled Belarus over the years. When it was under Lithuanian control, the Lithuanian Statutes of 1557 set forth property rights and reduced peasants to serfs. It was not until the 1860s, when Belarus was part of the Russian empire, that serfdom was finally abolished. **What is a *serf*, and how does a serf differ from a peasant?** A serf is bound to the land and subject to the will of his lord. A peasant is not under the direct control of a lord. A peasant is in the class of persons tilling the soil as small landowners or as laborers.

The largest surviving area of primeval forest lies in a nature reserve across the Belarus/Polish border. **What does *primeval* mean, and why did this forest survive?** *Primeval* means "ancient" or "primitive." The forest survived because it was the private hunting reserve of those in power—like kings and Soviet dignitaries—for centuries.

Europe

A sure thing: each and every one of you used plastic today. It might have been your toothbrush, telephone, computer, car, electric insulator, or even in a water bottle. Leo Baekeland, the man who produced the first commercial batch of synthetic plastic, was born in this country back in 1863. What's that you hear? Flemings in the north speaking Flemish (a form of Dutch), Walloons in the south speaking French, and in a small corner close to Germany, people speaking German. You want to be understood by everyone, and so you decide to communicate in a way another native son made possible: on the saxophone. *Where on Earth are you? Can you find your place?*

Belgium

Almost like two countries in one because of linguistic and cultural differences, Belgium is a densely populated country in Western Europe. Adolph Sax (1814–1894) invented the saxophone, saxhorn, saxtuba, and the saxtromba. Sax made flutes and clarinets in his father's music workshop. When Sax invented the saxophone, a single reed woodwind instrument, he had trouble persuading people to take the new instrument seriously. Today, it is very popular and holds a special place in jazz bands. **Can you name some other woodwinds?** Characterized by wooden or metal tubes with finger holes or keys, woodwinds usually end in a slightly flared bell. Tones are produced by the vibration of one or two reeds in the mouthpiece or by the passing of air over a mouth hole. Clarinets, flutes, and oboes are all woodwinds.

saxophone

Belgium is a land of polyglots. **What is a *polyglot*, and what does that have to do with many international corporations setting up offices here?** A polyglot knows many languages. Most Belgians know two or three. In fact, every child is required to learn a second language in school. Brussels is a bilingual city, and so children must learn Flemish and French. Outside of Brussels, some children learn German. It behooves international corporations to have offices in Belgium because they do not need to hire translators.

Believe it or not, lace making was once a political issue. Labor intensive (meaning it takes a lot of labor or work to produce one piece), lace first became popular in the 16th century when men and women wore it to demonstrate their wealth. Children started learning the craft from a young age, and when lace was really in fashion during the 17th and 18th centuries, the lace industry employed thousands of women and provided them with needed income. It was then that the Belgian emperor Philip II tried to stop any girl over the age of 12 from working in the industry. He did not do this because of concern for children; he did it because girls were choosing to work as lacemakers rather than servants! At the same time in England, the government was trying to ban the buying of Belgian lace because of how much money was being spent on it. Both the Belgian and British campaigns had little success, but the problems solved themselves when lace went out of fashion. **Was it right for the governments to try and interfere with the marketplace? What is in fashion today that might be out of fashion tomorrow?**

Europe

You are in place where no rivers within the country are navigable. You like birthday parties, but you don't want to be the one to blow out the candles on this cake: the nation is over 1300 years old. You have been conquered by Alexander the Great, ruled by tzars and kings, and when the Communist Party was in control, state ownership was the order of the day. In 1990, the first free elections occurred. Today, private farming has been restored; and the literacy rate, 95%, is one of the highest in the world. *Where on Earth are you? Can you find your place?*

Bulgaria

Occupying a pivotal location in the Balkan Peninsula in southeastern Europe, Bulgaria is separated from Romania by the Danube River, a body of water that is, unlike Bulgaria's 490 internal rivers, navigable. One of the oldest settled lands in Europe, Bulgaria marked its 1300th birthday as a nation in 1981. **How many years old is Bulgaria today?**

When one thinks of farming, growing flowers doesn't normally come to mind. But these flowers are grown commercially in Bulgaria because the seeds, rich in fat and protein, are fed to poultry and livestock, crushed to make oil, or eaten as a treat by humans. The rest of the plant is used as fodder. **What is the name of the flower, and what is** *fodder?* Sunflowers are grown commercially throughout Bulgaria, and fodder is coarse food used for animals such as cattle, horses, and sheep. The stalks of sunflowers grow from 6–10 feet (1.8 to 3 meters) high, so each plant produces a significant amount of fodder! Productive farmland covers over half of Bulgaria; and a variety of fruits, flowers, grains, and vegetables are grown.

Proverbs are old sayings. One proverb from Bulgaria goes like this: "An empty bag weighs more than a full one." **What does this mean?** It means that when one has nothing, one feels a heavier weight on themselves—there is more to worry about. **Can you think of another proverb?** "Where there is smoke, there is fire" is a common proverb in the United States.

After seventh or eighth grade, students in Bulgaria have to choose a high school and take an exam to get in. If students go to a vocational high school, one where students spend three years learning a trade, they cannot go on to a university. **Should career choices be determined at this age? What type of school would you like to go to? How would you study for the entrance exam?**

Throughout the 1990s, Bulgaria suffered from a "brain drain." **What is a "brain drain"?** "Brain drain" is a phrase used to describe the moving of skilled and professional people to another country. It is usually a country that is more developed, where people will be paid more for their skills and have a higher standard of living.

How many of the 48,000 Bulgarian Jews were sent to concentration camps in WWII? Despite being an ally of Nazi Germany, Bulgarians refused to turn over their Jews when ordered. Church officials and ordinary farmers threatened to lie down on the railway tracks to stop the deportation trains. Every Jew was saved.

Ethnic hostilities have torn apart this newly independent nation. Cities were destroyed, and millions of dollars of damage was done. Tourism was a major source of funding, but now the industry is almost nonexistent. People of this nation feared that the Kingdom of Serbs, Croats, and Slovenes, and its later successor, Yugoslavia, were part of a plan to create a "Greater Serbia." *Where on Earth are you? Can you find your place?*

Europe

Croatia

Located in the northwest Balkan Peninsula, Croatia, along with the other five republics and two autonomous provinces that made up Yugoslavia, began to reassert its individual identity as communism fell apart in Eastern Europe and the Soviet Union disintegrated. When Croatia declared independence in 1991, intra-ethnic troubles started immediately. There was a mass dismissal of some 600,000 Serbs from public service jobs, and a predominately Serb area declared independence from Croatia. Serbia supported the Serbs with armed intervention. It wasn't until 1995 that the Dayton Peace Agreement confirmed Croatian control within the current boundaries of the country.

What is an example of a public-service job, and how do you think it should be distributed? A public service job is one paid for in part by government—for example, workers in public transportation systems, parks, libraries, government offices, and schools. **Should "slots" anywhere—whether it be in schools or the work force—be reserved for certain ethnic groups or sexes? What if past history has created inequalities?**

The Croatian Diaspora has a long history. What is a *diaspora*? A diaspora is the breaking up and scattering of a people. The Croatian Diaspora started back in the 14th and 15th centuries when many young men left for Italy and elsewhere in the pursuit of higher education. It has continued in response to invasions, world wars, and recent hostilities. Despite their departure, Croatians have maintained strong ties back to their ancestral land, and dollars sent back to relatives have helped the Croatian economy. Currently, overseas Croatians may retain their citizenship and vote for members of the House of Representatives.

Croatian historians feel that despite popular belief, the famous explorer Marco Polo (1254–1324) is not Venetian. Croatian historians claim that he was born on the island of Korcula in Dalmatia, part of Croatia. At the time Polo journeyed to China, Europeans did not bathe often. Polo was amazed that the Chinese bathed almost daily, and he described in his book how the water was heated with "black stones existing in veins in mountains, which they dig out and burn like firewood." **By reading Polo's book, many Europeans were learning about what for the first time?** Answer: Coal. **What does your encyclopedia say about Polo's nationality?**

One export—both legal and illegal—is small and shriveled. **Dogs have been specially trained to hunt out this export. What could it be?** Truffles, said to be one of the world's most delicious mushrooms, grow wild in Croatia's forests and are not cultivated. They are in season only from October to January, and it is believed that many truffles are smuggled illegally to Italy.

Europe

On January 1, 1993, one country became two. You are in one of the two. When this division occurred, it became known as the "Velvet Divorce." The "Velvet Divorce" followed soon after the "Velvet Revolution," the bloodless overthrowing of communism. Despite this country's youth, its culture is old—over 1,000 years old. The famous composer Antonin Dvorak heralded from this country. Is it flooding again? Hopefully it is not as bad as 1977, when over one-third of the country was affected. *Where on Earth are you? Can you find your place?*

Czech Republic

Formerly Czechoslovakia, or the Czechoslovak Socialist Republic, the beginning formation of the present day Czech Republic occurred during the Velvet Revolution. Starting in 1989, people began to demonstrate against the communist government that had come into control after WWII with the military backing of the Soviet Union. Over half the population stopped working for two hours in the strike that finally precipitated the resignation of the communist chairman. The process of restoring democracy became known as the "Velvet Revolution" because it was a peaceful process, without any blood being shed. Just a few years later, during the "Velvet Divorce," Czechoslovakia decided to separate into two republics: the Czech Republic and Slovakia. The military was divided up, with both sides agreeing it would be illegal to station troops on the shared border. **Do you think this was a wise decision?**

Antonin Dvorak (1841–1904) left an abundant heritage of musical compositions. When Dvorak visited the United States, he composed his "Symphony in E Minor, From the New World." It is said to exuberantly convey Dvorak's impressions of American scenes and folk music while at the same time evoking nostalgia for his native land. To earn money for his music studies, Dvorak played the violin in his father's inn. Later, he played the viola in a symphony. **Could you tell a violin and a viola apart, and do you think music can convey emotions like nostalgia and exuberance?** The viola is a bit larger than a violin, and it is tuned a fifth lower. Both the violin and viola are supported by the shoulder and held firmly under the chin.

Prague church

Why does Prague, the capital city, have so many beautiful old buildings? Prague was one of the few European cities that was not bombed during WWII. In fact, there are still some early 18th century homes where *cartouches*—signs or ornamental frames made of metal, stone, or wood—above the main door indicate the social rank and the profession of earlier inhabitants. **Would you like a cartouche above your door that indicated your profession and social rank to all passers-by?**

Czechs have been renowned for centuries for their cut and engraved glass and crystal. **What is crystal?** Crystal is a type of glass with the key ingredient of limestone. The limestone gives the glass a greater brilliance, providing a more striking contrast when it is engraved.

Europe

You didn't arrive in the Viking boats of old, but you are in a country with one of the highest standards of living in the world. Today, there is a state welfare system where health care and education are available free of charge. Providing such service is expensive, and the money comes from high taxes. Back in the Viking period, from the ninth to 11th centuries, the Vikings didn't think about a state welfare system—they were too busy raiding, sailing up major rivers of Europe to plunder cities in England, France, and Germany. As a matter of fact, kings from this country occupied the throne of England until 1042! *Where on Earth are you? Can you find your place?*

Denmark

A small country in northern Europe, Denmark is considered to be part of Scandinavia. **Can you name another Scandinavian country?** Scandinavia is comprised of Norway, Sweden, Denmark, Finland, and Iceland.

It is unusual to find weather differing very much from one part of Denmark to another. Why? Denmark's climate is strongly influenced by the sea. There is not one place in Denmark that is more than 32 miles (52 km) from the sea. In addition, there aren't any mountains in Denmark. It is one of the flattest countries in the world. Thus, winds blowing in from the sea can quickly sweep across the entire country.

The world's largest island is considered part of North America. Politically though, this island is part of Denmark, on the European continent. **What island is this?** The world's largest island is Greenland. 85% of Greenland is covered by a permanent icecap. The ice cap is up to 5,000 feet (1,500 m) deep. Greenland has had a home-rule government under normal Danish rule since 1953. The Faeroe Islands are also self-governing regions that are still possessions of Denmark.

Can you name one of Denmark's greatest writers? (Hint: think of fairy tales like "The Little Mermaid," "The Ugly Duckling," and "The Emperor's New Clothes.") Hans Christian Anderson (1805–1875) wrote stories that made him famous around the world. His stories have been translated into more than 100 languages. Anderson once wrote of himself, "His nose as mighty as a cannon/ His eyes are tiny, like green peas." **Do you think Anderson put some of his feelings about his own appearance into the story "The Ugly Duckling"?**

One of the world's greatest toys comes from Denmark. Can you guess what it might be? (Hint: interlocking building blocks.) Legos®. In the 1930s a carpenter was having trouble selling his furniture so he started to make sets of toy bricks out of wood. After WWII, he set up a factory and began to mass produce his bricks from plastic. There are now Legoland® amusement parks where everything is made of these plastic bricks!

Denmark is a constitutional monarchy. With the royal family line dating back to King Gorm in 930, Denmark has the oldest unbroken royal line in all of Europe. **What do you think makes a person royal?**

As you sit and enjoy your afternoon tea, you look at a policeman standing nearby. He is not carrying a firearm. Except for specific cases such as anti-terrorist work, police do not carry firearms. In fact, special authorization is required. You are at 0 degrees longitude, and the prime meridian runs through this country. *Where on Earth are you? Can you find your place?*

England

England, Wales, and Scotland lie on Great Britain, the largest of the 2,000 or so islands that make up the British Isles. Great Britain is part of the United Kingdom, which includes Northern Ireland, the Isle of Man, and the Channel Islands. **What is the prime meridian?** The prime meridian runs through the original site of the Royal Greenwich Observatory at Greenwich, England, and all other longitudes are reckoned from this site. Navigators need to know both longitude and latitude if they are to figure out their location. **What is England's latitude?** Between 50 and 60 degrees north latitude.

England is as far north as Newfoundland, Canada, but England's winters are much milder. In fact, daffodils can bloom in February. **Why?** Ocean currents. Fifty miles (80 km) wide and more than 2000 feet (610 m) deep, the warm Gulf Stream flows out of the Gulf of Mexico and merges with the warm North Atlantic Drift current. These currents warm England and influence the climate of Western Europe.

England's most famous writer is William Shakespeare (1564–1616). **Can you match these lines to his plays *Romeo and Juliet*, *Hamlet*, and *Richard the Third*?** 1. "My kingdom for a horse!" (*Richard the Third*). 2. "O Romeo, Romeo! Wherefore art thou, Romeo?" (*Romeo and Juliet*). 3. "To be, or not to be, that is the question…" (*Hamlet*).

The United Kingdom is part of the European Union (EU). **What is the EU, and why would someone join?** In 1986, France, Belgium, Germany, Italy, Luxembourg, and the Netherlands joined together to create the European Economic Community, or Common Market. In 1992, Denmark, Ireland, the United Kingdom, Greece, Spain, and Portugal joined, and the organization became known as the EU. In 1995, Austria, Finland, and Sweden became members. There are no trade barriers between these countries and together, they form one of the world's largest and most powerful economic trading blocs.

England has been ruled by Celts (about 2,600 years ago from Northern Europe), Romans, German-speaking Anglos and Saxons, Vikings from Scandinavia, and French-speaking Normans. Many kings and queens followed, but in 1936 King Edward VIII chose to abdicate because he was not allowed to marry the woman he loved. She had been divorced twice, and this made her unacceptable to the royal family. The throne went to Edward's brother, the current Queen Elizabeth's father. **Would you have abdicated?**

When Henry VIII (1509–1547) was told he could not have his marriage annulled so that he could marry Anne Boleyn, Henry did not abdicate. Instead, he started a new church: the Church of England. Anne was beheaded later, and Henry married six times. **Is it right to advance one's personal desires under the guise of public policy or moral right? Do some leaders do this today?**

You are visiting Lapland, and you are watching a Sami (as these people like to be called) family take care of their reindeer herd. Reindeer are very important to the Sami because they make dairy products from its milk, eat its meat, and use its hide for leather. Reindeer even pull their sleds! As you look at the snow-covered ground, you wonder what reindeer eat. *Where on Earth are you? Can you find your place?*

Europe

Finland

From the Middle Ages to 1809, Finland was part of the Swedish kingdom. It was ceded to Russia after Sweden was defeated in war, but Finland was able to gain its independence in 1917 when the chaos of the 1917 revolution in Russia enabled it to break free. **How long has your country been independent compared to Finland?**

Reindeer eat lichen. **What are lichens?** Lichens are simple plants that can withstand great extremes in temperature. They consist of algae that live *symbiotically* with fungi. A symbiotic relationship is one in which two very different organisms live together in a mutually beneficial relationship. With lichens, the fungi obtain food from the algae, but the fungi absorbs and retains the water that is used by the algae for photosynthesis.

An entire one-third of Finland lies north of the Arctic Circle, making it one of the most northerly countries in the world. **What are the Arctic Circle, the winter solstice, and the midnight sun; and what is the connection between all three?** The Arctic Circle is an imaginary line on Earth's surface at 66° 31'N latitude. It marks the northernmost point at which the sun can be seen at the winter solstice and the southernmost point of the northern polar regions at which the midnight sun is visible. The winter solstice (about December 22) is when the sun is directly overhead at noon at the Tropic of Capricorn. The midnight sun is the term for the sun when it is visible for 24 hours or longer.

Tundra is a Finnish word that today is part of the English language. **What is a tundra?** A tundra is a spongy mixture of soil and vegetation with a permanently frozen subsoil (permafrost). **Would you expect trees to grow on a tundra?** Trees cannot grow there. For most of the year temperatures are below freezing, winters are long and severe, and the subsoil is permanently frozen. The tundra is a fragile and easily destroyed ecosystem, but dwarf shrubs, lichens, and mosses can grow there.

Finland is one of the world's biggest suppliers of paper. **From that bit of information, what can you guess about Finland's natural resources?** Two-thirds of Finland is covered in forest, and due to a conscious reforestation program, this great natural resource is not being depleted.

Finland is bilingual. Why? Finnish and Swedish are Finland's two official languages. Very few people in the world speak Finnish. Very few outsiders learn it because it is extremely difficult and shares little in common with other European languages. Out of necessity, Finlanders must be bilingual.

You could go to the largest museum in the world or you could visit a very special cave. This cave is an exact replica of another cave discovered in 1940 by four boys playing in a forest. The cave the boys found contained over 600 paintings on, and 1,500 engravings carved into, the walls by Cro-Magnon artists over 17,000 years ago! At first the cave was open to the public, but in 1963 it was closed because the visitors' breath and body heat were damaging the paintings. The solution was an exact replica, opened in 1983. Do you approve of that solution? While you ponder how to save artifacts and share with new generations, you wonder where the entrance to a new type of "cave" is: the Chunnel. *Where on Earth are you? Can you find your place?*

France

The largest country in Western Europe, France is shaped like an irregular hexagon. **How many sides does a hexagon have?** A hexagon has six sides.

The Lascaux Cave is a natural cave filled with ancient art. The Chunnel is manmade, and it connects France to England. An underwater tunnel that opened in 1994, it enables one to travel from one country to another in about 35 minutes. Before, by ferry, it took several hours. **Do you think this changes the way some people do business and with whom they have transactions?**

One of France's most famous leaders was Napoleon Bonaparte (Napoleon I). A brilliant military strategist, Bonaparte founded the French legal system and reorganized education. After leading his army to victory over Europe's strongest nations, Napoleon was defeated in Belgium at Waterloo. **Did Napoleon come before or after the French Revolution and the "Reign of Terror"?** It was during the "Reign of Terror," that thousands of French nobles were beheaded, including King Louis and his wife, Marie Antoinette. Napoleon was emperor of France from 1804–1814 and again in 1815. Napoleon took control after the French Revolution and the ensuing "Reign of Terror."

When was the French Revolution, and did Marie Antoinette really say the famous words, "Let them eat cake?" On July 14, 1789, a Paris mob stormed and captured a royal fortress-prison called the Bastille because King Louis XVI would not draft a new constitution reducing the monarchy's power. Today, France celebrates July 14, Bastille Day, as their independence day. Although Marie Antoinette led an extravagant life and involved herself in several scandals, she has been unjustly credited with the famous line, "Let them eat cake" when told there was no bread for the peasants. It is true that there was a bread famine and peasants were starving.

The Louvre in Paris is the world's largest museum. French artists have had a great influence on art. When they started the style of French Impressionism, many people were furious. Impressionist paintings are not strict realistic depictions. They stress color and composition, giving an "impression" of a subject. Today, these paintings sell for huge amounts of money. **Can you name some Impressionist painters, and do you think new art forms often create controversy?** Monet and Renoir were founders of the Impressionist movement.

Europe

There was a man born in this country in 1397 who invented something that changed the world: a press with moveable type. Before, books had to be copied by hand. They were so precious and rare that only rich scholars or priests had copies. With this man's press, a printer could print in one day what a scribe could write in one year. This invention lowered barriers; the masses could get their hands on books. Years later, another barrier—a wall that divided a city into eastern and western sectors—was lowered in this country. *Where on Earth are you? Can you find your place?*

Germany

One of the largest and most populous countries in north central Europe, Germany has a rich cultural history. The inventor of the printing press was Johann Gutenberg. Unfortunately, he died poor and destitute because of dishonest partners, but he left the world a richer place.

The wall that was disassembled was the Berlin Wall. After Germany's defeat in WWII, the United States, the Soviet Union, Britain, and France occupied the city of Berlin. The city was divided into two sectors, with East Berlin becoming the capital of Communist East Germany, and West Berlin remaining part of West Germany, even though it was cut off from the rest of that country. In 1961, the Communists built a massive wall around West Berlin to prevent people from Communist East Germany from fleeing to freedom in West Germany. The wall was protected with barbed wire and armed guards. The wall was destroyed in 1989 when East Germany opened its borders, and the two Germanys reunited in 1990.

When this great German composer went to the performance of the Ninth Choral Symphony, one of his last compositions, he followed along with written pages of music. When the performance ended, one of the singers tugged on his arm to get him to stand. It was only when the composer turned to the audience that he "saw" the thunderous applause. He could not hear it because he was deaf. **Do you think you could compose a piece of music if you could not hear.** It was agony for this composer to not be able to hear, and yet he was still able to produce a masterpiece, with parts for solo singers as well as a large orchestra and chorus. **Who was this great composer: Robert Schumann, Johann Sebastian Bach, Felix Mendelssohn, Ludwig van Beethoven, or Richard Wagner?** All the composers mentioned were German composers of the highest caliber. Beethoven (1770–1827) was the one who lost his hearing.

Germany was involved and defeated in both WWI and WWII. **Do you know when either war started or ended?** WWI, also known as the Great War, dates from 1914–18. WWII dates from 1939–45.

Despite strict laws about replanting when trees are harvested, Germany still has had problems with diminishing forests. **Why?** Air pollution (mainly from cars and factories) is causing many trees to lose their foliage and die.

It is the tradition in one part of Germany that newly married couples saw a piece of wood. It is meant to show how they will manage to accomplish tough tasks together. **How do you think traditions get started? Can you think of other traditions that are involved with wedding ceremonies?**

Europe

One is never more than 60 miles (96.5 km) from the sea in this country—not just on the over 2,600 islands, but on the continent, too! There is the Aegean Sea, the Mediterranean Sea, and the Ionian Sea. Perhaps all this water helps explain why this nation's merchant fleet is one of the largest in the world and its ships can be found traveling on every ocean. This country is home to the first marathon. Back during the Persian Wars in 490 B.C., a runner was sent to Athens to report that the battle of Marathon had been won. To commemorate the whopping distance (about 26 miles; 41.9 km) that he ran, a marathon race was included in the revival of the Olympic Games in 1896. *Where on Earth are you? Can you find your place?*

Greece

Greece is a country whose ancient civilization has impacted even the modern world. Its legacy of democracy, theater, philosophy, and literature has helped to shape current governments, educational processes, and the arts.

Today, marathons are exactly 26 miles, 385 yards (42,195 m). Why? The Olympic Committee standardized the marathon distance in 1924, based on the 1908 British Olympic Committee's decision to start the race that year from Windsor Castle and finish it in front of the royal box in the stadium at London.

What do you know about the Olympic Games? The first Olympic Games took place around 776 B.C. in Olympia, near one of the temples built to honor Zeus, king of the gods. The ideal man was not only athletically fit, but he could write poetry, thus ensuring that Olympic athletes were well-rounded. Events expanded, and the games became so much a part of life that four-year periods were referred to as "olympiads." The games stopped in A.D. 393 for 1,500 years when the current emperor banned all pagan festivals. In 1896, the games were revived in Athens by Baron Pierre de Coubertin to bring athletes from around the world together and build friendship among countries.

Today, there are many Greek words in our vocabulary, as well as words based on Greek roots. **Do you know the meanings of these roots: *autos*, *biblios*, *logy*, *philos*, and *dynamis*? Can you name some words they provide a base for?** *Autos* means "self." An autograph is your signature, done by yourself. An automobile travels by itself. *Biblios* means "book." A bibliography is a list of books used. *Logy* means "the study of." Zoology is the study of animals, and geology is the study of the earth. *Philos* means "love," and a philanthropist loves man, donating money or time to help mankind. A bibliophile loves books. *Dynamis* means "power," and dynamite is a powerful explosive. Someone with a dynamic personality has a personality filled with power.

What are the *Illiad* and the *Odyssey*? The *Illiad* and the *Odyssey* are narrative poems that tell about heroic deeds of gods and men. Written by Homer around 800 B.C., the *Illiad* is the story of the Trojan War, and the *Odyssey* is the story of the Trojan War hero Odysseus and his adventures traveling home to Ithaca. Among others, he meets with Cyclops, a one-eyed giant, and Sirens, sea nymphs whose song lured men to shipwreck and death.

Europe

For thousands of acres, as far as the eye can see, the fields are covered in pepper plants. If you wanted, you could even go to the Spice Pepper Museum, the only museum in the world that honors the fiery red pepper paprika. You could look at the beautiful Blue Danube River that flows through the capital of Budapest, but you don't have time. You're too busy trying to figure out the Rubik's Cube, a game invented here where one tries to make the sides of a cube all one color. *Where on Earth are you? Can you find your place?*

Hungary

Paprika is considered a uniquely Hungarian spice, and nowhere else in the world does it grow so well. This pepper even helped a Hungarian win a Nobel Prize (Albert Szentgyorgyi, in 1937, for his work dealing with the Vitamin C properties of peppers). Paprika is one of the richest sources of Vitamin C. **Why is Vitamin C important, and what is the name of the disease one is afflicted with if they don't get enough of it?** Vitamin C (ascorbic acid) is water soluble and can't be stored in the body, so we need to constantly replenish our supply. We can eat citrus fruits, tomatoes, peppers, cabbage, potatoes, and berries to satisfy our requirements. Vitamin C protects one from scurvy, a disease characterized by weakened capillaries, internal hemorrhaging, anemia, and general debility. Many early explorers died from scurvy because of lack of fresh food on the long sea voyages.

Located between the Alps and the Carpathian Mountains, Hungary lies in the Carpathian Basin. In 1920, at the end of WWI, Hungary lost about two-thirds of its territory in the Treaty of Trianon. Hitler returned some of the territory when Hungary aligned itself with Germany during WWII, but at the end of the war, the land was taken away again. Students complain that they don't want to learn history. **But how would you feel if all of a sudden your borders changed? Wouldn't it affect how you felt about your neighbors?** If you were in Slovakia or Romania today, you might be angry if a Hungarian considered your land to be rightfully theirs. Our past makes a tremendous difference in how we view the world. **Is there something in your past that affects the way you look at the world?**

Hungary was controlled by the Soviet Union after WWII, and it became a communist state. In 1989 Hungary declared its independence, and in 1990 free elections were held. When the Communists came to power, they renamed streets, squares, and even whole towns. The new names were famous names in Communist history. After the fall of communism, everything was renamed. But people didn't want to get lost! The old street signs were kept up, but a red line was painted through them. The new signs went next to the old. **If every name was changed around you, how long would it take for you to get used to it? What is your city, school, and street named for?**

Hungarian Dr. Ignac Semmelweis (1818–1865) proposed a procedure that reduced death during childbirth (to both mother and child) dramatically. It's common sense today. **What is it?** Dr. Semmelweis insisted doctors wash their hands between patients and sterilize instruments.

Europe

It is time for lunch, but you are in the dark. Even though the sun cannot be seen and it is winter, you bathe outside in the Blue Lagoon. Its waters are warm, heated naturally with geothermal energy. While swimming, you are told that this country has harnessed various forms of geothermal energy. In fact, geothermal energy provides the heat for 86% of all households! *Where on Earth are you? Can you find your place?*

Iceland

Iceland is an island in the North Atlantic Ocean that is growing about an inch a year. **How is this possible?** Iceland sits at the point where two tectonic plates are parting. These tectonic plates are vast masses that float on the Earth's central magma. As the plate that supports North America pulls away from the plate supporting Europe and Africa, earthquakes and volcanic eruptions occur. Lava fills in the gap, and thus, Iceland grows an inch.

Have you ever seen a volcano erupt? Iceland experiences about one volcanic eruption every five years. When one volcano erupted on the ocean floor, between November 1963 and June 1967, a new island was born. Scientists had the unique opportunity of studying the creation of new land. They have been able to observe and document how life forms slowly become established.

In 1973, during one surprise volcanic eruption on the island of Heimaey, the entire population had to be evacuated to safety by boats. The volcano spewed out 33 million tons of debris over the course of five months. The lava flow threatened to block the island's harbor, and in an attempt to stop it, cold seawater was sprayed onto the 500-foot high wall of lava that was advancing 100 feet per day. Even though a third of the town was buried under lava, the end result was that the harbor was not blocked. Instead, a more sheltered entrance was created.

Iceland is just south of the Arctic Circle. **How does this affect the length of daylight?** In summer, Iceland is a land of midnight sun. A brief period of twilight is the only sign of night in June and July. Everyone stays up late, and activities abound. Yet one has to take the good with the bad! In winter, daylight is limited to only a few hours of twilight in the middle of the day. If one happens to live surrounded by steep fjords, one may actually see no sign of the sun at all for the entire winter—not until February or March!

Is it possible to be too good a fisherman? Much of Iceland's economic life depends on fishing. The cold waters of the Arctic are warmed by the flow of the Gulf Stream, and this provides a perfect breeding ground for many different species of fish. With the development of modern fishing methods, Icelanders actually became too good at what they did. They caught so many fish that they threatened its stocks. Government quotas are now assigned, and Iceland does not allow rival countries to fish 200 nautical miles from its shores.

Europe

You are very glad that it is not 1845. If it were 1845, you would most likely starve to death. The staple food for this country at that time (and it is still important today) was the potato. In 1845, the nation was afflicted with a potato blight, and the entire crop failed. The blight lasted for at least three more years. At least a million people starved to death while another million emigrated to avoid starvation. But you wouldn't be much better off on the emigrant ships. The conditions were so inhumane that sometimes as many as one-fifth of the passengers died during the voyage to the United States! *Where on Earth are you? Can you find your place?*

Ireland

Ireland is an island in the far west of Europe. Its landmass consists largely of pasture and agricultural land. It rains a lot in Ireland, between 175 and 200 days per year. Often the rain is not heavy, and it falls as a gentle mist.

Much of Ireland consists of a raised bog. This land is useless for agriculture, but it provides peat. **What is a *bog*, and what was *peat* used for?** A bog is wet spongy ground. It is poorly drained and rich in plant residues. Over thousands of years, the bog plants accumulated and turned into peat, a form of fuel used by millions of Irish families over the centuries.

Is Northern Ireland different from Ireland? Northern Ireland is part of the United Kingdom, as is England, Scotland, and Wales. Northern Ireland takes up one-sixth of the Irish island. The Republic of Ireland takes up the remaining five-sixths. For centuries, the Irish island was one country, Ireland, with Northern Ireland being known as Ulster. In the 1920s, Britain determined that six of the nine counties of Ulster should have separate status. These six counties became Northern Ireland. At that time, the majority of the people in these counties were Protestant, and they chose to remain under British rule. The Republic of Ireland, with the majority of people being Catholic, fought to become self-governing, and their constitution states that the "national territory" includes the entire island.

Why are there troubles in Northern Ireland? Both Protestants and Catholics live in Northern Ireland. Many of the Protestants want to retain their place in the United Kingdom. Many of the Catholics would like to see Northern Ireland united with the Republic of Ireland. There are many places in the world where both Protestants and Catholics live together peacefully side by side. **Do you think it is possible in Ireland?**

Some people think that neat and legible handwriting is not that important. With computers, there are some who even think that spelling isn't that important because spell check programs will pick up errors. There is one country that is spelled exactly like Ireland except for one letter. **Can you think of it?** The answer is Iceland. **What if you were buying an airline ticket to Ireland, and the ticket agent made a mistake?** The computer would not find a spelling error, and you might find yourself on the wrong island!

Europe

You and your friend are going to tour some palaces, art galleries, and churches. You can't walk or ride a bike. You can't even ride in a car or a train. The only vehicle allowed is a motorless water taxi. How could a city be built in the middle of a lagoon at the northern rim of the Adriatic Sea? *Where on Earth are you? Can you find your place?*

Italy

Venice is a city in Italy that was built on 118 tiny islets (very small islands) within a lagoon back in the 9th century. Houses are built on thousands of heavy wooden pilings, and the "streets" are canals. Gondolas and other boats are the only way people can travel. The city is connected to the mainland by bridges.

Italy is shaped like what article of clothing? A high-heeled boot kicking a rock. Several islands belong to Italy, with Sicily and Sardinia being the two largest. Sicily is the "rock" being kicked.

Because of Italy's location and shape, about 75% of it is surrounded by water. **Can you name the four seas that surround it?** Answer: the Adriatic, the Ionian, the Tyrrhenian, and the Liturian. (How many of you answered the Mediterranean?)

There are two independent states within Italy's boundaries. One is 24 square miles (62 sq. km.) and the other is even smaller. **Can you name them?** The Republic of San Marino is one of the smallest republics in the world and claims to be the oldest state in Europe. Thought to have been established in the 4th century, San Marino has remained independent except for a few brief periods. Vatican City, given sovereignty in 1929, is small but powerful. Located in the middle of Rome, it contains the world's largest church as well as its own prison, stamps, newspaper, army, library, and radio station. The Pope lives in Vatican City.

It has been said that there are more masterpieces per square mile in Italy than any other place in the world. One of these masterpieces is the ceiling of the Sistine Chapel. Michelangelo spent four years on his back atop a scaffold to paint the ceiling. When the grease and layers of soot that accumulated over the centuries from the burning of candles was removed from the Sistine Chapel in a major restoration effort, it was discovered that Michelangelo had not painted his masterpiece in muted colors. Instead, the colors were bright and even gaudy. Some say that the restoration went too far—removing the dark shadows Michelangelo intended. Others say Michelangelo needs to be restudied. **Is there anything you have studied that later was changed?** (Dinosaur theories have changed, and the theory of plate tectonics has become established.)

Leonardo da Vinci's most famous painting is the *Mona Lisa*. **Why do you suppose Mona Lisa didn't smile?** One explanation is that Mona Lisa may have been hiding her black and rotting teeth. Leonardo da Vinci lived from 1452–1519, and during that time, it was very common for people to have rotten teeth. **What would your teeth look like if you did not have proper dental care?**

Europe

You are in the exact geographical center of Europe. Despite undergoing centuries of domination by Poland, Sweden, Germany and Russia, you have successfully preserved your language, religion, and traditions. Just recently, you became an independent nation once again. Your inclusion into the Union of Soviet Socialist Republics was forced in 1940, but in 1991 you were recognized by the United Nations as a fully independent sovereign state. Perhaps to celebrate your freedom you will visit the only island castle still standing in northeastern Europe. *Where on Earth are you? Can you find your place?*

Lithuania

Lithuania was once a large and powerful country, and during the Middle Ages, between 1362 and 1382, a castle was built in Trakai by the Grand Duke Jaunutis. The castle was built on an island in the middle of a lake. On a nearby peninsula, there is a complex of defensive fortifications. **What were the advantages and disadvantages of having your home on an island in a lake during that time?**

Lithuania is often referred to as a Baltic state. **Where do you think that name came from, and can you name two other Baltic states?** (Hint: look for the Baltic Sea) Former soviet republics, Lithuania, Latvia, and Estonia all border the Baltic Sea. Lithuania is the largest of the Baltic states, but all three share similar topography—low lying lands with many lakes and swamps—as well as many cultural elements.

Can you figure out the answer to these Lithuanian riddles? "Though it bends, it breaks not." (*smoke*) "It burns without fire and beats without a stick." (*the heart*).

Why would a Lithuanian attach a wagon wheel to his or her rooftop? The cart wheels are there for storks to nest on. It is considered a good sign to have a stork (the national bird) nesting on one's house, for it is supposed to indicate that a good person lives there. **Swallows nesting under the eaves are believed to protect the house from lightning, but do you think it prudent to invest in a lightning rod, too?**

At a Lithuanian meal, would you be more likely to be offered white, brown, or rye bread? Rye bread is a dark bread made from rye, a cereal grass whose seed or grain is used in making flour and as feed for farm animals. Rye bread is typically eaten at every meal.

Often, saunas are built near streams or lakes in Lithuania so that one can plunge from the sweltering sauna into icy cold water. **Would you consider this fun?**

During Soviet rule, religious freedom was severely limited. Believers were often sent to prison or denied access to higher education. Churches were converted to other uses, but today they are being restored. **Do you think it is justifiable to deny someone the right to practice his or her religion? What if you do not agree with his or her religion?**

Europe

Fields and fields of tulips surround you. Their beauty is outstanding. Brought to this country in 1593 from Turkey, tulips quickly became an obsession. Rare bulbs were changing hands for dazzling sums. Investors were using gold to pay for premium bulbs, and single flowers were being sold for more than the cost of a house. Fortunes were made overnight, but so too were they lost. When the market crashed in 1637, men who had been the richest faced bankruptcy and ruin. It seems impossible that the land you are now standing on was once covered by the ocean. *Where on Earth are you? Can you find your place?*

Netherlands

Often called Holland, the Netherlands is one of the smaller countries in northern Europe. People from the Netherlands are known as Dutch, as is their language. A saying from the Netherlands explains that the Lord created the land, except for Holland, which was created by the Dutch. This is because of the ceaseless battle the Dutch have had with the North Sea. **How do the Dutch battle the sea?** Answer: They have to constantly reclaim the land from the sea. To do this, dikes are built around the area to be reclaimed. The water in the enclosed area is pumped out (in the past with energy provided by windmills). A network of canals is constructed so that water can be pumped back into the ocean. Pumping has to be maintained every day. To eliminate the salt residue, course grass is planted and left to grow for several years. Finally, the land is ready for settlement and agriculture.

Anton van Leeuwenhoek (1623–1723) was known as the "Father of Microbiology." **What tool did this Dutch man make that helped him gain this title?** Van Leeuwenhoek ground lenses so that he could magnify what he was looking at. He made over 247 of the world's first microscopes. In van Leeuwenhoek's time, many people did not brush their teeth. Van Leeuwenhoek looked at scrapings from mouths of people who had never brushed their teeth and compared them to people who had. He always saw more creatures from the scrapings of those who had never brushed their teeth. Van Leeuwenhoek surmised that it was these creatures that caused "stinking" breath.

The Netherlands is a highly industrialized, trading nation; and its capital, Amsterdam, is known as the diamond center of the world. Diamond cutting has been practiced in Amsterdam since the 16th century. **What are diamonds used for?** Amsterdam produces 80% of the world's industrial diamonds, those diamonds used for cutting tools and drills. Diamonds are also cut and polished and sold for jewelry.

Why is the Netherlands a great trading nation? Answer: location. More than one-third of all seaborne goods loaded or unloaded in European Union countries pass through the Netherlands. The busiest port is in Rotterdam, and it is the largest human-made harbor and port complex in the world. It extends for 21 miles (35 km).

The land is flat, but roads are constructed with gentle bends. Why? To keep drivers awake. The flatness may be part of the reason the Netherlands is known as the land of the bicycle. There are three times more bicycles in the Netherlands than cars.

Europe

Skiing originated here, in this land of over 150,000 islands and 160,000 lakes. However, only about 2,000 of the islands are inhabited. The lemming lives here, a small rodent with a population surge every few years. When this happens, the crowded lemmings start to migrate. The myth is that the lemmings march to cliffs and purposefully jump off to drown in the ocean below. The truth is that many lemmings do die during the migration, providing a feast for hungry fish and birds of prey, but they don't purposely drown. They try to avoid water if they can't see the other side, but many drown while swimming because they run out of energy before they reach the opposite shore. *Where on Earth are you? Can you find your place?*

Norway

With one-third of its area lying north of the Arctic Circle, Norway is a land created by ice. Together, Norway, Sweden, and Denmark, are sometimes referred to as Scandinavia. Scandinavia was the name for this area during the time of the ancient Norsemen or Vikings. Norway is filled with fjords. **What are *fjords*?** Fjords are narrow inlets in which the sea penetrates the land between steep cliffs. Created by glaciers, some of the fjords are deeper than the sea from which their water flows.

fjord

Norway is at about the same latitude as Greenland, but Greenland has a permanent ice sheet covering all but its coastal fringes. **What makes Norway different?** The Gulf Stream is a huge current of warm water that crosses the Atlantic from the Caribbean Sea. Because the air above the current is also warmer, Norway has warmer weather along the coast than one would expect at that latitude.

King Olav V ruled Norway from 1957 to 1991. King Olav V believed in setting an example. He was a Resistance hero during WWII, and during the oil crisis in 1972, the king rode the trolley and insisted on paying his fare. Instead of hiding his handicap—dyslexia, a condition that often interferes with reading—King Olav simply explained to his people that he might have trouble when he gave speeches. **How do you think people reacted to King Olav?** The king was admired and is remembered fondly as "the people's king." Because of the way the king was so forward about his handicap, people saw him as a symbol of human strength.

It was a race to the South Pole! The Norwegians beat the English. Yet because the Englishman died, many people remember his party better than the Norwegian one! **Who knows the name of the Norwegian and the English explorers?** On December 14, 1911, Roald Amundsen became the first man to reach the South Pole. Robert Scott arrived there a month after Amundsen, and he and his party perished on the way back. A master planner, Amundsen was first because of his work beforehand. Amundsen trained with the Inuit, people accustomed to living and thriving in Arctic conditions. He learned how to use dogs (Scott used ponies) and what type of clothes to wear.

Europe

You are in a country that has been erased two times! The first time this country was wiped off the map was in 1795. Prussia, Austria, and Russia divided it up, having started taking territory in 1772. After an absence of 132 years, at the end of WWI, it was finally put back on the map. During WWII, it was taken over by Russia and Germany. The Germans were expelled in 1945. The Russians, after forcing communistic rule, left in 1956. The country suffered economically. Despite being initially outlawed, the Solidarity movement, the first free trade union in the Communist bloc, finally came to power in 1989 when the first free elections were held in over 40 years. *Where on Earth are you? Can you find your place?*

Poland

During WWI, starving soldiers killed the last herd of European Bison in Poland and ate them. In 1929, three pairs of bison were purchased from other European zoos and returned to the forest. Today, there are about 300 bison. Some people feel zoos are cruel and should not exist. **What is your opinion?**

Can you name the professions of these three famous Poles: Nicolaus Copernicus, Marie Curie, and Frederick Chopin?

➤ Copernicus (1473–1543) was an astronomer whose work supported the theory that Earth was round and that it revolved on an axis, an imaginary line through its middle. Copernicus kept his work a secret for many years because he was worried about opposition from the church and the government.

➤ Curie (1867–1934) was the first person to win a second Nobel Prize. She won one in physics and one in chemistry. Curie worked with radioactive materials at a time when the dangers of radioactive materials were not known. For many years after Curie's death, her notebooks and the chair that she sat in while she worked in the lab were highly radioactive. **Is it no wonder that Curie felt too ill to attend the awards ceremony?**

➤ Chopin (1810–1849) was a composer who published his first score when he was only eight years old. He wrote one piece that listeners said sounded "like guns hidden in flowers." He died of tuberculosis.

What happened to the Jews in Poland during WWII? Hitler's "Final Solution" was to exterminate the Jewish people, as well as the Romas (Gypsies) and others he did not consider to be pure Aryans. He wanted to murder every man, woman, and child. Concentration camps such as Treblinka, Majdanek, Auschwitz, and Birkenau (also called Auschwitz II) were built. Jews were tortured, shot, and gassed. Ovens were built at Birkenau that could incinerate nearly 200 bodies per hour. Poland was turned into a mass graveyard. Over 6 million Jews from Poland and other German-controlled countries were systematically murdered.

Would you ever expect a Pole to wear an insect? Insects are worn in special cases. Amber from the Baltic is increasingly precious, and if one can find a piece of it with a fossilized insect trapped in the resin, it is even more precious. Amber beads can be made into necklaces.

This small rectangular strip of a nation on the southwestern corner of the Iberian Peninsula once led the world in exploration. With Prince Henry the Navigator spurring the country on, it opened up the African coast to European traders, found the Cape route to the Indies, colonized Brazil, and secured a trade monopoly in India and the East Indies. Explorer Vasco Da Gama hailed from here, as did Ferdinand Magellan, the skilled navigator who led the Spanish sponsored voyage that was the first to successfully circumnavigate the globe. *Where on Earth are you? Can you find your place?*

Portugal

Today, all that remains of Portugal's once vast empire are the islands of the Azores and Maderia. They are located in the North Atlantic Ocean off the western coast of Africa. Although Portuguese territories, both the Azore and Maderia archipelagos are autonomous regions with their own legislatures and governments. The Azores are about 1,000 miles (1,600 km) from Lisbon, Portugal's capital.

What does it mean to secure a trade monopoly? *Mono* means "one"; and when one has a monopoly, there is only one in control. If one has a trade monopoly, one has exclusive possession or control over trade for that region. **Do you think prices would be higher or lower if there was a trade monopoly? If you were the producer, would you be paid more or less if there was only one buyer to whom you could sell?** Some governments have enacted laws that limit monopolies. **Do you agree? How would you feel if you could only buy one brand of car, medicine, or toy?**

There is a canine in Portugal that has webbed feet for better swimming and a tail curved up over its back that serves as a rudder. The Spanish waterdog is an ancient breed from the Iberian coast. It has very curly hair that does not molt. Able to swim up to five miles, waterdogs can dive 12 feet down to pull up fish and nets. They are useful in the fog—they bark when danger is close. Also excellent herders, these dogs are able to transverse wet ground and are more commonly used in that capacity today.

Father Fernando Oliveira wrote in 1555, "We were the inventors of such a vile trade, never previously used or heard of among human beings." For daring to publish such an opinion about the slave trade, Father Oliveira was imprisoned by the Inquisition. **What was the Inquisition?** The Inquisition was a tribunal of the Roman Catholic Church formed to suppress heresy. *Heresy* is an opinion, doctrine, or practice contrary to accepted truth—in this case what the Roman Catholic Church dictated.

Spanish waterdog

Portugal has a law that says that cork bark can be stripped from a tree only once every 11 years. Cork, which brings in millions of dollars in exports, is used for such things as bottle stoppers, fishing floats, and table-tennis paddles.

Europe

The majority of the people around you can trace their origins to the Romans who occupied this country from A.D. 106 to A.D. 271, and the name of this nation reflects this Latin heritage. Although this Balkan country has been around for centuries, it was only in 1989 that its present form was founded. That was when the people successfully revolted against the cruel dictator who had ruled them since 1965. You know the history—how after WWII this nation became a Russian-dominated communist state—but right now, you're interested in more recent events. For instance, what is perhaps the world's only ecosystem that does not rely on sunlight, discovered in 1986? *Where on Earth are you? Can you name your place?*

Romania

A Balkan country in Eastern Europe, Romania borders the Black Sea.

How could there be an ecosystem in Romania that does not rely on sunlight? Sealed off from the rest of the world for 5.5 million years, the Romanian Movile Cave was only discovered in 1986 when engineers were drilling for a new construction site. Located 80 feet (24 m) below ground, the cave's only connection to the outside world is oxygen that flows in through tiny cracks in the rock. Leeches, millipedes, scorpions, and spiders—48 different animal species in all—comprise an ecosystem that does not rely on photosynthesis. **What is *photosynthesis*?** Photosynthesis is the natural process in which plants turn sunlight into energy, and it was once believed to be the basis of every ecosystem on Earth. In Molive Cave though, the base of the food chain is a thick layer of bacteria that floats on top of the water at the bottom of the cave. **Do you think there could be other ecosystems not based on photosynthesis on Earth?**

scorpion

Romania has produced some amazing athletes and is perhaps best known for its gymnasts. For example, Nadia Comaneci earned seven perfect scores and three gold medals in the 1976 Olympic gymnastic competition, and she became the all-around champion when she was only 14 years old. In Romania, there are special schools for athletes run by the government. Nadia started training in one of government programs when she was only six years old. **Do you think there should be government schools for athletes, and at what age should children start training?**

The Roma people—once know as Gypsies—are descendents of people who came to Europe from India and Iran over 1,000 years ago. A nomadic people, the Romas usually travel in groups, moving to different locations as they look for work and the resources they need to survive. History has not been kind to the Romas. In the early 1800s, many Romas were slaves to wealthy Romanians, and they were not emancipated until 1848. Part of Hitler's Final Solution during WWII was to murder all the Romas, as well as the Jews. Even today Romas are often mistreated and blamed for anything that goes wrong. By saying to someone, "He gypped me" or "I was gypped," one is reinforcing the negative stereotype of the Romas. One is suggesting that Romas always steal.

Europe

People have claimed for years that a monster ("Nessie") lives in the depths of Loch Ness. You're pretty sure that despite the photographs, the whole "Nessie" thing is a hoax. It's a good one though—tourists flock to Loch Ness hoping for a sighting. Even if you can't spot "Nessie," you're not leaving disappointed. There are over 600 castles and towers to see, and you've always wanted to see a moor. *Where on Earth are you? Can you find your place?*

Scotland

Scotland has over 790 islands, including the Hebrides, Orkney, and Shetland island groups, but the majority of Scotland's land mass lies on the island of Great Britain. England and Wales are also part of the island. These three countries, along with Northern Ireland, make up the United Kingdom.

What is a *loch*, a *moor*, and "Nessie"? A loch is a lake, and a moor is a boggy, treeless area. "Nessie" is the name given to the dinosaur-like creature that lives in Loch Ness, but is it no surprise that scientists, even with special equipment, have found no trace of her? **Have you ever seen a monster, only to discover that it is a shadow or a friend tricking you?**

What can one tell about someone by the patterns on their kilts? Scotland was once ruled by different clans, each with their own area and chief. Each clan had a *tartan*—a colorful patterned cloth of crisscrossed stripes—that was exclusively theirs. Tartans were used for *kilts*, knee-length pleated skirts traditionally worn by Scottish men. Men wear short black pants underneath their kilts.

In 1922 a Scottish man named Alexander Fleming blew his nose and changed the world. How? Fleming blew his nose, looked at the mucus in his handkerchief, and out of curiosity put some on a culture jelly in which colonies of microbes were breeding. Fleming discovered that the mucus contained an antiseptic that killed some of the microbes. For six years he looked for more germ-killing substances that would help human beings fight internal infections. When a mold from a plant blew in from an open window and landed on one of the jelly cultures that he had just happened to take the lid off of, Fleming did not view his experiment as ruined. Good thing, because he had just discovered penicillin! It took nine years and two chemists to purify the drug, but a new era of medicine had begun.

What musical instrument is often associated with Scotland? The bagpipes. A player blows air into a leather bag that is then forced with the arm through several pipes to make shrill tones. The earliest bagpipes used sheep or goat bladders. Bagpipes are thought to have originated in the Near East; and different versions are found throughout Europe, North Africa, the Arabian Peninsula, and India.

For generations, eating out in Scotland meant going out and buying bags of hot, deep-fried food like chips (thick French fries). Until recently, chips were put in a greaseproof bag and wrapped in newspaper. Newspaper is no longer allowed with the new European Union regulations. Styrofoam® boxes and paper wrappings have taken its place. **Why would there be regulations against newspapers?** Answer: sanitation control.

Europe

When there is turbulence, there is wild commotion, disturbance, unrest, and perhaps violence. This nation has certainly been witness to turbulence—in the past and the present. Once part of a great Slav kingdom, this country has seen its territories expand and shrink over the centuries. At one point, it was defeated by the Turks and made part of the Ottoman Empire, and then in turn, years later, during the Balkan Wars, it and other Balkan countries gained back territory. WWI started when Austria declared war on this nation, whom it blamed for the assassination of Archduke Francis Ferdinand and his wife in 1914. *Where on Earth are you? Can you name your place?*

Serbia

A mountainous country, Serbia is located in the heart of the Balkans. **What nations make up the Balkans?** The Balkans, or Balkan States, are Slovenia, Croatia, Bosnia and Herzegovina, Macedonia, Yugoslavia, Romania, Bulgaria, Albania, Greece, and Turkey.

What is Serbia's connection to Yugoslavia? After WWI, this nation became part of the Kingdom of the Serbs, Croats, and Slovenes, whose name was changed to Yugoslavia in 1929. There might have been one name, but it didn't change the fact that the country was made up of different groups, with disagreements between the Croatians and the Serbians (making up the majority of the population) being especially strong. During WWII, Croatia, supported by Italy, sought to get rid of all Serbs, Jews, and Romas (Gypsies). Yugoslavia was only held together after the war by a communist dictator named Tito, and past resentments between ethnic groups and the six republics were never healed. When Yugoslavia broke up in 1991, there was fighting between Serbs, Muslims, and Croats. In 1992, Serbia joined with Montenegro to form the Federal Republic of Yugoslavia.

Unlike most languages, the Serbian language can be written in two alphabets: Roman and Cyrillic. Since the split with Croatia, there is the tendency to use the Cyrillic alphabet more, but both alphabets are taught in school. There is only one sound to go with each letter, and each word is spelled exactly as it sounds, with the emphasis or accent on the first syllable. **Would it have been easier to learn how to read if a vowel was always long or short and there weren't any silent letters like the "gh" in "might" or the "e" in "gate"?**

When Nikola Tesla (1856–1943) arrived in the United States, he had in his pocket just four cents, calculations for a flying machine, and some poems he had written. Truly a man of the world, Tesla was born in Croatia but is considered Serbian-American because his parents were Serbian and he became an American citizen. Tesla worked for a short time with Thomas Edison. **Though Edison called Tesla "a poet of science," the two became rivals. About what?** The answer is *current*. Tesla's idea of connecting alternating current (AC) to a motor—eventually leading to the development of power stations in the U.S. and around the world—bested Edison's direct current (DC) systems. When hydropower was harnessed for the first time at Niagara Falls to supply power to the city of Buffalo in 1896, the machinery installed bore Tesla's name and patent number. Over time, Tesla received 112 U.S. patents, many of which are still in use today.

Europe

It's early morning, and you are in your swiftest running shoes, ready to go. A rocket goes off, and you take off. So do the bulls. The bulls are fighting in the ring that afternoon, but you, you're just trying to get to the ring before the bulls get you. As you race down the streets, between the wooden barriers, you try not to think about the people who are hurt every year. Instead, you think about everyone cheering you on as they look safely down at you from their windows. Safe at last, you feel you are a changed person. This country has certainly changed over the years, what with the Romans, the Visigoths, and the Moors. In this century alone it has gone from one supreme ruler to a democracy. *Where on Earth are you? Can you find your place?*

Spain

The third largest country in Europe, Spain is a parliamentary monarchy. The king is the head of the state, but the prime minister is the head of the government. Elections are held for members of the legislature. Before the current king, General Franco ruled the country from 1939 to 1975. Franco gained power by rebelling against the government and winning the civil war that followed. Franco chose the grandson (who was living in exile) of the last reigning monarch to succeed him. Franco expected the king to continue his strict ways, but the king led his country through democratic reforms.

Spain was conquered and ruled by the Romans for over 300 years, as well as by Germanic tribes like the Visigoths. The Moors, the name given to Muslims by Christians, entered Spain in 711. In 1492 King Ferdinand and Queen Isabella reclaimed all the territory conquered by the Arabs.

What was the Spanish Inquisition? Part of Ferdinand and Isabella's drive was due to their religious crusade to make all of their subjects followers of the Catholic faith. They created the Inquisition, a religious court with unlimited power. It tortured, imprisoned, and killed anyone suspected of not believing in the Catholic religion. It was a terrible time, when many innocent people were executed. **Is it ever right to force religion on anyone?**

At the height of the Spanish Empire, Spaniards traveled all over the world. It was a Spaniard, Father Junipero Serra, who in 1769 planted the first palm tree in California. It was the Spaniards who introduced oranges, lemons, limes, peaches, pears, apples, and apricots, as well as horses, to the U.S.

Each year in Pamplona, thousands of people participate in the Running of the Bulls, during which a group of bulls are led from their corral to a bullring 860 yards (790 meters) away. Runners dressed in red and white prod the bulls forward. **If you fall while running in front of a bull, what should you do?** Expert runners advise you to curl up into a ball. Whatever you do, don't try to get up until someone taps you on the shoulder, signaling that the bulls have passed. **Would you ever take part in such a dangerous tradition?**

The famous Spanish master Pablo Picasso (1881–1973) was one of the first producers of cubist art. **What is cubist art?** Cubist art is a style where shapes such as squares, circles, and triangles represent people and objects. One of Picasso's most famous works is a large painting called *Guernica*, which depicts the agony caused by the German bombing of that city. Picasso would not allow the picture to enter Spain while Franco was alive. It is in Spain today, hanging behind layers of bulletproof glass.

Europe

It's private land you see and private land you are walking on. You're not worried about anyone saying you aren't allowed there because, even though the land is privately owned, it's *allemannsratten*—or "everyman's land." Without asking for permission, you may camp, hike, and pick berries and mushrooms. You can't go to someone's house, cut down trees, or hunt, though. Alfred Nobel, whose legacy is the invention of dynamite and the creation of the prestigious Nobel Prize, hails from this country, as did another man who changed the world. His invention may not have been as explosive as Nobel's, but you've probably had hands-on dealings with it. He put milk in a carton. *Where on Earth are you? Can you find your place?*

Sweden

The fourth largest country in Europe, Sweden is most heavily populated in the south where the beautiful city of Stockholm, Sweden's capital, is located.

Taxes are high in Sweden where basic medical and social services are paid for by the state. Taxes do not pay for Nobel prizes, though; Nobel's fortune does. **What are the Nobel Prizes?** Alfred Nobel, a Swedish inventor and industrialist, left money for those who had "conferred the greatest benefit on mankind." Nobel Prizes have been awarded annually since 1901 in physics, chemistry, physiology or medicine, literature, and peace. The discoverers of penicillin and X-rays were awarded Nobel Prizes. An economics award was added in 1968 in Nobel's memory.

In Nobel's nitroglycerine factory, workers sat on one-legged stools. **Why?** Nitroglycerine is an incredibly dangerous explosive. No one sitting on a one-legged stool would be able to nod off. **Should your school switch to one-legged stools?**

When Sweden granted women suffrage in 1912, it was one of the first countries to grant this right to females. **What does *suffrage* mean, and when was it granted in your country?** *Suffrage* means the right to vote.

Sweden has a constitutional monarchy. There is a parliament and a monarchy. In 1979, the Act of Succession was amended so that the crown no longer goes to the first-born son, but rather the first-born child. Political power rests within the parliament, and its members are elected by proportional representation. **What does this mean?** Parliament seats are allocated among the parties in proportion to the number of votes they get, but a party must gain at least 4% of the national vote to get a seat. For example, if different parties got 5%, 15%, 25%, and 55% of the vote, they would get 5%, 15%, 25%, and 55% of the parliament seats respectively. Some feel this is the best way for all people to be heard because it is not "winner takes all"—even small parties can join coalitions and negotiate their desires. **What do you think?**

Ruben Rausing invented a packaging machine in 1952 that produced a long paper tube. After being filled with milk, it could be cut off and sealed at both ends. Today, juice, cream, and other foods are packaged this way, as well. **How was milk packaged before?** Typically in glass bottles or cans. **Which way is more convenient? Why?**

High in the Alps, the largest mountain system in Europe, you realize you are lost. You're not interested in climbing the Matterhorn. You are only interested in getting back. You look at your watch, a locally constructed and fine instrument so well built that cold, heat, and water won't affect its precision. You think about William Tell, and you want to be as brave and fearless as he was. What is that you hear? Could it be a St. Bernard dog is coming to rescue you? *Where on Earth are you? Can you find your place?*

Switzerland

Located in central Europe, Switzerland is a landlocked country with the Alps taking up three-fifths of its landmass. Although Switzerland has to import 60% of its food, Switzerland has a thriving economy because of its emphasis on quality. For example, the Swiss are known for their superb timepieces. For most watches, the metals and parts needed for construction cost only 5% of what it costs to pay the watchmaker. **What does this mean about the money made on the watch?** Most of the money remains in Switzerland. Only a negligible amount goes back out to buy more materials.

Is it fact or fiction that William Tell shot an apple off his son's head? The historical facts are disputed, but it's a great story. For refusing to remove his hat when he passed the tyrannical governor's hat that had been placed on a pole, Tell was ordered to shoot an apple off his son's head. Tell took out two arrows from his quiver, but he only used one to shoot the apple. When the governor asked what the other arrow was for, Tell replied, "For you if I had missed." Tell was arrested, escaped, and later killed the governor. He is known as a Swiss symbol of freedom.

How did St. Bernard dogs get their names? When the St. Bernard monks were responsible for keeping the St. Bernard Pass open in the winter, these intelligent dogs were used to help rescue people. Their colossal size helped them to push snow out of the way and clear paths. These dogs rescued over 2,000 people from 1750–1900.

What international aid society was started in Switzerland? The Red Cross was started by Jean Henri Dunant. In 1859, he passed by a battlefield in Italy and saw 40,000 dying and critically injured men. Dunant found volunteers to help the wounded soldiers. Later, he pleaded that there be permanent societies of volunteers who would help the wounded in times of war, regardless of nationality. The first meeting of the Red Cross was held in 1863 in Geneva. Dunant shared the first Nobel Peace Prize in 1901. Today, the Red Cross helps victims of poverty and natural disasters as well as war.

Historically, Switzerland is known for its neutrality. It does, however, have a citizen's army, where all able-bodied men go through basic training and, between the ages of 20 and 50, are permanently on call. **Why would the Swiss have an army, especially because of their stance on antiviolence?** The Swiss never attack with their forces. They only protect their neutrality. For example, during the battle of France in 1940, the Swiss shot down German airplanes that had violated their air space. They remained ready to blow up tunnels and passes through the Alps.

Europe

Known as the "breadbasket of Europe," flat fertile plains called steppes make up much of this nation that is the largest country entirely located in Europe. Two independence days are celebrated here, one on January 22, when independence from Russia was declared in 1918, and one on August 24, when independence from the Soviet Union was declared in 1991. *Where on Earth are you? Can you find your place?*

Ukraine

Located in southeastern Europe, north of the Black Sea, Ukraine became a province of Russia after the Russians helped the Cossacks (Ukrainian peasant fighters known for their fierceness) in their struggle against Poland. After the Russian revolution in 1917, Ukraine did not want to become part of the Soviet Union, and they declared their independence in 1918. It was short-lived though, for in 1921, the communist army took control of Ukraine and it became a part of the U.S.S.R. in 1922. In the 1930s there was a terrible famine where as many as 10 million people died. **How could this happen in a country covered with fertile black earth where crops such as wheat, corn, rye, sugar beets, and potatoes grow in abundance?** Under U.S.S.R. leader Joseph Stalin's communist regime, privately owned farms were turned into collectives, large farms owned and run by the government. Ukrainians resented their land being taken from them, and they tried to resist collectivization. Stalin created a famine by taking away all of the grain. Stalin even outlawed Ukrainians from writing in their own language.

You are told that you are going on a field trip to see Ukrainian eggs. You don't go to a farm; you go to a museum. **What's so special about Ukrainian eggs?** The ancient art of decorating eggs is called *pysanka*, and Ukrainian painted eggs are world famous. Long ago, it was believed that the painted eggs held magical powers and helped ensure a bountiful harvest and personal good fortune. The eggs were given to family members and special friends. Today, people know that the painted eggs hold no magical powers, but they are still used to celebrate Easter and the arrival of spring.

In 1945 near the end of WWII, several world leaders met on the Crimean Peninsula on the Black Sea in the Ukrainian town of Yalta to discuss the fate of Germany. **Can you name the Russian, American, and British leaders who met there?** Premier Joseph Stalin, President Franklin D. Roosevelt, and Prime Minister Winston Churchill, respectively.

***Borscht* is often served in Ukraine. What is it?** (Hint: one needs a spoon to eat it.) Borscht is beet soup.

On April 26, 1986, radiation hundreds of times greater than the atomic bombs that exploded over Japan in WWII was unleashed in Ukraine. **What happened?** A reactor at the Chernobyl nuclear power plant exploded. Land still remains contaminated, and people are still suffering from the effects of radiation contamination.

Welcome to
North and Central America!

Map of North and Central America

The countries are numbered according to the page number on which you will find them. Not all countries are covered in this book. Use tape or glue to connect page 128 to page 129 at the tab.

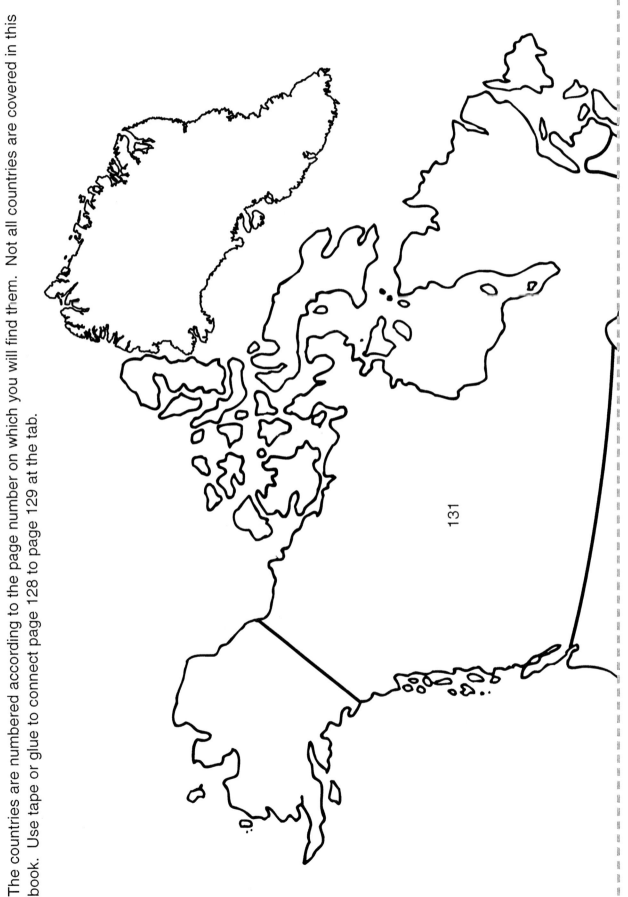

131

Map of North and Central America *(cont.)*

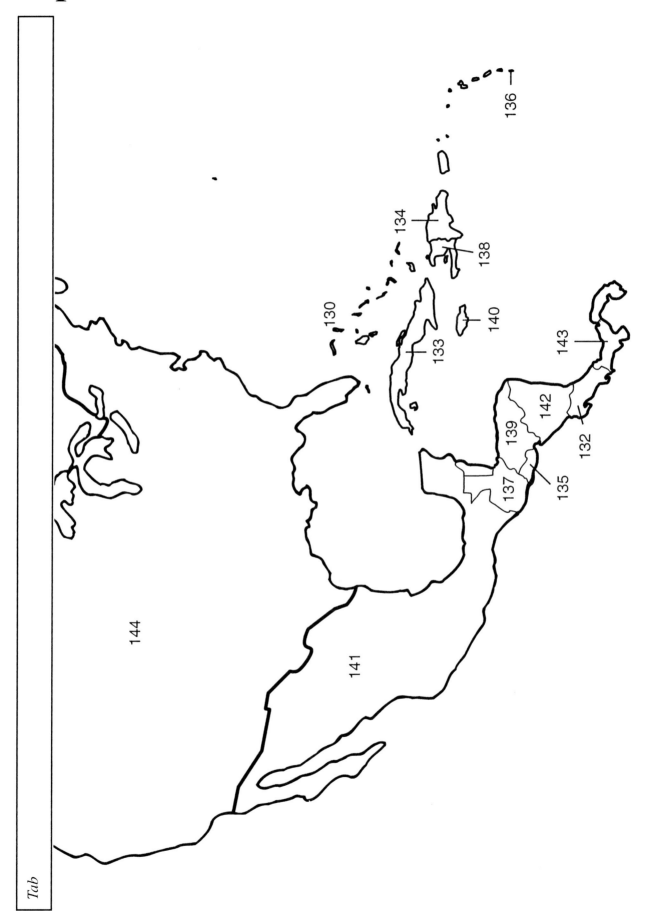

There are no permanent rivers or streams on this land where the flamingo is the national bird and Christopher Columbus first landed in the New World in 1492. The overland journey to India and China from Europe was long and dangerous, and Columbus was looking for a faster and easier route. He didn't find India, but he did find lands that Europeans were unaware of. For 250 years, this nation was a British colony, but finally, in 1973, it became an independent country. Watch carefully when you step out onto the street: people still drive on the left side of the road here, just as they do in England. *Where on Earth are you? Can you find your place?*

The Bahamas

More than 2,000 islands make up the North Atlantic Ocean nation of the Bahamas, but the majority of the people live on just 23 of them. Columbus landed on the island of San Salvador, inhabited by a peaceful group of Arawak Indians called the Lucayans. Columbus wrote in his journal that these friendly people would make excellent servants. He even kidnapped some to take back to Spain. (The kidnapped Lucayans never made it back home.) **How would it make you feel if someone viewed you only as servant material? Does this type of perceived superiority still happen today?**

A flamingo's plumage is mainly pink, tinged with light vermilion. **What color is vermilion, and is the flamingo *garrulous* or *gregarious*?** Vermilion is bright red. A flamingo is gregarious. If one is gregarious, one tends to be social. Flamingoes are gregarious—there were 60,000 birds in one flock alone on the Bahamian Great Inagua Island! If one is garrulous, one tends to talk a lot. **Are you garrulous? How about gregarious?**

When were women finally given the right to vote in the Bahamas: 1881, 1901, 1921, 1941, or 1961? Women were given the right to vote in 1961. **When were women allowed to vote in your country?**

There are no income taxes in the Bahamas. **What type of tax is an income tax, and what tax do you think the Bahamas imposes instead?** An income tax is a tax on what one earns. A sales tax, on the other hand, has nothing to do with one's income. One pays a set percentage of the price of the item to the government. Money is raised in the Bahamas by taxing goods shipped into the country. A great many items are imported into the Bahamas because tourism is its number one industry, and it does not have a large manufacturing or agricultural base. **Do you think corporations take into consideration a nation's tax laws when they decide to move their head offices there?**

During what two time periods in the United States were the Bahamas used as starting off points for blockade-runners? During the Civil War, southern blockade-runners carried cotton—which could then be sent on to English mills—to the Bahamas. Medicine and other supplies were carried back on their return. In 1919, the United States added the 18th Amendment to the U.S. Constitution. This amendment prohibited the manufacture and sale of alcohol. Whiskey and rum were brought in through the Bahamas during the 1920s, and the government collected taxes on every bottle!

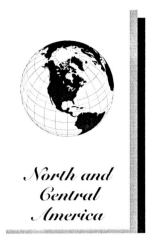

North and Central America

Watch out for the language police! Your outdoor sign is in French (as is required), but on your indoor sign, the French words are not twice as big as the English ones. Even worse, they are not a "stronger" color. Better to face the language police than a bear, especially because there are three types here: the black, the grizzly, and the polar. You've had enough of worries. You're going to get on your snowmobile—invented here—and find a perfect place to watch the Northern Lights. There are certainly plenty of places to ride to. After all, you're in the second largest country in the world. *Where on Earth are you? Can you find your place?*

Canada

Stretching from the Atlantic to the Pacific, Canada is immense, and it makes sense that there is some of everything—rocky and forested mountains, rolling prairies, fishing villages, sophisticated cities, and arctic snow and ice. The largest province in Canada is Quebec, and the mainly French population there makes it unique. Some inhabitants of Quebec want Quebec to secede from Canada and become an independent country. To hold on to their traditions, Quebec has language laws. French is their official language, while it is English for the remainder of Canada. There are English- and French-speaking schools, but if your grandfather went to a French school or you are a child of an immigrant, you must go to a French school. **Is this fair?**

Everything about a polar bear is big except its ears. Why does it have tiny ears? The ears would freeze if they were much larger. Polar bears rely on their keen sense of smell. It is believed that a polar bear can smell a seal from more than 3 miles (5 km) away. A polar bear can also smell a seal's birth lair under the snow, even when there is 3–4 feet (1 to 1.2 m) of snow and ice above it. The polar bear pounds on the roof until it caves in and then jumps in head first. **Why do polar bears sometimes cover their nose and mouth with a paw?** While stalking its prey, a polar bear will sometimes cover its dark nose and mouth with a paw so that it can't be seen as easily.

What are the Northern Lights, and do you know what else they are called? The Northern Lights are also known as the aurora borealis. Caused by solar particles hitting the Earth's atmosphere, they are a brilliant spectacle. Different colors, though usually white or blue, they dance across the sky in bands or billowing sheets.

The world's highest tides flow in and out of the Bay of Fundy between Nova Scotia and New Brunswick. **How high do you think the water measures?** Believe it or not, these powerful tides have cut away mountainsides to form towering cliffs and caves. They reach 48 feet (almost 15 m) each day!

The magnetic north pole is in Canada. **What is the magnetic north pole versus the North Pole?** The North Pole rests on ice and sea water at the "top" of the world. There is both a north and south magnetic pole. The poles are where every compass needle points from any direction throughout the region. A compass is useless if it is close to a magnetic pole. The horizontal intensity is too small to determine direction.

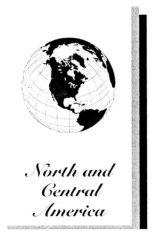

You are in the middle of a Cloud Forest in a nation with lots of parks and reserves but no army—it was abolished in 1948. The wildlife around you is astounding—there are jaguars, ocelots, pumas, and over 400 species of birds. On one tree alone, entomologists found over 950 different species of beetles, and there are more species of butterflies in this one nation than all of Africa. For this region, you have one of the lowest birth rates and the highest standard of health and literacy rate. Part of the Pacific "Ring of Fire," you are familiar with volcanoes and earthquakes. *Where on Earth are you? Can you find your place?*

Costa Rica

With species from both North and South America, Costa Rica lives up to its name when it comes to animal, insect, and plant life. *Rica* means "rich" in Spanish, and Costa Rica means "rich coast." With its presidential elections in 1890, Costa Rica was the first country in Central America to hold truly democratic elections. Today, Costa Rica exports coffee and bananas, but it is also known for its ecotourism. Ecotourists can see smoking volcanoes, beautiful beaches, and cloud forests. **What exactly is a cloud forest?** A cloud forest is a forest where the trees are almost permanently shrouded in mist. The forest floor is usually dark and damp because there is almost no sunlight reaching it, but insects, spiders, and small frogs abound.

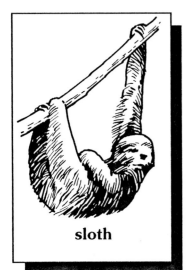

sloth

The slowest animal in the world is found in Costa Rica. What is it? The sloth. Sloths usually stay in trees, often hanging upside down, because they cannot walk. They pull themselves along the ground with their claws at an average speed of 6–8 feet per minute (1.8–2.4 meters) and are easy prey for jaguars and other predators. In the trees, although they are still slow—accelerating to just 15 feet per minute (4.6 meters)—they are well camouflaged. In fact, during the rainy season, a green alga grows on their stiff, brownish hairs and helps them to blend into the leaves.

It is illegal to capture many animals, but, unfortunately, a black market exists. Someone comes to you and says, "I am a reputable dealer. I have a license to collect these animals. This monkey is a rare find. I didn't steal it from Costa Rica. I got it from the Congo, in the middle of Africa." Taking a careful look at the monkey, its tail wrapped around a bar of its cage, you say suddenly, "Stay right here. I'm turning you in." **How did you know the dealer was not being honest?** Monkeys in Costa Rica are New World monkeys—they are the only ones with prehensile tails. Old World monkeys, those found in Africa and Asia, do not have prehensile tails. Not all New World monkeys have prehensile tails, but not one Old World monkey has a prehensile tail. **What do you think *prehensile* means?** *Prehensile* means adapted for seizing or grasping, especially by wrapping around. **Are your toes prehensile?**

Randomly dotting the southwest region, there are 1,000-year-old perfectly round stone balls carved out of hard granite. Some stand more than 6 feet (2 m) high! The perfect spheres are a mystery!

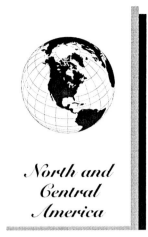

You are on the largest island in the Caribbean, and you are going to be visiting the largest wetlands area in the Caribbean. Crocodiles are long time inhabitants of this swamp, and you're going to be seeing them close up at the Crocodile Farm where 10,000 of them are being raised for meat and leather. You're going to be on a close look out for things small too, for the world's smallest bird, frog, and scorpion live here. One thing you're not going to be worrying about is polio. This country was the first in the world to eradicate the disease. The best beaches have been reserved for tourists. You enjoy them, but you wonder how the people who live here feel about that. *Where on Earth are you? Can you find your place?*

Cuba

A Spanish colony for over 350 years, Cuba became an independent country in 1902. Cuba is known for its revolutionary leader, Fidel Castro, who took power in 1959. Castro received help from the Soviet Union, but when the U.S.S.R.'s communist government collapsed in 1989, Cuba's economy was devastated. Before, Cuba traded sugar for oil and machinery. Castro worked hard to improve people's lives by training doctors and providing schools, but people were not allowed to speak or travel freely. Today, there are lines for bread and other essentials. Cuba is hoping to develop tourism, but everyone wonders, "What will happen when Castro dies?" **How does transition of power work in your country?**

The United States has a trade embargo against Cuba, but there is a U.S. naval base at Guantanamo Bay. **How did the U.S. get a naval base in Cuba?** After defeating the Spanish in 1898 in the Spanish-American War, a U.S. military government ruled Cuba from 1899–1902. The Americans left, but with the condition that they could interfere in Cuban affairs and build a naval base. When Castro's revolutionary forces took over in 1959, relations with the U.S. deteriorated. Many Cubans did not like Castro's friendship to the Soviet Union and his take-over of privately owned businesses and properties. These Cubans fled to the United States. The U.S. banned trade with Cuba in 1961.

Often mistaken for an insect, the Cuban bee hummingbird is about the size of a bumblebee. It is about 2 inches (5 cm) long, but half of that is the beak and the tail! It weighs less than one-fifteenth of an ounce (2 g). The tiny banana frog measures only .44 to .48 inches (1.1–1.2 cm), and the biggest the world's smallest scorpion ever gets is 2.5 inches (6.4 cm) long. **How does a hummingbird survive the night without food?** Hummingbirds expend lots of energy flying and keeping warm. In order to survive cold nights, hummingbirds go into a deep sleep called *torpor*. They put their heads against their chests, fluff their feathers to create an insulating pocket of air, and slow their heartbeats. Sometimes their body temperatures may drop more than 30°F (17°C).

Since 1970, school children must spend time working in the fields. This was to make students aware of their social responsibilities and reduce prejudice against manual labor. **Is there a prejudice against manual labor?**

The Columbus brothers, Christopher and Bartholomew, played a big part in this nation's history. On Christopher's second voyage, he established the first permanent European colony in the New World here in 1493. In 1496, Bartholomew moved the capital to Santo Domingo, where it became an important Spanish base for trade and exploration. Today, Santo Domingo is still the capital, and it holds the distinction of being the oldest surviving European city in the Western Hemisphere, as well as housing the first university founded in the New World. Baseball anyone? Today, many men from this country—Sammy Sosa, for example—are stars in the United States. *Where on Earth are you? Can you find your place?*

Dominican Republic

Covering the eastern two-thirds of the island Hispaniola, which it shares with Haiti, the Dominican Republic was founded in 1844. It broke away from the harsh Haitian dictatorship that controlled it, first in 1801 and then again in 1822. Over the years, it became a Spanish colony again (1861–1865) and was occupied by American troops in a state of near-anarchy (1916–1924). **What does *anarchy* mean?** *Anarchy* is the complete absence of government and law. Today, the Dominican Republic is a republic with a two-house legislature, and the two most important industries are sugar and tourism.

From December through March, humpback whales visit a section of the Dominican coast. All whales are cetaceans and can be divided into two groups: Odontoceti and Mysticeti. **Can you figure out which group the humpback whale belongs to if you are told that *Odontoceti* means "toothed whales," and *Mysticeti* means "whales with mustaches"?** The humpback whale belongs to the Mysticeti group, often called the baleen whales. The baleen in a whale's mouth hangs down like a mustache, and the whale filters (or strains) small animals from the ocean water through it. **What do you call a male, female, and baby whale?** Male whales are bulls, females are cows, and young whales are calves.

Cashews are grown in the Dominican Republic. **Are they a native species, and why must someone be very careful when dealing with the nut?** The cashew plant is native to the Dominican Republic. While it is a characteristic ingredient of numerous chicken and vegetarian dishes in India, it was not introduced to India and East Africa until the 15th century when Portuguese missionaries brought it there from Central and South America. The cashew species is related to poison ivy and poison sumac, and the brown oil between the outer and inner shells causes blisters on human skin. Nuts are roasted so that the outer shells will burst open. The oil can catch fire and give off fumes injurious to the eyes and skin. In places where roasting methods have been improved, the poisonous properties are dispelled in roasting cylinders. **Have you ever wondered who the first person was to figure out that something so hard to obtain was edible?**

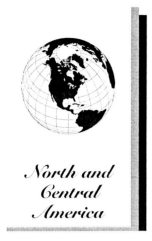

It is important not to waste firewood here, so as soon as you have finished cooking your tortillas, you take the sticks of wood out of the fire and extinguish the flames and deaden all sparks by banging the burning wood against the floor. This way you can cook another meal or two. Things are precious here in this tiny tropical country that is still recovering from a destructive civil war. This nation has the distinction of being the smallest country in Central America and the only one without an Atlantic seaboard. *Where on Earth are you? Can you find your place?*

El Salvador

Spaniards first came to El Salvador in 1524 and divided the land into large estates. In 1821 it declared independence from Spain and joined the United Provinces of Central America. This federation collapsed, and El Salvador became an independent country in 1841. From the very beginning, there were terrible land inequities. When El Salvador was first given to the Europeans, the indigenous people were given right along with the land! They became the property of the landowner and had to work for him. The first major export crop was natural dyes, including indigo, harvested from the leaves of the xiquilite plant. This was a profitable crop for the Europeans, but it was not profitable for the Salvadorans. The dye is toxic, and it caused many workers to become deathly ill. The market for indigo fell off in the early 1800s, but indigo was still a popular color. **What happened?** Artificial dyes were invented.

When the landowners switched to growing coffee in the 1840s, they needed even more land and more workers. The government made it so that people were forced to work on coffee plantations and not allowed to grow their own food. Many people think that this action contributed to the civil war over 100 years later because it started a system wherein the government did not take care of the poor. If a president tried to instigate land reform, he was overthrown by the military. During the civil war (1980–1992), government forces killed thousands of people. Many people fled, becoming refugees, while others simply disappeared. It is still dangerous to live in El Salvador, but hopefully true peace will come and people will be able to support their families. In 1996, volunteers went to a site that had been destroyed by bombs and started planting a Reconciliation Forest. Seventy-five thousand trees will be planted, one for each person killed in the war. **What does *reconciliation* mean?** *Reconciliation* is the action of restoring friendship or harmony.

Some children don't start school until they are 10 or 11 in El Salvador. Why? Schools, especially in the rural areas, can be few and far away. Parents have to wait until their children are old enough to make the long trip alone before they can send them. **How do you get to school?**

The Mayan city of Joya de Ceren, discovered by accident in 1976, has been called the Pompeii of the Americas. Just as the Italian Pompeii was covered in volcanic ash, so too was Joya de Ceren. Pompeii was destroyed in A.D. 79, and Joya de Ceren in A.D. 260. Because life was arrested so suddenly at both places, archeologists have learned much about the daily life of ordinary people.

There is no summer or winter here on this island nation that produces one-third of the world's nutmeg. There is only a wet and a dry season. Within 10 years of gaining independence from the British in 1974, a combined force of the OCES (Organization of Eastern Caribbean States) and the United States invaded this tiny country. *Where on Earth are you? Can you find your place?*

Grenada

The nation of Grenada is made up of three main islands—Grenada, Carriacou, and Petit Martinique—as well as more than 20 other small islands or cays. The island of Grenada is part of the Windward Islands which, together with the Leeward Islands, make up the Lesser Antilles. Carricou and Petit, though part of the nation of Grenada, are also part of the Grenadines, a chain of smaller islands between the islands of Grenada and St. Vincent.

If you were told that Grenada's weather is "balmy," would you hazard a true or false guess? "Balmy" means soothing and mild, and because Grenada lies south of the Tropic of Cancer, it has a balmy climate all year, with the average daily temperature measuring 80°F (27°C).

Five years after Grenada gained independence, its elected leader was overthrown in a bloodless coup by a group of armed rebels led by Maurice Bishop. In 1983, Bishop, who had adopted a communist-style government, was, in turn, overthrown and executed by even more left-wing members of his party. The rebels were defeated and Grenada's constitution was restored in six days, so that leaders are now chosen by election rather than by force. Several conditions precipitated the U.S. and OCES invasion, including the U.S. concern that the Cuban-built airport could become a missile base for Cuba. There were also some American medical students studying in Grenada. **What is a bloodless coup?** A bloodless coup is an overthrow of the government without bloodshed.

What spice besides nutmeg is harvested from the nutmeg tree? Round and yellow, the mature fruit from the nutmeg tree splits open to reveal a dark brown shell. The nutmeg is in the shell, but it is the lacy membrane covering the shell that is a spice on its own: mace. Mace is used to season foods and is also used by pharmaceutical industries. Allspice comes from Grenada, too, but it is produced from the dried berries of the pimento tree.

Animal life on Grenada is limited because few animals were able to cross the water from South America. Mongooses were brought to Grenada by sugarcane farmers to help get rid of the cane rat. **It is true that mongooses are active, bold predators, but the plan did not work?** Cane rats are nocturnal (active at night) and mongooses are diurnal (active during the day). The mongoose flourished and is commonly found in Grenada today, but to the detriment of native plantlife.

You are on top of a pyramid that is 229 feet (70 m) high. It's a massive and imposing structure, and it seems impossible that it was built without the use of iron tools, wheels, or even pack animals to cart materials. There is no sand or desert around you. Instead, you are surrounded by lush green jungle. You can hear spider monkeys and lots of birds. *Where on Earth are you? Can you find your place?*

Guatemala

Located in Central America, Guatemala was one of the countries where the great Mayan civilization flourished. The Mayans' Golden Age was between A.D. 250 and A.D. 900. During that time, they built great cities. One of the largest and oldest of these cities was Tikal. Pyramids, palaces, temples, markets, and shrines can all be seen today at this site excavated by archeologists. The archeologists also found aqueducts that the Mayans had built. **What is an aqueduct?** An aqueduct is a large pipe or channel for bringing water from one place to another.

The Mayans developed an accurate yearly calendar of 360 days. They divided their year into 18 months of 20 days each, and every year had five extra days. **How does this contrast to our calendar?** Our year consists of 12 months and 365 days, and every four years, we have what we call a leap year. On a leap year, one extra day is added to February. It takes the Earth 365 ¼ solar days to make one complete revolution around the sun. We make up for the ¼ day every leap year.

The Mayans thought that their extra days were unlucky, and because of this, on those days, they would have special ceremonies and fast (*not eat*). **Do you consider February 29th unlucky?**

The Mayans developed a picture language. **What is the special word we use for this type of language?** The answer is *hieroglyphics*.

The Mayans were incredible astronomers. Even though they did not have telescopes, the Mayans were able to predict solar and lunar eclipses, as well as trace the path of planets. **What is the difference between a solar and a lunar eclipse?** A lunar eclipse occurs when Earth blocks the sun's light from the moon. A solar eclipse occurs when the moon blocks the sun's light from some areas of the Earth. **If you did not understand what an eclipse was or know one was coming, might you be afraid that the world was coming to an end?**

Guatemala has only two seasons, the wet and the dry. Because of its climate, different flowers bloom all year. Guatemala has over 8,000 different types of plants, including 600 species of orchids. Today, Guatemala's economy is based on agriculture. Agricultural exports include coffee, bananas, and sugar. Most of the rural houses do not have any electricity or running water, and poverty is a way of life. **Are coffee and bananas native to Guatemala?** Coffee was known in Ethiopia before A.D. 1000, used in Arabia by the 15th century, and had reached Europe and been introduced to North America by the 17th century. Bananas are native to tropical Asia.

North and Central America

Poverty surrounds you, for you are in the poorest country in the western hemisphere. Many young children are more likely to work in the fields than go to school: a family needs to grow food, and when one is short of food, school is a luxury. Despite the dire conditions, this place has a unique history: it has the distinction of being the first black independent republic in the Americas. It won its independence less than 30 years after the United States won theirs. *Where on Earth are you? Can you find your place?*

Haiti

Haiti lies on the western side of the island of Hispaniola. The Dominican Republic is on the other side. Hispaniola was the name given to this island by Christopher Columbus when he landed there in 1492. *Hispaniola* means "Little Spain. Haiti was ceded to the French in 1697, while Spain kept the other side. So many slaves were brought to Haiti that the blacks outnumbered the whites, ten to one. At first, the French used the slaves to help grow indigo, a valuable plant that produces a vibrant blue dye. With their consistent planting of a single crop, the French depleted the soil and growing sugarcane on vast plantations took the place of growing indigo. The Haitian revolution, led by mulatto (mixed color) and black rebels was initially launched in 1791. The French withdrew in 1804, but still, the violence continued. Over the years, Haiti has been ruled by dishonest leaders and cruel dictators. Only recently has there been an elected president.

One of the original leaders of the slave rebellion was a man named Toussaint. Toussaint's owner had allowed him to learn to read. **Do you think this added to his leadership abilities?** Although Toussaint had to work in the fields, by borrowing books he learned about other lands where slavery was not allowed. Toussaint had never gone to military school but, because he had read about different military tactics, he made a great leader. He knew how to take his enemies by surprise and outmaneuver them. In some countries, teaching slaves to read and write was outlawed. People knew that education led the way to being free. **Is this still true today?**

Thousands of Haitians have crowded into small and unsafe boats and fled for their lives. By the 1990s more Haitian doctors lived in Canada than in Haiti. **Haiti needs doctors, but should someone be forced to live in a country with extreme poverty, political turmoil, and possible death? What would you do?**

Haiti is one of the most densely populated countries in the world. What does this mean? When one calculates the density of a population, they take the land size and divide it by the number of people. In the late 1990s, it was calculated that there were 600 people per square mile (238 per sq km) in Haiti. Contrast this to 74 people per square mile in the United States. **Do you think Haiti's population density adds to their deforestation problem?** Haiti's land is overused, and the situation is only becoming worse. Before, there were acres of forests and swamps. Today, there is parched and eroded earth.

North and Central America

Because of its complex topography and its many habitats, this nation, making up less than 1% of the world's surface area, harbors over 10% of the world's biodiversity. With nearly 50,000 species of insects alone, it's a good thing there are lots of bats—70 different types, 68 of which are insect-eaters and two that are blood-drinkers. Off one coast lies the second largest barrier reef in the world. Craving hot chocolate? Just remember that cacao beans, the source of chocolate, are native to this area. European explorers and traders were so enamored with their first drink that they took it back home with them. *Where on Earth are you? Can you find your place?*

Honduras

The second largest and most mountainous country in Central America, Honduras was once known as a "banana republic." **How did this term originate?** Honduras gained its independence from Spain in 1821 and banded with other Central American countries to become the United Provinces of Central America. In 1838, Honduras decided to go it alone. Close to 50 years later, in 1899, the first boatload of bananas from Honduras was shipped to the United States. There was a high demand for bananas, and U.S. traders saw Honduras as an excellent location to build up production and diversify supply away from Costa Rica. U.S. fruit companies eventually owned 75% of Honduras's banana plantations and possessed great influence on Honduras' politicians. The U.S. owners built railroads and seaports, but little of the fruit companies' wealth remained within Honduras. Bananas are still important to Honduras' economy, but coffee is their chief export.

Should you be afraid of vampire bats? Vampire bats are found only in Latin America, and you really have nothing to fear. They typically feed on the blood of large animals, like cows or horses. Most times, these animals never even know they provided dinner! The bat lands near the animal, "walks" up to it, and then makes a tiny cut in the animal's skin. The bat does not greedily suck up blood. Instead, it takes tiny laps with its tongue.

Some bromeliad plants in Honduras are called "tank" or "cistern" bromeliads because they can hold up to two or three gallons of rainwater. This creates a tiny ecosystem of insects, amphibians, and even small mammals. The problem: weight. Many bromeliads live on the surfaces of other plants. Their water weight, combined with the water weight of other bromeliads, can cause a tree to come crashing down. **What defensive measures have trees come up with?** Rapidly peeling bark, weak branch connections (which allows a limb to fall off with minimal damage to the trunk), and chemical defenses.

What is an example of an environmental policy affecting the outcome of a hurricane? Unchecked deforestation leads to erosion. When Hurricane Fifi struck in 1974, deforested hillsides collapsed, sliding down into rivers, causing temporary dams. When they broke, entire villages were washed away. Today, Honduras is still recovering from 1998's Hurricane Mitch. Eighty percent of Honduras' agriculture was destroyed, as were factories, bridges, and homes. Entire hillsides collapsed, and once again damage was most extensive in deforested areas.

Every one likes to get presents. How would you like to receive a country? The king and queen of Spain gave this island nation to Christopher Columbus' family. The English wanted this present for themselves, so in 1655, they invaded and took over. Full independence from the English came in 1962. Today, this West Indian country is known for its beautiful beaches; exports of sugarcane, bananas, coffee and cocoa; and reggae music. *Where on Earth are you? Can you find your place?*

Jamaica

The third largest island in the Caribbean Sea, Jamaica's population is made up of descendents of African slaves brought over to work the sugarcane plantations (over 80%), and Indian and Chinese laborers who were brought in to work the plantations after the emancipation of Jamaica's slaves in 1838. (Slavery was actually abolished in 1807, but it wasn't until the slaves rebelled in 1838 that they were all freed.) The entire native population of Arawaks had completely disappeared by the 18th century. Their numbers were drastically reduced after the Spanish enslaved them. Some of the Arawaks were able to flee the island, but many died of overwork while others died from diseases like the common cold.

What is reggae music? Reggae music developed in the '60s and '70s, with nearly all of the early reggae musicians coming from the slum areas of Kingston, Jamaica's capital. Possibly, its name came from the *patois* (a dialect other than the standard or literary one) words *streggae* (rudeness or rude-boy) or *regge-regge* (quarrel). With a regular bass-dominated sound, reggae is characterized by a springy, offbeat rhythm. Many reggae songs are political or emphasize peace, love, and reconciliation—the tenets of the Rastafarian religious movement. Because of its association with "rude-boy" music and its political elements, Jamaican radio stations in the 1970s were hesitant to play reggae. Famous reggae musicians include Jimmy Cliff and Bob Marley. Today, Bob Marley's house in Kingston is a museum, and his songs are played all over the world. **What are some other new music forms? Would it be more difficult for a song to become popular if radios refused to give it airtime?**

Many tourists go to snorkel and scuba dive in Jamaica because of its beautiful coral reef and its extremely clear water—sunlight can penetrate up to a depth of 80 feet (24 m). Tourists may look for the parrotfish that protects itself at night from predators by wrapping itself in a mucous cocoon, but if they look for a Portuguese man-of-war, it is only to stay away from it. **What is a Portuguese man-of-war?** A Portuguese man-of-war is actually a colony of organisms, each with a specialized function. One part of it secretes gas into a translucent bladder-like organ known as the "float." This allows the colony to drift on ocean currents. Beneath the float are three different types of clusters of polyps: one is responsible for capturing prey, one for reproducing, and one for feeding. Hanging from the polyps are tentacles covered with stinging structures that can extend down as far as 165 feet (50 m). The sting is very painful to people and can cause serious effects.

The mining of bauxite is one of Jamaica's most important industries. **What is bauxite used for?** Bauxite is used to produce aluminum.

Corn is one of the world's most widely distributed food plants. It is second in the world when it comes to number of acres planted. (Wheat is first.) You are in the country that first cultivated corn. Christopher Columbus and other explorers brought it back to Europe. At that time, in the 16th century, Europe still suffered from famines. The introduction of corn helped make famine less frequent. *Where on Earth are you? Can you find your place?*

Mexico

When corn was first cultivated in Mexico around 7000 B.C., the stability that came from farming allowed people to develop advanced civilizations. Pre-Columbian civilizations included the Olmec, Maya, Toltec, and Aztec. Perhaps the greatest city built by these people was Tenochtitlan, constructed by the Aztecs in 1325. There were towering pyramids, perfectly straight streets, and canal thoroughfares for the transport of crops. It is estimated that 60,000 people bought and sold goods in the city marketplace. The Spaniards came to this city in 1519, and when they fought to conquer the Aztecs, the city was reduced to rubble. Spain ruled Mexico for the next 300 years, only relinquishing control in 1821 after a successful revolt. During the two-year battle with the Aztecs, the Spaniards had the help of neighboring Indian nations who disliked the powerful Aztecs. They also had an ally so dangerous that within 30 years of the Spaniard's arrival, the Indian population in Central Mexico had been cut in half. **Who (or what) was the ally?** Disease. Europeans had lived with smallpox, measles, diphtheria, and other diseases for hundreds of years, and they had built up immunities. The Indians had no built up immunities, and thus they died in large numbers.

Today, Mexico City alone has a larger population than many countries, and almost one out of every four Mexicans lives in Mexico City. With 25% of the people living on less than 1% of the land, Mexico City is one of the most polluted cities in the world. The situation is exacerbated (made worse) by the high mountains surrounding the city because they prevent the polluted air from escaping. Many people in the city live without access to sewer facilities, and their waste flows untreated into rivers and waterways. Hundreds of families live in Mexico City's garbage dumps, searching through the refuse for items to sell. Mexico City's problems are overwhelming. **What is one small thing that each individual could do to help?**

In 1994, Mexico, the United States, and Canada signed the North American Free Trade Agreement, called NAFTA for short. This agreement will, over 15 years, dismantle trade barriers, creating one of the largest free trade areas in the world. Some people are angry at the signing of NAFTA. Others feel it will make North American trade stronger. **Can you think of a situation or someone who might lose business by NAFTA, and then think of a situation or someone who would be helped?** Even before NAFTA, there were factories built in Mexico because the cost of labor was so much cheaper than in the US. **Will more factories move to Mexico? Will people in the U.S. lose jobs? Will the cost of items come down? Will business owners profit? Will people be paid enough to live good lives? Will North American markets be more competitive with European ones?**

Feel like going to the coast? You have your choice of two: the Pacific or the Caribbean. Coffee production produced a monoculture here, with disastrous results for poor peasants who worked the plantations. Coffee is still one of the major crops, but today cotton and sugar are also exported. The United States has intervened militarily in this poor nation, stationing Marines there from 1912–1925 and again in 1926–1933, as well as financing attacks against the government in the early 1980s. *Where on Earth are you? Can you find your place?*

Nicaragua

A tropical country in the center of Central America, Nicaragua gained independence from Spain in 1821, but it did not achieve full sovereignty over its English-speaking Mosquito Coast (a swampy region on the Caribbean coast) until 1894. In 1823, Nicaragua, Guatemala, El Salvador, Honduras, and Costa Rica joined together to form the United Provinces of Central America, but the group broke up into separate nations in 1838 after years of dissension. Many indigenous people died in battles against the European conquerors, and diseases like influenza and measles devastated entire populations. Native Americans were also taken as slaves. Thousands of Nicaraguans were captured by the Spanish and taken to other parts of the Spanish Empire in the Americas to work as slaves. The slaves that were taken to Peru to work in the gold and silver mines in the 1530s were treated especially brutally. If they were not in the number that died on the slave ships, they were literally worked to death within a few years.

What were some of the reasons the United States became so involved in Nicaragua's affairs? The U.S., who built and controlled the Panama Canal, did not want a canal built in Nicaragua. To prevent competition, the U.S. gained exclusive canal-building rights in Nicaragua in the 1916 Bryan-Chamorro Treaty. This agreement was not annulled until 1970. Nicaragua had a series of brutal dictators who grew rich off their countrymen. In 1977, conditions in Nicaragua were so deplorable that it was identified as the country with the worst human rights record in the whole of Latin America. A civil war ensued, and in 1979 Sandinista rebels took control. The U.S. felt that the new government was too aligned with communist countries like the Soviet Union and Cuba. Though the Sandinistas started literacy and health brigades, the U.S. financed attacks against them. Nicaragua is still recovering from the revolution and the civil war. **Do you think it is right for an outside country to try and bring down a government in another country? Under what conditions?**

Nicaragua has the largest freshwater lakes in all of Central America, and some very unique sharks live in them. Long ago, it is believed that these lakes (Nicaragua and Managua) formed part of the sea. Due to volcanic eruptions, they became inland basins. Oceanic animal life adapted as the water gradually turned from salt to fresh. **What is the difference between a fish skeleton and a shark skeleton?** Most fish have skeletons made of bones, as you do. Sharks and their close relatives have skeletons made out of cartilage, the same material that is in your nose and ears. Cartilage is hard, tough, and easier to bend than bone.

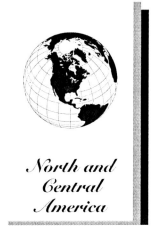

North and Central America

You stand on an isthmus—a narrow neck of land that connects two larger landmasses—between North America and South America. At the narrowest part of the isthmus, a mere 50 miles (81 km) separates the Atlantic Ocean from the Pacific. The oceans are separate bodies of water, but one doesn't have to travel all the way to the tip of South America to reach the other. Instead, one can go through a canal, one of the most amazing feats of construction engineering in the world. *Where on Earth are you? Can you find your place?*

Panama

Panama is a country whose geographic position has influenced its history and economy. Even before the canal was built, travelers could save incredible amounts of time by getting off a boat on one side, crossing the 50-mile (81 km) "bridge," and catching another boat on the other side. Many prospectors on their way to California during the 1848 gold rush did this. With the canal, however, huge boats, not just people, can save time. For example, without the canal, a boat sailing from New York to San Francisco, California, would have to travel 13,135 miles (22,268 km) further.

Each ship has to pay a toll to use the canal. **Why would a captain choose to pay a toll?** Time is very important. By using the canal, a captain can make more trips. He or she might be carrying fresh cargo that needs to be delivered quickly. He or she might find more things to trade if they could reach faraway ports more often.

Who built the canal? Excavation started with the French in 1882, but they didn't get very far. Because of the heavy rain, it became too muddy to work. Between 16,000 and 20,000 men died from yellow fever and malaria that they had contracted from mosquitoes. The work stopped in 1889 with very little accomplished. The United States took over in 1904, and the canal was completed in 1914. Mosquitoes were eradicated from the Canal Zone, and then a dam was built. Huge iron locks were constructed, and eight miles of rock were hacked out. It cost the United States 380 million dollars to build the canal.

Who owns the canal? The canal was controlled by the United States, but as agreed to in a treaty signed in 1977, Panama assumed control on December 31, 1999.

What is a lock? A lock is an enclosed part of a river or canal with gates at each end. Water can be let in or out so that the ship is raised or lowered to a certain level. Ships are lifted (or lowered) 85 feet (26 m) in the Panama Canal locks. Ships can travel through the canal by night or day, with each trip taking from 14–16 hours.

Panama includes over 1,600 islands. About 25,000 Kuna Indians live on 40 of the San Blas islands. The Kuna still use dug out canoes and live in their traditional manner. **Do you think that where they live aids in their maintaining their language and traditions?**

You see the words *"e pluribus unum"* on every coin. You wonder if they are related to the words you see on the Statue of Liberty, "Give me your tired, your poor, your huddled masses yearning to breathe free." Or, could they be related to the words written about the Battle of Lexington and Concord, "Here once the embattled farmers stood and fired the shot heard round the world." *Where on Earth are you? Can you find your place?*

United States

The United States is the fourth largest nation in the world, and it contains every type of landscape imaginable: mountains, deserts, plains, glaciers, and tropical beaches. *E pluribus unum* means "from many, one," and it is this very idea that helps define the United States. With a population made up of Native Americans and immigrants from around the globe, the United States is one of the most diverse nations on Earth. People may have been "tired," "poor," and "yearning to breathe free," when they first arrived, but they worked hard to better themselves.

What exactly did Ralph Waldo Emerson mean when he wrote "…the embattled farmers stood and fired the shot heard round the world"? Emerson was referring to the first battle of the American Revolutionary War. The success of the United States' fight for independence from England has encouraged worldwide movements toward democracy even today. The United States Declaration of Independence, written mainly by Thomas Jefferson, was adopted on July 4, 1776. It states that "all men are created equal," and that they are entitled to "life, liberty, and the pursuit of happiness."

A civil war is when a country fights internally. The U.S. Civil War (1861–1865) pitted the Northern states against the Southern states that wanted to secede from the Union. **What was the main issue behind the Civil War?** Slavery. The North (the Union) was opposed to slavery and secession.

When Ben Franklin (1706–1790), a famous American, invented the lightning rod, he did not patent it or try to make money from it. Franklin just wanted everyone to be safe. The lightning rod is placed on top of a house or building, becoming the highest point. If electricity hits, it strikes the rod and flows, channeled down to the ground by the rod, where it becomes harmless.

The son of a former slave, Garrett Morgan invented the first gas mask, as well as the first traffic light. No one thought Morgan's gas mask would work until there was an explosion in a tunnel in 1916 beneath Lake Erie. Several firefighters had already died in the effort to save trapped workers. Morgan and his brother were able to save 32 of the workers despite the smoke, poisonous gas, and dust.

What American said, "That's one small step for man, one giant leap for mankind"? When did he say it? Neil Armstrong said it in 1969 when he became the first man to walk on the moon.

Welcome to
South America!

Map of South America

The countries are numbered according to the page number on which you will find them. Not all countries are covered in this book. Use tape or glue to connect page 146 to page 147 at the tab.

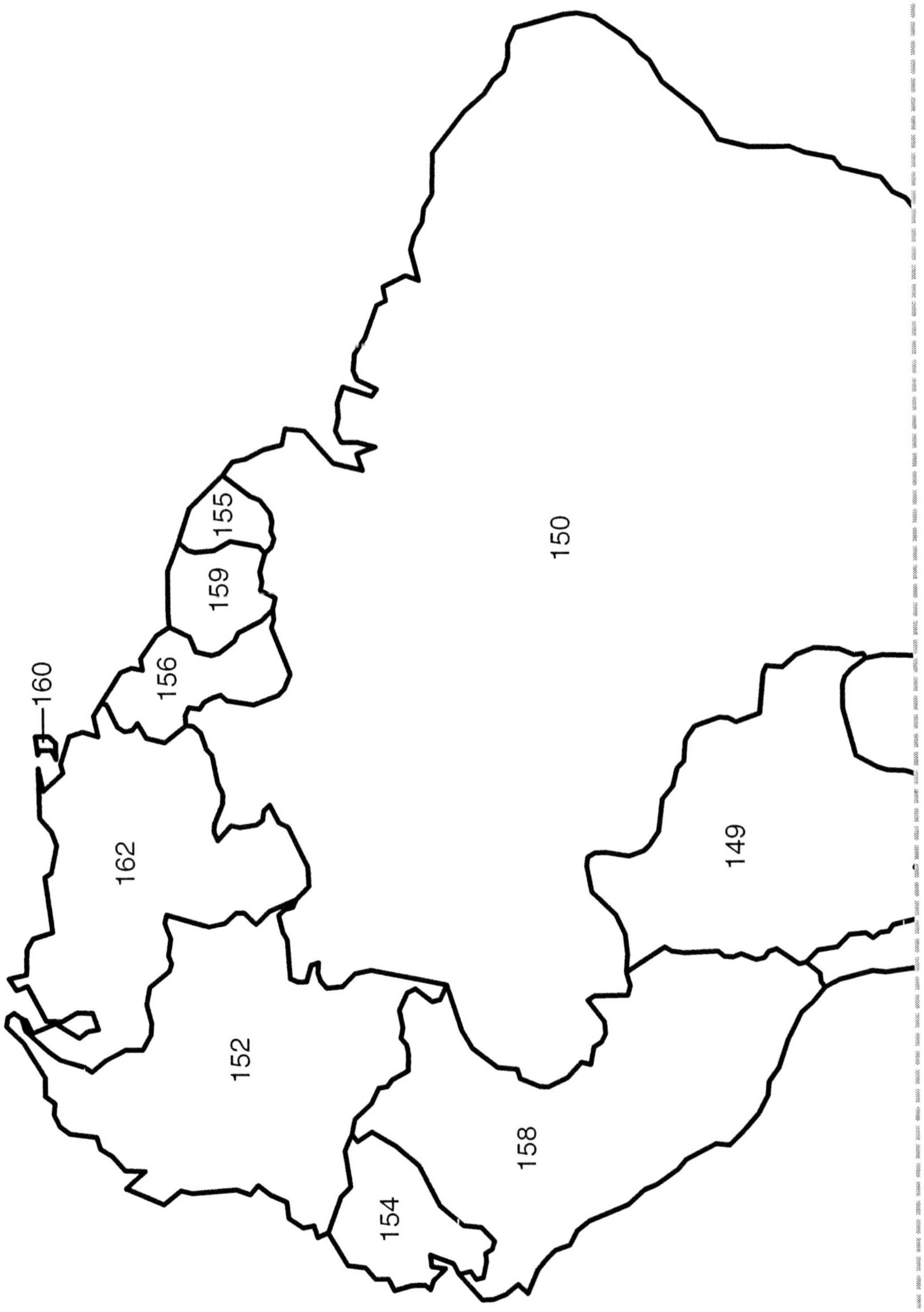

155

159

156

160

150

162

149

152

158

154

Map of South America *(cont.)*

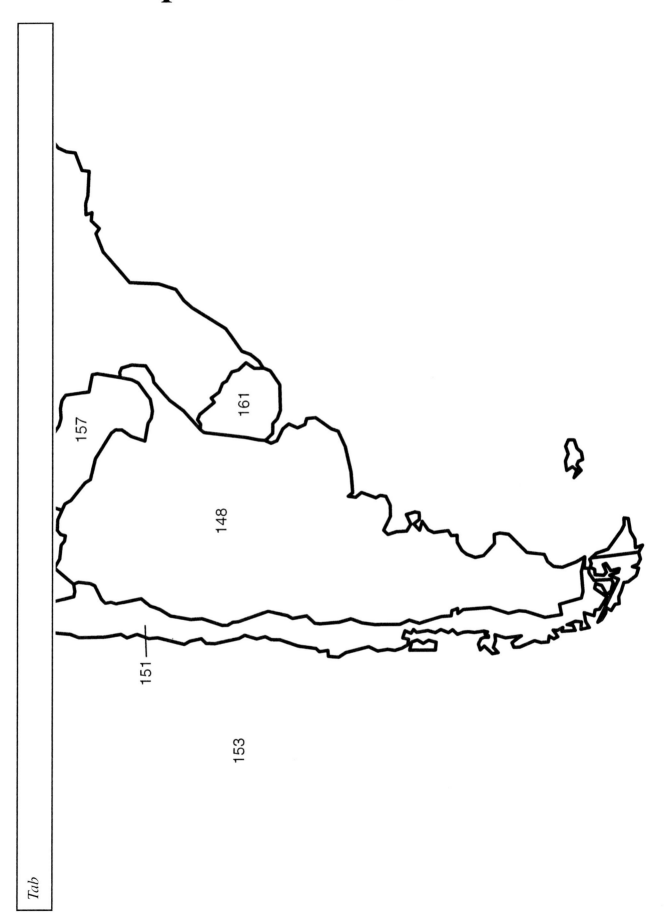

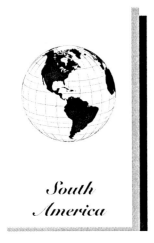

Without ever leaving this country's borders, you have traveled from Ushuaia, the southernmost town in the world, north to the Perito Moreno glacier, the only inland glacier in the world that is still growing. You've seen broad plains, towering mountains, vast deserts, and beautiful waterfalls. You've looked at cowboys (or *gauchos* as they are called here) and you are amazed at their skillful riding and rope throwing. Two things you are determined to see before you leave: a rhea and the tango. *Where on Earth are you? Can you find your place?*

Argentina

The eighth largest country in the world, Argentina was a colony of Spain from the 1500s until the 1800s. Argentina declared its independence in 1810, but Spain did not accept it. General Jose de San Martin, now honored as an Argentinean national hero, fought for liberation, and in 1816, Argentina became an independent country. San Martin felt that for Argentina to be really free, Spain would not only have to be removed from Argentina, but from the entire continent. San Martin led an expedition across the Andes where he helped drive out Spanish troops from Chile and Peru.

What is a rhea? A rhea is a large flightless bird that can grow up to six feet tall. It roams the open grasslands of South America. It looks and acts very much like an ostrich, but it is smaller. **How does it protect itself?** Like ostriches and emus, rheas protect themselves by staying in groups. There is safety in numbers, and they run fast!

The tango is the national dance of Argentina, characterized by the male and female dancer holding each other and taking long steps and striking dramatic poses. What is interesting is that, at first, the tango was considered vulgar by the upper classes. Today, it is very popular, no matter one's social status. **What does *vulgar* mean?** *Vulgar* means showing bad manners or taste. If something is vulgar, it is crude or coarse. **Can you think of something else that was once considered vulgar and is now acceptable?**

All Supreme Court and Federal Court of Appeals judges are appointed for life in Argentina. It is believed that a life appointment makes one more impartial—one doesn't have to worry about giving "unpopular" sentences that will make one lose the next election. **How long are judge's terms where you live? Do you think a judge appointed for life would be more likely to be impartial than one who is elected?**

You wouldn't know from its name that Argentina is famous for its beef production. **Why not?** *Argentum* is the Latin word for "silver," and *argintino* is the Spanish word for "silvery." When some of the first explorers returned to Spain, they brought back some pieces of silver they had found. This launched a silver rush to Argentina, but the fortune to be made was in agriculture. Argentina has flat, fertile, and temperate plains (called *pampas*) that cover one-fifth of the country. Wheat, corn, and alfalfa are raised in the wetter area, and vast herds of cattle graze on the drier. Hogs and flax are also raised here.

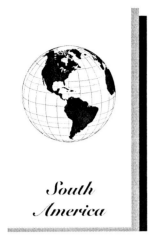

South America

You are surrounded by salt—4,674 square miles (12,000 sq km) of it. Salt, but no ocean. The country you are in is landlocked. Back at your hotel—made entirely of salt (the floors, walls, and even the chairs, tables, and beds!)—you think about all the amazing things in this country that is named for a famous liberator. Before you leave, you will make a special trip to see the ruins of a city of a people who lived before the time of the Incas and were so advanced that they performed brain surgery. You know there are llamas here, but can there really be bears? *Where on Earth are you? Can you find your place?*

Bolivia

Named after the famed liberator Simon Bolivar, Bolivia is a country rich with diversity, both natural and cultural. There are the rugged Andean Mountains and thick tropical rain forests. With Native Americans making up a little over half of the population, Bolivia has the largest percentage of indigenous people than any other Latin American country.

Who is Simon Bolivar? Simon Bolivar (1783–1830) was a revolutionary leader who liberated much of South America from Spanish rule. He became president of Gran Colombia (Panama, Venezuela, and Ecuador were part of Gran Colombia). Cooperating with Sucre and San Martin and other rebel leaders, Bolivar won victories against the Spanish in Peru and created Bolivia in 1825. Bolivar's vision of a unified South America was not to be, partly because of his dictatorial methods, but he is recognized today as a great hero and liberator.

The spectacled bear is the only species of bear in South America. **Does this rare bear hibernate? Would you change your answer if you knew that the bear is primarily a vegetarian?** Ninety-five percent of the spectacled bears' diet is vegetarian, and because its food sources are available throughout the year, it does not hibernate.

The salt in Bolivia is found in a salt pan. **What is a salt pan?** It is an accumulation of salt on the floor of a desert basin. It is estimated that the Salar de Uyuni salt pan has more than 10 billion tons (9,072 kg) of fine salt. Chainsaws were used to cut out the blocks of salt to make the hotel, but local farmers use pickaxes and shovels. In the middle of the salt pan, 50 miles (80 km) from shore, there is an isolated volcanic island with cactus growing 40 feet (12 m) tall and a stranded colony of *viscachas*, which are long-tailed rodents. **Would you rather be stranded on that island or one in the ocean?**

The Tiwanakans (1600 B.C.—A.D. 1000) were expert hydrologists. **What is a *hydrologist*?** A hydrologist is an expert on the property of water. The Tiwanakans were able to grow plants on a barren plain by raising fields that were 656 feet (200 m) long and 50 feet (15 m) wide. Below the top layer of rich organic topsoil, were three distinct layers of gravel for drainage, a layer of clay to retain water, and finally, cobblestones. Water irrigation canals were between the beds; and at night, the heat released from the canal water kept the plants from suffering from frost damage. The fields and canals covered 30,000 acres (12,146 hectares) and supported 50,000 people! Scientists think a long drought caused the Tiwanakans to abandon their city.

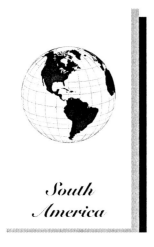

This may be the world's fifth largest country, but it's number one when it comes to one of the world's largest freshwater fish. The fish, known as the pirarucu or the paiche, is impressive—it can grow to a length of 10 feet (3 m) and a weight of 250 pounds (113 kg)—but its diet is what really sets it apart. It's a fruit eater, lunging out of the water to grab fruit from overhanging tree branches. This fish provides more than food. The indigenous people use its tough scales and bony tongue as tools. You hear Portuguese, not Spanish, being spoken. Portuguese is the national language for only one country in all of Latin America. *Where on Earth are you? Can you find your place?*

Brazil

Talk about having to get along with neighbors, Brazil has 10 of them! **Can you name some? Could you get along with so many?**

Brazil gained independence from Portugal back in 1822, but its present constitution wasn't approved until 1988. A vast country, Brazil has modern and developed cities to contrast its large tracts of Amazonian rain forest, where some inhabitants have never seen an outsider. **Is the Amazon the longest river in the world?** At 3,990 miles (6424 km), the Amazon comes in second. Although the Nile may be longer, the Amazon comes in first in volume of water (one-fifth of the freshwater that flows into the world's oceans comes from the Amazon), number of branches (there are over 1,000, with more than 200 in Brazil), and drainage area (the river drains into an area almost the size of Australia, including parts of Brazil, Peru, Ecuador, Bolivia, and Venezuela). Some sections of the river are several miles wide when floodwaters are high, and early explorers believed they were on a vast inland sea rather than a river.

Most of the Amazon's drainage basin is covered in jungle, making up one-third of the world's natural forests. Today, rainforest is being cut down for logging and farming at an alarming rate. **What does this have to do with the Greenhouse Effect?** A greenhouse traps warm air inside. When we burn fuels such as petroleum, carbon dioxide is released into the atmosphere, creating a layer of gas that traps the sun's heat. In photosynthesis, rain forests take in large amounts of carbon dioxide. Every year we release more carbon dioxide, but we are cutting down more trees. Some scientists estimate that if we destroy the Amazon jungle, the Earth's temperature will increase by 5°F (3°C), and the polar ice caps will melt enough to raise ocean levels to the point where coastal lands will become submerged.

Brazilian Indians collected latex, a milky white substance that dripped from V-shaped slashes cut into certain trees. They used the latex as insect repellent and a waterproof covering for their feathered robes. The first to process rubber, the Indians would form shoes, bottles, and balls out of boiled latex. In the late 1800s and early 1900s, there was a tremendous demand for rubber, and rubber plantations were established. Many Indians became virtual slaves. Schools were not allowed on the plantations, and Indians were forced to start collecting latex even before the sun came up. **Why was there a higher demand for rubber?** There was a boom in the automobile industry, and rubber was needed for tires.

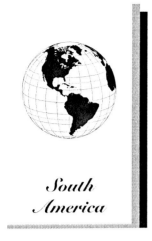

South America

You have traveled to the longest and narrowest country in the world to see the largest picture of a person in the world. A land of fire and ice, there are volcanoes, glaciers, mountains, the driest desert on Earth, and a vast ocean to the west. There are no bears or poisonous snakes here, and the flora and fauna are more like that of Australia and New Zealand than the vegetation and animal life on the rest of the continent. *Where on Earth are you? Can you find your place?*

Chile

With the natural barriers of the Andes mountains to the east, the Pacific Ocean to the west and south, and the Atacama Desert to the north, Chile is a relatively isolated country in South America. Every part of it is close to the ocean and the mountains. Because of its lack of humid tropical forests common to other South American countries, its flora and fauna are quite different from the rest of the continent. For example, it doesn't have the colorful birds that Brazil does, but it has penguins. All of Chile is located in the Southern Hemisphere. **What does that tell one about its seasons?** Seasons south of the equator in the Southern Hemisphere are the opposite of those north of the equator in the Northern Hemisphere. In Chile, spring begins in September, summer in December, autumn in March, and winter in June.

How large do you think the world's largest picture of a man is? Created between the 11th and 14th centuries A.D., there is a picture of a man called "The Giant of the Atacama" that is nearly 400 feet (122 m) long. To draw this man, Indians scraped away a top layer of brown stones to expose the light sand underneath on the side of a huge sand dune. There are other geoglyphs, or giant murals, filled with geometric shapes and figures of animals. Archaeologists have found arrows in the geoglyphs, and some archaeologists feel that this supports the notion that the pictures were roadside maps for caravans. Other archaeologists feel that the figures had religious significance.

Down at Cape Horn, glaciers abound, some as much as a millions years old. Your friend takes one look at an iceberg (a broken off piece of a glacier) floating near by, and he or she says, "That iceberg is really old." **How could your friend tell?** Icebergs in this region are often a deep, clear, blue. The blue color indicates that the iceberg is old. It's very compressed and nearly all the oxygen has been squeezed out. **What word do scientists use to describe it when a piece of a glacier breaks off to form an iceberg?** It is called "calving."

What is the Strait of Magellan? Named after the 15th century Portuguese explorer Ferdinand Magellan, the Strait is a stormy and dangerous passageway connecting the Atlantic and Pacific Oceans in southernmost South America. Although he died before the journey was completed, Magellan is credited with leading the first expedition to sail around the world. He started off with five ships, and only one, with just 17 crewmembers alive, made it back. Only one person has ever swum across the Strait—a woman named Lynne Cox. **Why do people do things like that?**

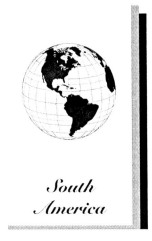

South America

Named for Christopher Columbus, this country is the only one on the continent to have both a Caribbean Sea and Pacific Ocean coastline. There are a record number of species of birds in this country, about 20% of the world's total! Think about this: the entire continent of Africa has only about 15%. Colombia is also one of the world's wettest places. The average annual rainfall in this region is 324 inches (823 cm), but one record year it rained more than 585 inches (1,500 cm). There are also snow-capped mountains and frogs you definitely should not touch. *Where on Earth are you? Can you find your place?*

Colombia

The fourth largest country on the South American continent, Colombia gained its independence from Spain in 1819 when Simon Bolivar joined forces with General Francisco do Paula Santanda. Bolivar became president and Santanda was vice-president of a new nation made up of Colombia, Venezuela, Panama, and Ecuador. Together, they were called Gran Colombia. Gran Colombia split up in 1830.

Parts of Colombia are covered in tropical jungle. Unfortunately, many of these forests are being cut down and the way of life for many indigenous tribes threatened.

Why might it be dangerous to touch a frog there? Poison-dart frogs, found throughout much of the wetter South and Central American tropical forests, have poisonous skins. They are brightly colored, and their gaudy color acts as a warning to any animal that might think it a tasty morsel. Indians dip their arrows in poison harvested from these frogs.

poison-dart frog

In the regions of Colombia over 5,000 feet (1517 meters), recipes that work at sea level have to be altered. Why? There is less pressure at higher altitudes so water begins to boil at lower temperatures. For example, water boils at 212°F (100°C) at sea level, but it boils at 203°F (95°C) at 5,000 feet. At 15,000 feet (4550 meters), water boils at 185°F (85°C). In addition, leavening agents (such as yeast and baking powder) have to be reduced. If you put in the "normal" amount, the cake or bread will rise too much and then collapse.

Colombia is known for its coffee, which was introduced in 1700. It became an important export in the 1800s. Grown on hilly slopes at altitudes from 3,000–6,000 feet (914 to 1,829 m), most of the cultivation is done by hand because the terrain is not conducive to mechanized farming. Entire families use hoes and machetes and pick the coffee beans by hand. **How much coffee do you think a mature tree yields?** A mature tree can produce about 2,000 beans per year (remember they are all handpicked!). Processed, these beans, can fill a 1-pound (.4 kg) coffee can. Often these beans are carried by mule and donkey to the nearest mill.

What is green and is mined in Colombia? Emeralds, including the world's largest.

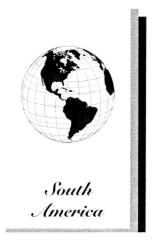

You are on a tiny speck of land in the southeast Pacific. A million square miles of empty ocean surrounds you. One thousand stern-faced stone statues seem to stare at you. The tallest stretches to 60 feet and the heaviest weighs 90 tons. Carved on the inside of a volcanic cliff with nothing but small crude picks made of hard black obsidian, the statues were somehow moved to where they now stand. How were they raised on to their altars—some as high as 15 feet!? And how was it possible that red stone topknots were placed on top of some of the statues? Some topknots weighed 30 tons! How had these ancient islanders done it? *Where on Earth are you? Can you find your place?*

Easter Island

Easter Island is about 63 square miles. It is 2,200 miles west of Chile and belongs to Chile. Triangular shaped with a volcano on each corner, Easter Island was created when the volcanoes erupted many years ago. Lava stones riddle the center of the island. There is not one single stream on the entire island. **How is the absence of a stream connected to Easter Island's volcanic origins?** The soil on Easter Island is made up of volcanic ash. The soil is so porous that rainfall quickly seeps away.

It is believed that Easter Island was initially inhabited about A.D. 400, and that the statues were erected sometime between A.D. 1000–1600. The original inhabitants were Polynesians from the Marquesas. **Can you find this group of islands on the map?**

Though the population could never have exceeded three or four thousand, the Easter Islanders developed a unique form of hieroglyphic writing, the only indigenous script in Oceania before the 20th century. The writing was not decoded or deciphered until 1994 by Steven Fischer. **What does** *indigenous* **mean?** *Indigenous* means produced, growing, or living naturally in a particular environment. **Who and what are indigenous in your country?**

When one thinks of the slave trade, one does not think of tiny Pacific islands. Yet the slave trade changed life on Easter Island dramatically. In 1862–63, one third of the islanders were abducted by Peruvian slave raids. Every person that knew how to read the hieroglyphics was taken, and every one of them died. Only a few people were ever able to return, and unfortunately they returned with small pox and tuberculosis. These diseases further decimated the population. **How would our world change today if everyone who could read was taken away? Would our culture change?**

Some of the stone statues that were knocked down have been lifted again, using the original method that had been passed down in an oral tradition. **How were the stones lifted?** Poles, acting as levers, are pressed under the statue face, and the face is then lifted up a fraction. Stones are shoved into the space. This dangerous procedure is continued until the statue is almost upright. Then while poles act as levers on the statue's chin, ropes are used to pull the statue upright. The topknots were raised with the same stones used to raise the statues.

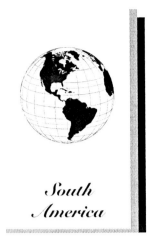

Named for its location, this country is famous for its Galapagos Islands, one of the world's most famous wildlife sanctuaries. During thousands of generations of isolation, finches on these islands adapted to fill specific needs. For example, two finch species use tools. They take cactus spines to probe for grubs. A scientist named Charles Darwin recorded his observations about these islands, and his ideas made people think about adaptations and how life evolves. You were impressed by the giant 440 pound (200kg) tortoises on the islands, but now you want to go to the mainland to see if you can spot an Andean condor, the largest flying bird in the Americas. *Where on Earth are you? Can you find your place?*

Ecuador

Ecuador's name comes from its location: the country straddles the Earth's equator. The diversity of life found on the Galapagos Islands is amazing, but so too is the ecological diversity found on the mainland. With the Andes Mountains as the backbone of the country, there is Amazonian jungle on one side and coastal lowlands, mountains, and river valleys on the other. Spain colonized Ecuador around the 1530s, replacing the ruling Incas. To escape Spanish subjugation, nearly one-fourth of the native population fled to the jungles. With the help of "The Great Liberator," Simon Bolivar, Ecuador gained independence in 1830.

The Andean condor was the choice of the Ecuadorians for their national bird. **How large is the condor, and is it an eagle or a vulture?** From wingtip to wingtip, the Andean condor can easily reach 10 feet (3.3 meters). A vulture, meaning it eats carrion (dead animals and fish), the condor breeds every other year at altitudes above 10,000 feet (3333 meters).

Panama hat

The Panama hat is an indigenous product of Ecuador. **How did it get so misnamed?** (Hint: think gold rush and trade centers.) During the California gold rush in the mid-1800s, exports from the west coast of South America were transported across the Isthmus of Panama for shipment to North America and Europe. Gold miners, traveling from the east coast to the west coast of the United States via Panama, brought the hats to the United States. They erroneously thought the hats were from Panama since they purchased them there. Panama hats range in quality from coarse to superfine. The finest can hold water, with a weaver spending as many as 15 days on the first six inches and three weeks on the crown. **Can you think of anything else that is misnamed?**

Malaria is a disease that can be contracted by humans when bitten by mosquito carriers. Powdered bark from an Amazonian rain forest tree helps to prevent malarial attacks. When the Europeans were introduced to this powder (called *quinine*), it became in great demand, especially in tropical areas where malaria was rampant. Entire plantations in India were planted from seeds gathered from the Amazon to produce quinine. Synthetic alkaloids have been produced to replace natural quinine, but natural quinine is still needed because some organisms in malaria have become resistant to the synthetics. **How does this example show why it is necessary to protect the rainforest?**

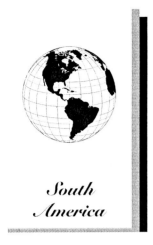

An advanced hi-tech space station is situated on the coast of this country, from which commercial rockets and satellites are launched. In contrast to this recently built modern facility is the rest of the country—more then 90% of the land is covered in tropical forest, very little of which has been disturbed. This country once served as a penal colony where prisoners were so brutally treated that it is estimated that more than 10% of all prisoners died every year. Prisoners had little food and were often placed in solitary confinement for years. Escape was impossible, since the surrounding waters were filled with sharks and the ocean currents were strong and treacherous. *Where on Earth are you? Can you find your place?*

French Guiana

Located on the north coast of South America, French Guiana was colonized by France. Today it has regional status, meaning that although it is represented in the French Parliament (by one deputy in the Senate and two in the National Assembly), it has a regional council with economic, social, and cultural responsibilities. Over a period of 80 years, France sent some 80,000 convicts to French Guiana. The last prisoners were not returned to France until 1954. Perhaps two of the most famous prisoners were Henri Charriere and Captain Alfred Dreyfus. Charriere was the only man known to escape. His book *Papillon* describes his harrowing experience in excruciating detail, including the year spent in solitary confinement and compulsory total silence. Dreyfus was innocent, convicted for a crime he never committed. He spent four miserable years in prison, sometimes chained to a bed in total isolation. Today, Dreyfus is honored as a symbol of police injustice. **Are inhumane prison conditions justifiable? How can a person wrongly imprisoned prove his case if he/she is in forced silence?**

French Guiana's coast extends the full breadth of the country along the Atlantic Ocean. **From what you know about South America, would you expect beautiful sandy beaches?** Sandy beaches are a rarity in French Guiana. Instead, one is met with mangrove swamps. This is because the Amazon and other rivers carry enormous quantities of particles of sediment. When this sediment is deposited at the coast, it forms mud banks, some as long as 25 miles (40 km). As the banks move and grow northward with the general ocean current, mangroves colonize them. In just a decade, one mangrove grove advanced 1.5 miles (2.4 km). Even in the capital city of Cayenne, encroaching mangroves have to be cut back.

Many of French Guiana's indigenous people's cultures were devastated as a result of disease brought by the Europeans. Today, the majority of the Wayana tribe lives in the zone interdite, or "prohibited" zone. To travel there, one needs a permit and a medical certificate ensuring that one is not a carrier of any infectious disease. One traditional custom of the Wayana still retained today is the *marake*, or ant test. To signify the beginning of adulthood, stinging ants enclosed in a wicker frame are applied all over the child's body. Both males and females take this test. Despite the pain, one is expected to remain silent. **Could you? Would it be easier to do if you anticipated the test and wanted to become an adult?**

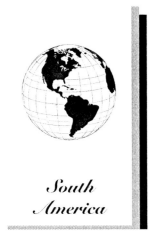

A British colony for 150 years, this country gained independence in 1966. Initially settled by Dutch and British in 1616, it is a land whose cultural diversity is largely due to economics. There are miles of waterways, but only a fraction are navigable because of strong currents, dangerous rapids, sandbars, mudflats, and waterfalls. There is a water lily here, the Victoria Regia, whose leaves grow six feet (1.8 m) wide! Sir Walter Raleigh was executed after returning from this country, unsuccessful in his attempt to find the fabled gold city of El Dorado. *Where on Earth are you? Can you find your place?*

Guyana

Is Guyana located just north of the equator on the northwestern or northeastern coast of South America? Guyana is located on the northeastern coast.

How did economics affect the cultural diversity of Guyana? As sugarcane plantations were developed, considerable labor was needed. Slaves were imported from Africa, and soon, the slave population outnumbered the Europeans in many areas. When slavery was outlawed, indentured laborers were brought in. Today, the majority of the population (about 52%) is East Indian (descendents of settlers from the Indian subcontinent), and people of African descent make up about 40%. The remainder of the population is made up of Amerindians, Europeans (mainly Portuguese and English) and mixed race peoples.

There are four distinct geographical regions in Guyana: coastal plain, hilly sand and clay belt, interior savannas, and highlands. **From what you know about populations and resources, what region do you think is the most populated in Guyana? Would you change your answer if you knew that much of the coastal plain lies below sea level at high tide? Would you change your answer again if you knew that the earliest settlers were Dutch?** The narrow coastal plain runs from Suriname to the Venezuelan border and measures only 2 to 30 miles (3.2 to 48 km) wide. Despite the fact that the northwestern portion has infertile soil, 90% of the population and almost all Guyana's agricultural products come from a 180-mile (290 km) stretch of coastal plain. Much of the coastal plain is only farmable because Dutch settlers built a system of drainage canals, seawalls, and dikes. Georgetown, Guyana's capital, sits below sea level.

Your friend says, "I just bought this plant. I am going to give it to my sister as a present. You say, "You better get it into some dirt soon, otherwise it will die." Your friend says, "No, I'm not going to plant it or water it. I don't need to." How can this be? Epiphytes are plants that seem to live on nothing but air. It is true that epiphytes live on or are attached to other plants, merely for physical support, but they obtain water and minerals from rain and from debris that collects on the supporting plants. Epiphytes are primarily tropical, and Guyana, with its lush tropical forests covering over ¾ of the land, has plenty. Some familiar tropical epiphytes are orchids, ferns, and members of the pineapple family. Familiar temperate epiphytes are lichens, mosses, liverworts, and algae.

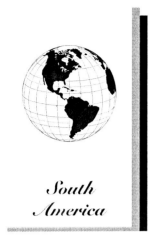

South America

In the heart of a New World continent, you are in a country where one of the two national languages is a Native American language so widespread that at least 90% of the people can speak it at some level. About half of the population knows both national languages, the indigenous one and the European import. Less than 10% of the population knows only the European import. The flag in this country is unique—the only one in the world in which two sides are different. A cat that swims lives here, as well as an animal that eats 30,000 insects a day. *Where on Earth are you? Can you find your place?*

Paraguay

Paraguay is one of only two landlocked countries in South America and has only one river route to the sea. It became the first nation on the continent to become an independent country when it declared its independence from Spain in 1811. Dictators followed, along with a disastrous war called the "War of the Triple Alliance" (Brazil, Argentina, and Uruguay). Paraguay lost territory and more than half of its population of 525,000 people. Before the war, males and females were fairly equal, but by the end of the war, only 106,254 women, 86,079 children, and 28,746 males survived. **How would such a dramatic change in population affect a country?**

There is currently a democracy in Paraguay, but times have been, and still are, very hard. Previous leaders, only concerned with individual gain, sold territory and land rights to foreigners and huge businesses. Part of Paraguay's poverty today is due to the fact that the majority of the land is owned by a tiny percentage of the population. **How would you institute land reform? Do you think it can happen without violence? How would you make it fair?**

What cat swims? Answer: the jaguar. **The coat patterns between jaguars and leopards are very similar. What distinguishes them?** The jaguar has black spots shaped like rosettes. (Even dark jaguars and leopards have spots. They are just harder to see.) A solitary predator, jaguars feed on deer, tapirs, capybaras, birds, and fish that it swats out of the water.

What animal can eat 30,000 insects a day? There are four types of anteaters, and it is the giant anteater that can grow up to seven feet long (2 m) long and weigh 100 pounds (45 kg) that needs to eat so many insects. Feeding primarily on ants and termites, anteaters use their long, sharp, curved claws to tear open insect nests. Then, they stick their long and worm-like tongues, covered with sticky saliva secreted from their large salivary glands, into the opening. Anteaters don't have any teeth, so they use their strong stomach muscles to grind up the insects.

About half of all the houses in Paraguay rely on outhouses or open sewers. Only about 10% have running water. **How much time and energy do you think you would save every day by having access to running water and a septic system? What health concerns arise from a lack of running water?**

Brazil and Paraguay built a huge damn together across the Parana River. Paraguay didn't have the cash, so Brazil paid with the understanding that Paraguay would sell much of its share of electricity to Brazil at a reduced rate. **Is this a good way of doing business?**

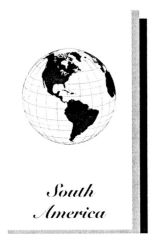

High in the Andes, the second highest mountain range in the world, you stand in awe at the ruins of Machu Picchu, an ancient Incan city. Perched atop a narrow saddle between two sharp peaks, this fortress city remained hidden from the Spaniards when they conquered the country. Only discovered in 1911, it is an amazing find because it is largely intact. There is a temple and a citadel (a fortress that commands a city) that were once surrounded by terraced gardens linked by more than 3,000 steps. There are stone blocks weighing more than three tons (273 kg) placed so carefully on top of the other that there is not even room enough for a sheet of paper to go between them! *Where on Earth are you? Can you find your place?*

Peru

The seat of the Inca Empire from around 1230, Peru is a country with spectacular landscapes: coast, desert, mountains, and rainforests. When the Spaniards came in the 1500s and conquered the Incas, Peru quickly became the most important region of all their colonies. The Spaniards stripped the Inca cities of their wealth, grew rich from gold and silver mines, and developed large land estates. Native Peruvians were forced to pay taxes, and entire families were made to journey hundreds of miles to work in underground mines. The population changed as people died by the thousands from overwork and diseases, such as small pox and the flu, brought by the Europeans. There were numerous revolts, and finally, in 1824, with the aid of General Simon Bolivar (Bolivar was also instrumental in liberating Venezuela and Colombia), independence from the Spanish was won. There have been many presidents since then, rule by a military junta, and back to civilian rule. **What is a military junta?** A group of persons from the military who control the government after a revolutionary seizure of power. A military junta ruled Peru from 1968–1980.

One of the most important food sources in the world came from Peru. What is it? The potato originated in the Andes, where there are over 200 different varieties. Europeans brought potatoes back to Europe where it quickly became an important food staple. **Believe it or not, some Peruvians freeze-dry their potatoes. How?** People in the highlands above 8,000 ft (2,500 m) grow potatoes that have adapted to that height and have become frost resistant. The potatoes freeze on the ground at night when the temperature is below zero, and then thaw out when the sun warms up the air. This process is continued until the potato becomes completely dehydrated, dry and cardboard like. The freeze-dried potatoes are good for about four years.

Coca was a "divine plant" to the Incas. The Spanish rulers and even the Spanish clergy liked it because it allowed them to work people more than normal; chewing the leaves suppressed hunger, thirst, and tiredness. Through its use, some natives were manipulated into working themselves to death in the mines. Today, cocaine is made from coca leaves. In Peru, cocaine is illegal, but coca leaves are not. It is a very profitable crop. **Why should a very poor farmer not grow coca?**

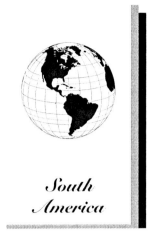

South America

You are in a country where swimming, despite all the rivers, is often not popular. Don't think this is because of the cold. It's actually quite warm here, with about three-quarters of the country covered in rainforests. The smallest independent country on the continent, 90% of the people live in 3% of the area. The yearly four seasons here are not spring, summer, fall, and winter. Rather, they are wet, dry, wet, and dry. Is that Dutch you hear being spoken? *Where on Earth are you? Can you find your place?*

Suriname

Located on the northeastern shoulder of South America, Suriname was a Dutch colony that only gained its independence from the Netherlands in 1975. Christopher Columbus was the first European to see Suriname. Settlements by the Spanish, British, Dutch, and French followed and failed until the 1650s. Experienced plantation owners from Barbados, a nearby Caribbean island ruled by the British, came with their slaves to develop Suriname. The slaves did all the backbreaking clearing and draining work and were horribly mistreated. The settlement became so prosperous that other Europeans came, and the Dutch began to fight with the British for ownership. The British gave Suriname to Holland in 1677 after the second Anglo-Dutch War. The British received, among other concessions, Manhattan Island in New York.

Have you figured out why swimming is not as popular in this region as one would think it might be? Piranhas are a type of fish that inhabit waterways of the Amazonian region. Although they measure only 10 inches (25 cm) in length, these small, razor-toothed fish kill more humans than any other water animal.

To keep from being enslaved by the Europeans, the Amerindians, members of the Arawak and Carib tribes, stayed in the forested interior. **How did these people deal with leafcutter ants (ants that can strip a tree in a single night)?** When ants moved in, people moved out. Immigrants tried poison, smoke, and explosives, but the Amerindian solution was the best. One could usually plant a field for several years before foraging ants found it, and then it was an opportunity to move on.

Before slavery was made illegal, about 300,000–350,000 slaves were imported to Suriname. Punishment was severe, and often slaves who tried to escape were killed. The selling of slaves was outlawed in Dutch territories in 1814, but the practice of slavery was not abolished until 1863. Even then, the freed slaves still had to work for 10 more years. **Who became the laborers?** Workers under contract were brought from China, India, and from the Indonesian island of Java, then a Dutch colony. Some of these people returned to their native countries, and others made Suriname their home. **How did different groups of people come to your country? How long does someone have to live in a new country before it is home?**

The largest rodent on the planet lives in Suriname. What is it? The capybara, or bush pig, looks something like a large gerbil. Capybaras can weigh up to 200 pounds (90 kilograms)!

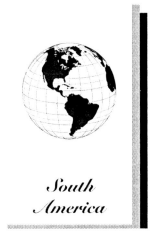

You have gone in search of the only nocturnal fruit-eating, echo-locating bird in the world. When people think of *echolocation*, the process of locating objects by means of sound waves, they usually think of bats. But these birds—oilbirds—avoid obstacles in the darkness of their cave-homes through echolocation. When there is adequate light, they use sight. To locate their food, they use their sense of smell. A twin-island republic, you are just off the South American coast and in the southernmost of the Caribbean countries. *Where on Earth are you? Can you find your place?*

Trinidad and Tobago

Do you weigh more than your parents? Oilbird babies stay in their nests a long time—between 95 to 120 days! At about 70 days, they may weigh up to 50% more than their parents! Obviously, the birds are fat, and this explains their name and why they were harvested by native islanders. Birds were collected from their nests on cave ledges and rendered down for their oil. The oil was used for cooking and fuel for torches and lamps. Oilbirds have become rare, and today they are protected by law in Trinidad and Tobago. Oilbird nests are used every year, and they are made primarily out of regurgitated matter. **What does *regurgitated* mean?** Regurgitated food is food that has been partly digested and brought back from the stomach to the mouth.

Trinidad and Tobago is part of the West Indies. It was claimed for Spain by Christopher Columbus in 1498 until it was taken by the British in 1797. Independence was granted in 1962, but Trinidad and Tobago remained part of the British Commonwealth, meaning they were ruled by a governor-general appointed by Britain. The cabinet and the bicameral (two houses) legislature were elected. In 1976, the islands became a republic and a new constitution was adopted, removing the governor-general.

Slavery was abolished in 1834, but starting in 1845, indentured Indian immigration began. It did not end until 1917. **What is *indentured immigration*?** An indentured immigrant is one that is bound by contract to work for a certain amount of time.

Is it possible to walk across a lake? Only if the water is frozen or if it is a pitch lake. It's a tropical climate in Trinidad and Tobago so water never freezes, but there is one of the world's three pitch lakes located in Trinidad. Of the three (the other two are in California and Venezuela), Trinidad's is the only one that is active. Oil oozes up to the ground, and the more volatile (changing readily into a gas or evaporating quickly) elements evaporate so that a residue of naturally occurring asphalt remains. Sir Walter Raleigh didn't walk across the lake, although he could have. Instead, he used the asphalt to caulk his boats in the 16th century and declared it the best he had ever used.

What crop was grown on plantations worked by slaves and indentured labor? The answer is sugarcane. Sugarcane is a labor-intensive industry, for it requires handcutting. Even today in Trinidad, some of the cane is brought to the refineries by ox-cart.

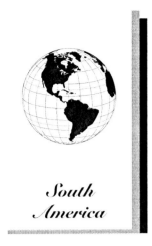

South America

Sandwiched between giants, you are in a country that was one of the first to have free, universal, compulsory education in Latin America (1877!). No wonder the literacy rate today is phenomenal. Independence was gained from Spain in 1828, but democracy is fragile today because the country is still recovering from a military coup that took place in 1973. Civilian rule did not return until 1985. It was a time of terror, when many people were tortured and killed. The demographics are not typical for Latin America in this country: 88% of the population are descendents of European settlers. *Where on Earth are you? Can you find your place?*

Uruguay

Demography is the statistical study of human populations, especially with reference to size, density, distribution, and vital statistics. **Why do descendents of European settlers make up such a large proportion of Uruguay's population?** Tragically, all of Uruguay's indigenous population disappeared because of disease, intentional extermination, and assimilation. Mestizos, the mixed descendents of Indian and Spanish during colonial times, make up 8% of the population. Descendents of slaves brought from Africa make up 4%.

One of the few mammals with a protective shell is indigenous to Uruguay. What could it be? Related to sloths and anteaters, the armadillo is a stout, short-legged creature with curved claws and protective armor. The armor covers most of the body, including the head and tail, and is composed of strips of hard material called *scutes* that are joined by flesh. When attacked, an armadillo draws in its feet and curls up close to the ground so that no soft flesh is exposed. It can also run, burrow, or claw at the attacker. Females give birth to genetic clones. Littermates (all females or males) develop from a single fertilized egg.

armadillo

Spanish is spoken in Uruguay, as it is in most of Central and South America. The easy answer to why is because Spain colonized much of the New World. During the 15th and 16th centuries, there were many languages spoken in Spain throughout its different regions, for example, Catalan, Galician, and Basque. **Why the dominance of a particular regional language in the colonies?** All the settlements for the New World were planned in central Spain, in the province of Castile. If one wanted to apply for the right to leave, one needed to learn enough Castilian to submit an application. If one's application was approved, one was sent to wait for a boat at either of two locations. As one waited (sometimes as long as a year), one became even more proficient in the local dialect. During the long trip and the necessary stop for restocking supplies at the Canary Islands (where Castilian was spoken), one gained further fluency. Meanwhile, Castilian Spanish became dominant in Spain because it was the language of the rulers.

People came to this country in search of El Dorado, a mythical man who was supposed to go about dusted in gold. There was gold of a different type—black gold, discovered in 1914. Simon Bolivar was born in this country where there is a waterfall that measures 3,212 feet (974 m), making it the tallest in the world. This waterfall was discovered by a pilot flying overhead in 1935. What was the pilot up to? He was looking for gold! *Where on Earth are you? Can you find your place?*

Venezuela

With half of Venezuela covered in forests and beaches, and the other half made up of mountains, plains, deserts, and grasslands, Venezuela is a magnificent land of amazing diversity and little gold. Colonized by the Spanish, Venezuela proclaimed independence in 1811. Independence, however, was not assured until 1821, when Simon Bolivar defeated the Spanish in the Battle of Carabobo. Bolivar united Venezuela, Columbia, Ecuador, and Panama into one nation called Gran Columbia. Venezuela became truly independent when it seceded from Gran Columbia in 1830.

During his presidential term starting in 1958, Romulo Betancourt started a policy of "sowing the oil." Oil is black gold, and what Betancourt did with all the wealth it generated was to put it back, or "sow" it back, into the country. He used oil profits to tackle the problems of illiteracy, poor living conditions and educational facilities, and the high infant mortality rate.

How are the names America, Venezuela, and Venice connected? Venice is a city in Italy filled with canals. When the Spanish explorer Alfonso de Ojeda traveled to northern Venezuela in 1499, he saw Indian huts built on stilts in Lake Maracaibo. This reminded de Ojedo and his mapmaker of Venice, so they named the country Venezuela or "Little Venice." De Ojedo's mapmaker was Amerigo Vespucci, and it is after Amerigo that America is named. Even today, the first to discover a new star, plant, microbe, or animal names it.

Venezuela's Orinoco River is the third largest river in South America and the eighth largest river in the world. The Orinoco connects to the Great Amazon River through a waterway called the Casiquiare Canal. This river system dominates more than a third of South America—approximately 2.5 million square miles. The Orinoco has 436 tributaries and diverges into 100 separate channels. When it hits the Atlantic Ocean 1,370 miles (2206 km) from its origins, it pours with such force that there is fresh water for miles out to sea. Amazing creatures live in the Orinoco, including a giant otter and crocodiles. You think you see a dolphin, but it's pink and the river is fresh water. Or is it a porpoise? **Are porpoises and dolphins the same animals?** Although both are small whales, they are different animals. All dolphins, including the freshwater ones that live in the Orinoco, usually have larger heads and longer snouts than porpoises. Dolphins have round, cone-shaped teeth; porpoises typically have flat triangular teeth. **The teeth on both show age. How?** There are rings on the inner parts of the teeth. Like trees, there is one ring for each year.

Writing Your Own Entry

There are too many places in the world to fit into this book! Now it is your turn to create an entry that would fit this text's format. Here are some hints that you might find useful for completing the task:

How specific do you want to be?

- country
- state or province
- city or county
- specific site such as fort, cave, mountain, battlefield, or building

Find something that makes your subject unique. For example,

- Was a famous person born in this country, state, or city?
- Is an interesting geographical feature (a mountain, a river, a cave, etc.) located here?
- When was this state or city settled? How old is it?
- Does a particular animal live here?
- What is the weather like?

Take one or two unique facts and tease your reader with them.

Examples:

> "A man from this state was blind, but he learned how to ride a motorcycle. Today, he is one of the greatest singers in the world."

> "The wheat that was in the cereal you ate for breakfast might very well have come from this state. Who would think that acres of sunflowers are grown here, too!"

Before you give the answers, ask the reader, *"Where on Earth are you? Can you find your place?"* Then, write the name of your place in bold or capital letters.

Write one or two lines about your place that answers the questions you posed in the beginning. For example, "Ray Charles was born in Florida. He was blind, but he learned how to ride a motorcycle. His friend would ride in front, and just the sound of the other motorcycle's exhaust was enough to guide Charles." Or, "Lots of wheat is grown in Kansas, but many people do not know that sunflowers are grown as a crop, too."

Continue with some other unique facts and some general information. For example,

- Is your site located by an ocean or river?
- Who are the neighbors?
- Would one ever see a particular animal like a grizzly bear, scorpion, or manatee?
- Where are people employed, or what is produced?

Remember, there is no right or wrong way of presenting your place. You decide if you want history, animal, or physical facts.

Use the form on page 164 to help you get started with your entry.

Writing Form

Name: _____

Date: _____ **Period:** _____

Introduction

_____

_____

_____

_____

_____

_____

_____

_____   _____

(place)

Answer to any questions in the introduction

_____

_____

_____

_____

General facts and questions

_____

_____

_____

_____

_____

_____

_____

_____

_____

_____

_____

_____

Bibliography

Achu, Kamala. *Nigeria.* The Bookwright Press, 1992.

Adeeb, Hassan, and Adeeb, Bonnetta. *Nigeria: One Nation, Many Cultures.* Marshall Cavendish, 1996.

Augustin, Byron. *Bolivia.* Children's Press, 2001.

Augustin, Byron, and Augustin, Rebecca A. *Qatar.* Children's Press, 1997.

Barnes-Svarney, Patricia. *Zimbabwe.* Chelsea House Publishers, 1999.

Beaton, Margaret. *Senegal.* Children's Press, 1997.

Beatty, Noelle B. *Suriname.* Chelsea House Publishers, 1999.

Berg, Elizabeth L. *Senegal.* Marshall Cavendish, 1999.

Biel, Timothy Levi. *Zoobooks: Deer.* Wildlife Education, Ltd., 1992.

————. *Zoobooks: Hummingbirds.* Wildlife Education, Ltd., 1991.

————. *Zoobooks: Polar Bears.* Wildlife Education, Ltd., 1992.

————. *Zoobooks: Tigers.* Wildlife Education, Ltd., 1992.

————. *Zoobooks: Turtles.* Wildlife Education, Ltd., 1988.

Billings, Henry. *Antarctica.* Children's Press, 1994.

Black, Eric. *Northern Ireland, Troubled Land.* Lerner Publications Company, 1998.

Black, Nancy Johnson, and Turck, Mary C. *Guatemala, Land of the Maya.* Dillon Press, 1999.

Blashfield, Jean F. *Norway.* Children's Press, 2000.

Blauer, Ettagale and Laure, Jason. *Ghana.* Children's Press, 1999.

————. *Madagascar.* Children's Press, 2000.

————. *Morocco.* Children's Press, 1999.

————. *South Africa.* Children's Press, 1998.

————. *Swaziland.* Children's Press, 1996.

————. *Uganda.* Children's Press, 1997.

Brill, Marlene Targ. *Algeria.* Children's Press, 1990.

————. *Guyana.* Children's Press, 1994.

Brill, Marlene Targ, and Targ, Harry, R. *Guatemala.* Children's Press, 1993.

Brook, Larry. *Daily Life in Ancient and Modern Timbuktu.* Runestone Press, 1999.

Brown, Roslind Varghese. *Tunisia.* Marshall Cavendish, 1998.

Brust, Beth Wagner. *Zoobooks: Dolphins and Porpoises.* Wildlife Education, Ltd., 1990.

Burbank, Jon. *Nepal.* Marshall Cavendish, 1991.

Burgan, Michael. *Belgium.* Children's Press, 2000.

Burke, Patrick. *Germany.* Thomson Learning, 1995.

Calhoun, Richard S. "Joya de Ceren." *Faces: El Salvador.* Cobblestone, November 1998, 20–24.

Carlsson, Bo Kage. *Sweden.* Thomson Learning, 1995.

Champion, Neil. *Portugal.* Thomson Learning, 1995.

Cheong-Lum, Roseline Ng. *Haiti.* Marshall Cavendish, 1995.

Cifarelli, Megan. *India: One Nation, Many Traditions.* Marshall Cavendish, 1996.

Clay, Rebecca. *Ukraine: A New Independence.* Marshall Cavendish, 1997.

Cooper, Robert. *Bahrain.* Marshall Cavendish, 2001.

————. *Bhutan.* Marshall Cavendish, 2001.

————. *Croatia.* Marshall Cavendish, 2001.

Creed, Alexander. *Uganda.* Chelsea House Publishers, 1988.

Bibliography *(cont.)*

Cunningham, Antonia (ed.). *Guinness World Records 2002.* Bantam Books, 2002.

Dash, Mike. *Tulipomania.* Orion Books Ltd., 1999.

Dhilawala, Sakina. *Armenia.* Marshall Cavendish, 1999.

Diamond, Judith. *Solomon Islands.* Children's Press, 1995.

Dramer, Kim. *People's Republic of China.* Children's Press, 1999.

DuBois, Jill. *Colombia.* Marshall Cavendish, 1992.

————. *Greece.* Marshall Cavendish, 1995.

————. *Israel.* Marshall Cavendish, 1994.

————. *Korea.* Marshall Cavendish, 1994.

Dunne, Mairead; Kairi, Wambui; Nyanjom, Eric. *Kenya.* Steck-Vaughn, 1998.

Elwood, Ann. Zoobooks: *Ostriches, Emus, Rheas, Kiwis, and Cassowaries.* Wildlife Education, Ltd., 1990.

Esbenshade, Richard S. *Hungary.* Marshall Cavendish, 1994.

Falconer, Kieran. *Peru.* Marshall Cavendish, 1995.

Ferroa, Peggy. *China.* Marshall Cavendish, 1993.

French, Richard. *A Guide to the Birds of Trinidad and Tobago.* Cornell University Press, 1991.

Fischer, Steven Roger. *Glyphbreaker.* Copernicus, 1997.

Foley, Erin. L. *Costa Rica.* Marshall Cavendish, 1997.

————. *Ecuador.* Marshall Cavendish, 1995.

Footman, Tim (ed.). *Guinness World Records 2001.* Bantam Books, 2001.

Foster, Leila Merrell. *Afghanistan.* Children's Press, 1996.

————. *Iraq.* Children's Press, 1997.

————. *Kuwait.* Children's Press, 1998.

————. *Oman.* Children's Press, 1999.

Foster, Ruth. *A Word A Week Vocabulary Program.* Teacher Created Resources, 1999.

————. *Take Five Minutes: Fascinating Facts and Stories for Reading and Critical Thinking.* Teacher Created Resources, 2001.

Fox, Mary Virginia. *Bahrain.* Children's Press, 1992.

————. *Cyprus.* Children's Press, 1993.

————. *Somalia.* Children's Press, 1996.

Fuller, Barbara. *Britain.* Marshall Cavendish, 1994.

Galvin, Irene Flum. *Chile, Journey to Freedom.* Dillon Press, 1997.

Gan, Delice. *Sweden.* Marshall Cavendish, 1993.

Garrard-Burnett, Virginia. "Chocolate to Dye For." *Faces: El Salvador.* Cobblestone, November, 1998, 14–15.

Gascoigne, Ingrid. *Papua New Guinea.* Marshall Cavendish, 1998.

Geography Department. *Armenia, Then & Now.* Lerner Publications Company, 1993.

————. *Uzbekistan, Then & Now.* Lerner Publications Company, 1993.

————. *Italy...in Pictures.* Lerner Publications Company, 1997.

————. *Georgia, Then & Now.* Lerner Publications Company, 1993.

————. *Germany...in Pictures.* Lerner Publications Company, 1994.

————. *Kazakhstan, Then & Now.* Lerner Publications Company, 1993.

————. *Lebanon...in Pictures.* Lerner Publications Company, 1992.

————. *Lithuania, Then & Now.* Lerner Publications Company, 1992.

————. *Malaysia...in Pictures.* Lerner Publications Company, 1997.

————. *Russia, Then & Now.* Lerner Publications Company, 1992.

————. *Sri Lanka...in Pictures.* Lerner Publications Company, 1997.

————. *Syria...in Pictures.* Lerner Publications Company, 1990.

Bibliography *(cont.)*

Gish, Steven. *Ethiopia*. Marshall Cavendish, 1996.

Gofen, Ethel Caro. *Argentina*. Marshall Cavendish, 1992.

————. *France*. Marshall Cavendish, 1995.

Gollin, James D. *Adventures in Nature: Honduras*. Avalon Travel Publishing, Inc., 2001.

Goodman, Jim. *Thailand*. Marshall Cavendish, 1993.

Gordon, Eugene. *Saudi Arabia in Pictures*. Lerner Publications Company, 1992.

Greenblatt, Miriam. *Cambodia*. Children's Press, 1995.

Griffiths, John. *Nicaragua*. Chelsea House Publishers, 1999.

Hansen, Ole Steen. *Denmark*. Steck-Vaugh Company, 1988.

Hassig, Susan M. *Iraq*. Marshall Cavendish, 1994.

————. *Panama*. Marshall Cavendish, 1996.

Haynes, Tricia. *Panama*. Chelsea House Publishers, 1999.

————. *Somalia*. Marshall Cavendish, 1997.

Heale, Jay. *Democratic Republic of the Congo*. Marshall Cavendish, 2001.

————. *Madagascar*. Marshall Cavendish, 1998.

————. *Poland*. Marshall Cavendish, 1994.

————. *Portugal*. Marshall Cavendish, 1995.

————. *Tanzania*. Marshall Cavendish, 1998.

Heinrichs, Ann. *Brazil*. Children's Press, 1997.

————. *Egypt*. Children's Press, 1997.

————. *Japan*. Children's Press, 1998.

————. *Nepal*. Children's Press, 1996.

————. *Niger*. Children's Press, 2001.

————. *Tibet*. Children's Press, 1996.

Hintz, Martin. *Argentina*. Children's Press, 1998.

————. *Haiti*. Children's Press, 1998.

————. *Hungary*. Children's Press, 1995.

————. *Poland*. Children's Press, 1998.

————. *The Netherlands*. Children's Press, 1999.

Hintz, Martin, and Hintz, Stephen. *The Bahamas*. Children's Press, 1997.

————. *Israel*. Children's Press, 1999.

Hirsch, E.D. Jr., Kett, Joseph F., Trefil, James. *The Dictionary of Cultural Literacy*. Houghton Mifflin Company, 1993.

Holmes, Timothy. *Zambia*. Marshall Cavendish, 1998.

Honeyman, Susannah. *Saudi Arabia*. Raintree Steck-Vaughn, 1995.

Hopkins, Daniel J. (ed.). *Merriam-Webster's Geographical Dictionary*. Merriam-Webster, Inc., 1997.

Jacobsen, Karen. *Laos*. Children's Press, 1991.

James, R.S. *Mozambique*. Chelsea House Publishers, 1988.

Janin, Hunt. *Saudi Arabia*. Marshall Cavendish, 1993.

Jermyn, Leslie. *Paraguay*. Marshall Cavendish, 2000.

————. *Uruguay*. Marshall Cavendish, 1999.

Kagda, Falaq. *Algeria*. Marshall Cavendish, 1999.

Kagda, Sakina. *Lithuania*. Marshall Cavendish, 1999.

————. *Norway*. Marshall Cavendish, 1995.

Kay, Rob. *Fiji: A Travel Survival Kit*. Lonely Planet Publications, 1993.

Bibliography *(cont.)*

Khng, Pauline. *Myanmar.* Gareth Stevens Publishing, 2000.

King, David C. *Kenya.* Marshall Cavendish, 1998.

Kizilos, Peter. *South Africa: Nation in Transition.* Lerner Publications Company, 1998.

Kohen, Elizabeth. *Spain.* Marshall Cavendish, 1995.

Kummer, Patricia, K. *Cote D'Ivoire (Ivory Coast).* Children's Press, 1996.

Laure, Jason. *Angola.* Children's Press, 1990.

Laure, Jason, and Blauer, Ettagale. *Mozambique.* Children's Press, 1995.

———. *Tanzania.* Children's Press, 1995.

Layton, Lesley. *Singapore.* Marshall Cavendish, 1990.

Lee, Tan Chung. *Finland.* Marshall Cavendish, 1996.

Lepthien, Emilie U. *Australia.* Children's Press, 1992.

Levey, Judith S., and Greenhall, Agnes (ed.). *The Concise Columbia Encyclopedia.* Avon Books, 1983.

Levy, Patricia. *Belarus.* Marshall Cavendish, 1999.

———. *Ireland.* Marshall Cavendish, 1994.

———. *Liberia.* Marshall Cavendish, 1998.

———. *Nigeria.* Marshall Cavendish, 1993.

———. *Scotland.* Marshall Cavendish, 2001.

———. *Sudan.* Marshall Cavendish, 1997.

———. *Switzerland.* Marshall Cavendish, 1994.

———. *Tibet.* Marshall Cavendish, 1996.

Lewington, Anna. *Mexico.* Steck-Vaughn Company, 1996.

Lieberg, Carolyn, S. *Suriname.* Children's Press, 1995.

Loveridge, Emma. *Egypt.* Raintree Steck-Vaughn, 1997.

Malcolm, Peter. *Libya.* Marshall Cavendish, 1993.

Mann, Peggy. *Easter Island, Land of Mysteries.* Holt, Rinehart, Winston, 1976.

Mansfield, Stephen. *Laos.* Marshall Cavendish, 1998.

McCulla, Patricia E. *Tanzania.* Chelsea House Publishers, 1999.

McNair, Sylvia. *Chile.* Children's Press, 2000.

———. *Finland.* Children's Press, 1997.

———. *Indonesia.* Children's Press, 1994.

———. *Thailand!.* Children's Press, 1998.

Merrick, Patrick. *Vietnam.* The Child's World, Inc., 2001.

Merrill, Tim L., (ed.) *Honduras: A Country Study.* Federal Research Division, Library of Congress, 1995.

Milivojevic, JoAnn. *Serbia.* Children's Press, 1999.

Mirepoix, Camille. *Afghanistan in Pictures.* Lerner Publications Company, 1990.

Mirpuri, Gouri. *Indonesia.* Marshall Cavendish, 1990.

Moiz, Azra. *Taiwan.* Marshall Cavendish, 1995.

Morrison, Marion. *Colombia.* Children's Press, 1999.

———. *Costa Rica.* Children's Press, 1998.

———. *Cuba.* Children's Press, 1999.

———. *Ecuador.* Children's Press, 2000.

———. *French Guiana.* Children's Press, 1995.

———. *Peru.* Children's Press, 2000.

Bibliography *(cont.)*

Nardo, Don. *France.* Children's Press, 2000.

Nash, Amy K. *North Korea.* Chelsea House Publishers, 1999.

NgCheong-Lum, Roseline. *Eritrea.* Marshall Cavendish, 2001.

———. *Maldives.* Marshall Cavendish, 2001.

———. *Tahiti.* Marshall Cavendish, 1997.

Oleksy, Walter. *The Philippines.* Children's Press, 2000.

O'Shea, Maria. *Kuwait.* Marshall Cavendish, 1999.

O'Sullivan, Marycate. *Scotland.* The Child's World, Inc., 2002.

Owhonda, John. *Nigeria: A Nation of Many People.* Dillon Press, 1998.

Pang Guek-Cheng. *Canada.* Marshall Cavendish, 1994.

———. *Grenada.* Marshall Cavendish, 2001.

———. *Kazakhstan.* Marshall Cavendish, 2001.

Pateman, Robert. *Belgium.* Marshall Cavendish, 1995.

———. *Bolivia.* Marshall Cavendish, 1995.

———. *Denmark.* Marshall Cavendish, 1995.

Popescu, Julian. *Russia.* Chelsea House Publishers, 1999.

Powell, Michael. "Overwhelmed: A small city wrestles with immigration." *Journal and Courier,* Oct. 14, 2002.

Resnick, Abraham. *Bulgaria.* Children's Press, 1995.

Richard, Christopher. *Brazil.* Marshall Cavendish, 1991.

Rogers, Barbara Radcliffe, and Rogers, Stillman D. *Canada.* Children's Press, 2000.

Rogers, Lura. *Switzerland.* Children's Press, 2001.

Rombauer, Irma, and Becker, Marion Rombauer. *Joy of Cooking.* Bobbs-Merrill Company, Inc., 1975.

Rowell, Jonathan. *Malaysia.* Raintree Steck-Vaugh, 1997.

Ryan, Patrick. *India.* The Child's World, Inc., 1999.

———. *New Zealand.* The Child's World, Inc., 1999.

Sayre, April Pulley. *Antarctica.* Twenty-First Century Books, 1998.

Schemenauer, Elma. *England.* The Child's World, Inc., 2001.

———. *Iran.* The Child's World, Inc., 2001.

Schwabach, Karen. *El Salvador.* Dillon Press, 1999.

Seah, Audrey. *Vietnam.* Marshall Cavendish, 1994.

Seward, Pat. *Morocco.* Marshall Cavendish, 1995.

———. *Netherlands.* Marshall Cavendish, 1995.

Sheehan, Sean. *Austria.* Marshall Cavendish, 1993.

———. *Cameroon.* Marshall Cavendish, 2001.

———. *Jamaica.* Marshall Cavendish, 1998.

———. *Lebanon.* Marshall Cavendish, 1997.

———. *Pakistan.* Marshall Cavendish, 1994.

———. *Romania.* Marshall Cavendish, 1994.

———. *Trinidad and Tobago.* Marshall Cavendish, 2001.

———. *Turkey.* Marshall Cavendish, 1993.

Shelley, Rex. *Japan.* Marshall Cavendish, 1990.

Bibliography *(cont.)*

Shepheard, Patricia. *South Korea.* Chelsea House Publishers, 1999.

Sioras, Efstathia. *Czech Republic.* Marshall Cavendish, 2000.

Smelt, Roselynn. *New Zealand.* Marshall Cavendish, 1998.

South, Coleman. *Jordan.* Marshall Cavendish, 1997.

———. *Syria.* Marshall Cavendish, 1995.

Spilling, Michael. *Georgia.* Marshall Cavendish, 1998.

Stanley, David. *Fiji Handbook.* Moon Publications, Inc., 1999.

Stark, Al. *Australia, A Lucky Land.* Dillon Press, 1997.

Stavreva, Kirilka. *Bulgaria.* Marshall Cavendish, 1997.

Stein, R. Conrad. *Austria.* Children's Press, 2000.

———. *Mexico.* Children's Press, 1998.

———. *The United States of America.* Children's Press, 1994.

Torchinsky, Oleg. *Russia.* Marshall Cavendish, 1994.

Urosevich, Patricia, R. *Trinidad and Tobago.* Chelsea House Publishers, 1999.

Wanasundera, Nanda P. *Sri Lanka.* Marshall Cavendish, 1993.

Wee, Jessie. *Taiwan.* Chelsea House Publishers, 1999.

Wexo, John Bonnett. *Zoobooks: Bears.* Wildlife Education, Ltd., 1991.

———. Zoobooks: Camels. Wildlife Education, Ltd., 1989.

———. *Zoobook: Elephants.* Wildlife Education, Ltd., 1986.

———. *Zoobooks: Giant Pandas.* Wildlife Education, Ltd., 1989.

———. *Zoobooks: Giraffes.* Wildlife Education, Ltd., 1991.

———. *Zoobooks: Gorillas.* Wildlife Education, Ltd., 1991.

———. *Zoobooks: Hippos.* Wildlife Education, Ltd., 1989.

———. *Zoobooks: Penguins.* Wildlife Education, Ltd., 1988.

———. *Zoobooks: Rhinos.* Wildlife Education, Ltd., 1991.

———. *Zoobooks: Sharks.* Wildlife Education, Ltd., 1988.

———. *Zoobooks: The Apes.* Wildlife Education, Ltd., 1991.

———. *Zoobooks: Whales.* Wildlife Education, Ltd., 1992.

Whyte, Mariam. *Bangladesh.* Marshall Cavendish, 1999.

Wilcox, Jonathan. *Iceland.* Marshall Cavendish, 1996.

Willis, Terri. *Libya.* Children's Press, 1999.

———. *Romania.* Children's Press, 2001.

Winter, Jane Kohen. *Italy.* Marshall Cavendish, 1992.

———. *Venezuela.* Marshall Cavendish, 1993.

Wolbers, Marian, F. *Burundi.* Chelsea House Publishers, 1989.

Wood, Linda C (ed.). *Zoobooks: Lions.* Wildlife Education, Ltd., 1989.

Wood, Linda C. *Zoobooks: Zebras.* Wildlife Education, Ltd., 1989.

Wood, Linda C., and Jenson, Cynthia L. *Zoobooks: Cheetahs.* Wildlife Education, Ltd., 1990.

Wood, Linda C., and Rink, Deane. *Zoobooks: Bats.* Wildlife Education, Ltd., 1989.

Woods, Geraldine. *Spain, Gateway to Europe.* Dillon Press, 1998.

Wright, David K. *Albania.* Children's Press, 1997.

Yin, Saw Myat. *Burma.* Marshall Cavendish, 1992.

Bibliography *(cont.)*

The following articles were referenced from Encyclopedia Britannica. Encyclopedia Britannica, Inc., 1990.

"anteater," (volume 1, page 441)

"armadillo," (volume 1, page 563)

"Avicenna," (volume 1, page 739–740.)

"bagpipes," (volume 1, page 795)

"Bo tree," (volume 2, page 305)

"buffalo," (volume 2, page 607)

"cashew," (volume 2, page 920)

"chamois," (volume 3, page 70)

"condor," (volume 3, page 522–523)

"corn," (volume 3, page 634)

"Easter Island," (volume 4, page 333–334)

"epiphyte," (volume 4, page 526)

"flax," (volume 4, page 824–825)

"hyena," (volume 6, page 196)

"hyrax," (volume 6, page 206)

"Iran," (volume 21, page 858)

"jaguar," (volume 6, page 471)

"kamikaze," (volume 6, page 704)

"Khwarizmi, al" (volume 6, page 848)

"leprosy," (volume 7, page 287)

"locust," (volume 7, page 438)

"Machu Picchu," (volume 7, page 631–632)

"malaria," (volume 7, page 725)

"Maldives," (volume 7, page 731–732)

"mamba," (volume 7, page 749)

"marathon," (volume 7, page 814–815)

"marten," (volume 7, page 884)

"mongoose," (volume 8, page 257–258)

"monkey," (volume 8, page 259)

"monotreme," (volume 8, page 266)

"Nicaragua, Lake," (volume 8, page 676–677)

"number system," (volume 8, page 826–827)

"plague," (volume 9, page 492–493)

"polo," (volume 9, page 570–571)

"Portuguese man-of-war," (volume 9, Page 634–635)

"Rafflesiales," (volume 9, page 899)

"Raleigh, Sir Walter," (volume 9, page 913–914)

"Semmelweis, Ignaz Philipp," (volume 10, page 627–628)

"sitatunga," (volume 10, page 849)

"sloth," (volume 10, page 883)

"tapir," (volume 11, page 554–555)

"tarsier," (volume 11, page 567)

"Tell, William," (volume 11, page 618)

"Tesla, Nikola," (volume 11, page 654–655)

Our World (Map)

Use tape or glue to connect pages 172 and 173 at the tab.

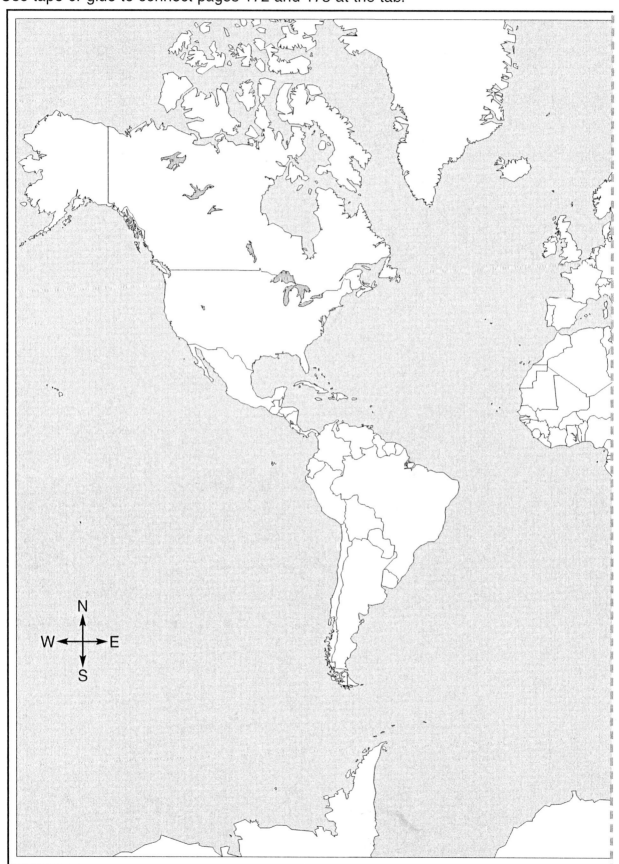

Our World (Map)

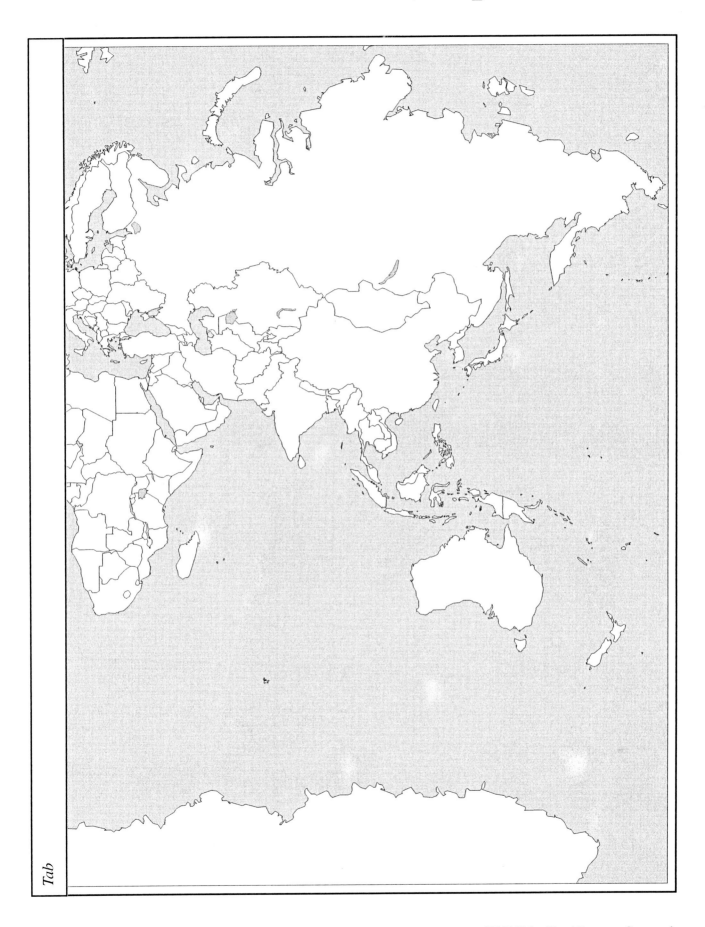

Tab

Index

Country	Region	Page Number
Afghanistan	Asia	46
Albania	Europe	98
Algeria	Africa	10
Angola	Africa	11
Antarctica	Antarctica	42
Argentina	South America	148
Armenia	Asia	47
Australia	Australia	93
Austria	Europe	99
Bahamas	North and Central America	130
Bahrain	Asia	48
Bangladesh	Asia	49
Belarus	Europe	100
Belgium	Europe	101
Bhutan	Asia	50
Bolivia	South America	149
Brazil	South America	150
Bulgaria	Europe	102
Burundi	Africa	12
Cambodia	Asia	51
Cameroon	Africa	13
Canada	North and Central America	131
China	Asia	52
Chile	South America	151
Colombia	South America	152
Costa Rica	North and Central America	132
Cote D'Ivoire (Ivory Coast)	Africa	14
Croatia	Europe	103
Cuba	North and Central America	133
Cyprus	Asia	53
Czech Republic	Europe	104
Democratic Republic of the Congo	Africa	15
Denmark	Europe	105
Dominican Republic	North and Central America	134
Easter Island	South America	153
Ecuador	South America	154
Egypt	Africa	16
El Salvador	North and Central America	135
England	Europe	106
Eritrea	Africa	17
Ethiopia	Africa	18
Fiji	Asia	54
Finland	Europe	107
France	Europe	108
French Guiana	South America	155
Gambia	Africa	19

Index *(cont.)*

Country	Region	Page Number
Georgia	Asia	55
Germany	Europe	109
Ghana	Africa	20
Greece	Europe	110
Grenada	North and Central America	136
Guatemala	North and Central America	137
Guyana	South America	156
Haiti	North and Central America	138
Honduras	North and Central America	139
Hungary	Europe	111
Iceland	Europe	112
India	Asia	56
Indonesia	Asia	57
Iran	Asia	58
Iraq	Asia	59
Ireland	Europe	113
Israel	Asia	60
Italy	Europe	114
Jamaica	North and Central America	140
Japan	Asia	61
Jordan	Asia	62
Kazakhstan	Asia	63
Kenya	Africa	21
Kuwait	Asia	64
Laos	Asia	65
Lebanon	Asia	66
Liberia	Africa	22
Libya	Africa	23
Lithuania	Europe	115
Madagascar	Africa	24
Malaysia	Asia	67
Maldives	Asia	68
Mali	Africa	25
Mexico	North and Central America	141
Morocco	Africa	26
Mozambique	Africa	27
Myanmar	Asia	69
Netherlands	Europe	116
Nepal	Asia	70
New Zealand	Australia	94
Nicaragua	North and Central America	142
Niger	Africa	28
Nigeria	Africa	29
North Korea	Asia	71
Norway	Europe	117
Oman	Asia	72

Index *(cont.)*

Country	Region	Page Number
Pakistan	Asia	73
Panama	North and Central America	143
Papua New Guinea	Asia	74
Paraguay	South America	157
Peru	South America	158
Philippines	Asia	75
Poland	Europe	118
Portugal	Europe	119
Qatar	Asia	76
Romania	Europe	120
Russia	Asia	77
Saudi Arabia	Asia	78
Scotland	Europe	121
Senegal	Africa	30
Serbia	Europe	122
Singapore	Asia	79
Solomon Islands	Asia	80
Somalia	Africa	31
South Africa	Africa	32
South Korea	Asia	81
Spain	Europe	123
Sri Lanka	Asia	82
Sudan	Africa	33
Suriname	South America	159
Swaziland	Africa	34
Sweden	Europe	124
Switzerland	Europe	125
Syria	Asia	83
Tahiti	Asia	84
Taiwan	Asia	85
Tanzania	Africa	35
Thailand	Asia	86
Tibet	Asia	87
Trinidad and Tobago	South America	160
Tunisia	Africa	36
Turkey	Asia	88
Uganda	Africa	37
Ukraine	Europe	126
United States	North and Central America	144
Uruguay	South America	161
Uzbekistan	Asia	89
Venezuela	South America	162
Vietnam	Asia	90
Zambia	Africa	38
Zimbabwe	Africa	39